THE SECRETS OF EARNING FREE GOVERNMENT MONEY

CLAIM A SHARE OF YOUR $32 BILLION THE GOVERNMENT HOLDS FOR YOU

DAVID BENDAH

David Bendah

New York   London   Toronto
Sydney   Tokyo   Singapore

David Bendah San Diego

This publication is designed to provide accurate and authoritative information in regard to the subject matter covered. It is sold with the understanding that the publisher is not engaged in rendering legal, accounting, or other professional service. If legal advice or other expert assistance is required, the services of a competent professional should be sought.

David Bendah books are available at special quantity discounts to use as premiums and sales promotions, in corporate training programs or for educational uses. For more information please write David Bendah, 914 E. 8th Street, Suite 110, National City, CA 91950-2564

Table Of Contents

Chapter 1

Your $32 Billion Dollar Opportunity

Would you like to stake a share of the $32,000,000,000 the government holds for you by surfing the internet then just making a few phone calls and then looking in some phone books? That is all you have to do to enjoy thousands of dollars. If you can read English and speak on the phone, you can make thousands of dollars overnight and you don't have to sell anything!

If you're tired of trying to sell products that don't appeal to the people in your city, here's a business for you. All you have to do is gather a little information about money owed to other people then tell them about their money. This plan is revolutionary and isn't well-known. And, the opportunity never ends as the government collects in their coffers more and more money every year. The huge pile of money that belongs to people in their state just keeps stacking up.

Let me tell you how I stumbled upon this plan. Many years ago I got involved in a bad business investment and lost $11,000. Everything I owned was lost. I needed money desperately to pay my expenses, so I was forced to toil as a waiter at the Sheraton Harbor Island Hotel in San Diego by night, and work in an office during the day. It was so exhausting that as soon as I got home I would sleep for several hours, wake up in a stupor, drink two cups of coffee and then scramble to my next job. I had no choice. It was the only thing I could do to pay the bills.

It was later that my friend Gary, told me a story that changed my life. He told me very excitedly, "I received a funny-looking letter. When I first saw it, I thought it was another creditor making a claim on me. The letter told me about money that was rightfully mine — it said that if I signed the enclosed form, I would receive $2,592.59. Things were so bad that I had nothing to lose, so I signed the form neatly and returned it to the company.

"Ten days later I received a check for $2,592.59. A distant aunt had died and left $4,320.98 in her savings account. The company that found me collected $1,728.39. The firm had no trouble finding out that I was related to her. Just for matching up people with the same last names, that agency was making millions of dollars every year.

It was just then that an amazing idea popped into my mind. I was overcome with excitement. This revolutionary system was so simple. I knew that anyone could do what this company was doing and make thousands of dollars for finding the rightful owners of lost money. All I had to do was come up with a system for finding people and getting the money to them. I worked out a plan. It was a spectacular plan.

It's a very simple plan. I put it into action. Let me tell more about this plan. I was never considered smart. I had a C average in high school and one year I received an F in English. But I did it. The amount of money I was making was incredible.

Now anyone can make thousands finding lost people. And, there is thirty two billion dollars just sitting out there waiting to be recovered. One out of ten Americans have forgotten or lost money in bank accounts, stocks, insurance premiums, etc. And, right now there are only 10 percent of these people getting their money back.

The states make no strong effort to contact the rightful owners. Why should they, when unclaimed property is their biggest source of revenue, second only to taxes? The states are required by law to make a list of unclaimed owners, but most of the people who are owed money don't know about these lists.

An Heir Finder

You could be an heir finder to enrich your income. You could unit lost fortunes with their families and make a hefty profit. Not just a small profit but a big profit. Huge fortunes have been left with no heirs. Find the person who is supposed to inherit the money and you can earn a huge finder's fee. Just imagine a person left ten million dollars with no heirs. Use this plan to find the lost heir. Let us say that you find the lost heir of this million dollar fortune. The person you found that inherited this ten million dollars then pays you a finder's fee. A finder's fee is a reward for finding lost money. At twenty five percent you would earn two and a half million dollars. Two and a half million dollars is a huge sum of money. You could buy a brand new home and a new car, and then retire with two and a half million dollars. You would not have to work again for anyone because you have millions of dollars. Listen carefully to my plan that could make you rich.

Locating People

How hard is it to locate an individual who owns unclaimed property? A California bank had an unclaimed property list with famous movie stars that are so easy to find.

Look at what someone who has never done a search was able to do. Bonnie Goldstein, a writer for the San Francisco Chronicle who doesn't know that much about finding people, located the owners of $4,100 in two-and-a-half hours with two telephone directories. She went to the Maryland Department of Miscellaneous Revenues, picked out 15 names and started making phone calls. When she made her first phone call, she reached the "lost money" owner's mother who told her that her daughter was still living there and had been for 33 years.

You will be able to do the same. All you need is a phone book, library references and maybe the internet, but most of all you need some time to make yourself a fortune. If you have the time you can start. I'll show you exactly how to find people on these unclaimed property lists.

To make your quest for unclaimed money easier, I have information about advanced systems of searching for people that only the top private investigators and government security organizations use. I will disclose many of them to you. You will be amazed at how easy it is to find anyone you want — no matter where this person is you will be able to find this person. Become a master sleuth with simple methods of finding people. Become rich by finding people and giving them their own money.

1922 SAN FRANCISCO CHRONICLE

C   SAN FRANCISCO CHRONICLE,

$750,000 Deposits Go Unclaimed in S.F. Banks

Neglected Riches for State After 20 Years

Figures Hide Stories of Human Tragedies

San Francisco banks rapidly are completing their respective reports of deposits unclaimed during the ten and twenty years preceding January 1, 1921. Banking authorities here say that the sum will approximate $750,000. This estimate largely is based on the fact that deposits unclaimed during the ten and twenty years preceding January 1, 1919, totaled $420,957.48.

The law provides that every bank in California shall make an annual report of deposits unclaimed during the twenty years preceding the date of said report. It also provides that, in odd years, the banks shall make additional reports, showing the deposits unclaimed during the preceding ten years.

PROVISION OF LAW

In this connection the law stipulates that:

"All amounts of money heretofore or hereafter deposited with any bank to the credit of depositors who have not made a deposit on said account, or withdrawn any part thereof, or the interest, and which shall have remained unclaimed for more than twenty years after the date of such deposit, or withdrawal of any part of principal or interest, and where neither the depositor nor any claimant has filed any notice with such bank showing his or her present residence, shall, with the increase and proceeds thereof, escheat to the State."

Pursuant to this provision, the Attorney-General of the State is charged with the duty of taking the proper steps to insure the turning over of this money to the State treasury. This means that through carelessness, neglect, death or some other exigency, something like $75,000, deposited more than twenty years ago in the banks of San Francisco, shortly will be paid over by these banks to the State. Each year the amount increases, indicating, if one cares to analyze the matter, increasing thoughtlessness on the part of people.

PENCHANT FOR WASTING

In these latter days, when thinking men and women throughout the country earnestly are seeking to impress upon the minds of every one—but especially the youth of the land—the value of thrift, the eloquent story told by San Francisco banks is one that should challenge undivided interest. Certainly there is much in the story told by these reports of deposits unclaimed to support the contention that

the American people, young and old, display a remarkable penchant for wasting.

Carelessness in handling what one has is on a par with the distinctly American characteristic of acting on the principle that want never can overtake one. If this brand of carelessness ever has been exemplified in San Francisco, it would seem to have been in the apparently utter disregard for literally thousands of accounts, small and large, forgotten in the banks of this city.

HUMAN INTEREST

What a hidden wealth of human interest essentially lies in the emotionless columns of figures comprising the San Francisco bank reports of deposits unclaimed during the last twenty years. Here, if anywhere, comedy must have stalked hand in hand with tragedy. It requires no effort of the imagination to speculate on the close relationship that must have existed between those forgotten deposits and the everyday life of the community as depicted in the newspaper accounts of those days.

Perusal of the reports submitted by the various banks brings to light much of interest. The forgotten accounts range in amounts anywhere from one cent to thousands of dollars. Obviously, before these reports are submitted every effort is made by the banks to locate the depositors. In some cases they are found to have died, leaving no trace of possible heirs, while in still other instances they simply have disappeared.

HEAVY TASK FOR BANKS

The work necessarily devolving upon the banks in caring for these forgotten accounts is tremendous. In times gone by, this work oftentimes was compensated for by the banks having been permitted to retain unclaimed deposits. While any of these banks gladly would have paid deposits to persons able to establish bona fide ownership, the sums that thus came into possession of various banks throughout the country were considerable. It is related that in Cleveland, more than one palatial bank building was erected solely through use of unclaimed deposits.

Not all deposits unclaimed during a period of ten years necessarily remain unclaimed during the ensuing ten years. Bank officials here declare that many deposits are claimed between the ten and twenty-year period. Most such deposits have been forgotten, but occasionally, so bank

officials say, men and women purposely have permitted their accounts to remain untouched for long periods of time.

VARIED ACCOUNTS

Analysis of the various reports shows that not all of the unclaimed deposits are personal accounts. Fraternal and political organizations are numbered among the depositors. Numerous accounts are shown in the name of trustees. Families widely-known in California are numbered among those depositors in San Francisco banks who apparently have forgotten the existence of their respective accounts.

In the Fresno branch of the Bank of Italy, for instance, are accounts credited to Mrs. F. Cartwright, George Barclay Hodgkin and George Shirley; In the Los Angeles branch the Non-Partisan City Central Committee, Myer Lissner, secretary, is credited with an account of $37.72. Los Angeles Tent No. 2, Knights of the Maccabees, is credited with a deposit of $796.38. Florence E. Dolph has an account of $1701.93 and Blanche L. Dolph has a credit of $2763.51.

The Wells Fargo Nevada National Bank of San Francisco shows an account of $13.50 credited to the American Bank of Mexico, while the Bar Association of San Francisco has an account of $3.80. The National Biscuit Co. still has a deposit of $1.88 that has not been touched during the last ten years.

BALANCE OF ONE CENT

In the Merchants' National Bank, Gus Bouquest still has an undisturbed balance of one cent that may go to the State unless prompt action be taken. The Swedish Christian Benevolent Society has a deposit of $23.59 that faces the same fate. John J. Ortner, trustee for Fred H. Ortner, has an account of $11.68 in the San Francisco Savings and Loan Society and Alexander McKenzie has $2223.64 in the same institution. In the Union Trust Company of San Francisco, A. L. Anderson has an undisturbed deposit of $2702.63 while Lillie B. Crocker, executrix of the estate of Mina D. Solomon, has $219.43 in this institution.

In the reports thus far received by the State Superintendent of Banks, the smallest unclaimed deposit is one cent, while the largest, $7883.66. For the most part the individual items shown in the various reports are for small amounts, the average being deposits of approximately $1.50.

A 1922 San Francisco Chronicle newspaper article that talks about unclaimed Money in San Francisco Banks.

You will be doing everyone a great service by first, finding people then second giving them money. This business could make you very rich. This people finding business could make you filthy rich.

Chapter 2

Getting
The Bills Rolling

It sounds hard to believe that people leave thousands of dollars in banks and other institutions and then forget about their own money. I know I would have a difficult time doing that. I don't forget money.   But the truth is that it happens all the time. Everyone forgets where they put their money. Some states have hundreds of millions of dollars in unclaimed property and some states have billions of dollars in unclaimed money. Some states have five hundred thousand dollars or more in just one account. $500,000 is like winning the state lottery.

Your goal is to return money back to the rightful owners. You would contact the owners of this unclaimed money and collect a fee for your services. There are people doing just that and are making a hefty profit every year. You could join these lucky business owners and make money on your own.

Every state has an unclaimed property office that has the sole responsibility of returning unclaimed money back to its owners. Every state has different laws and policies regarding the handling of unclaimed money. I have a list of the complete contact information for every state in this chapter. Check with each state to be familiar with their unclaimed property laws. Each state has different laws concerning money finders.   Let me first explain the process of how money is left unclaimed. A person, due to neglect, forgetfulness or death will leave behind money in an institution.   Everyone that dies leaves money behind. This always happens. The institution, whether it be a bank, insurance company, business (retirement fund), government office, or even a security company, must report unclaimed money to the state.   The unclaimed money must be claimed by the owner in a specified period of time. The amount of time varies from state to state.   Many states have laws that require banks and financial institutions three to five years to turn dormant accounts to the state treasury department. Some states have no time restriction for a person to claim his or her money once it is in the hands of the state, but some states do have time restrictions. States like Indiana allow owners 25 years to claim their own money. Twenty five years is just five years shorter than some mortgages. .

One more thing to remember is that the states have unclaimed money sitting patiently in their bank accounts some for even seventy years. Seventy years is a long period of time.   This lost money is waiting in a bank account for someone to claim it.   Maybe you could find the heir to lost money. Maybe you could unite the owner of lost money with their money.   You will make a lot of money for doing this.

Contacting the State Offices

The state offices contain a gold mine of information. They have lists of owners of unclaimed property. Some states will sell you a copy of the list. Some will let you view the records if you go to the department office.

THE UNCLAIMED PROPERTY PROGRAM

The Unclaimed Property Law is designed to return unclaimed property to owners or to their heirs. These people have either forgotten about the property, or in some instances did not even know of its existence.

The State does not receive any of this "abandoned" property until it has been held by the organizations reporting it for seven years after the last contact with the named owners.

The State begins its efforts to contact the owners as soon as the property is reported to us. The State Controller publishes the names of owners in a newspaper in the county of their last known address. In addition, the State Controller also mails a notice to the named owners at their last known address.

Current lists are also distributed to main libraries and interested TV and radio stations.

Microfilmed records of all accounts that have not been claimed are maintained in our office and are open for public review on Wednesdays and Thursdays from 8:00 to 4:30 p.m. These microfilmed records have also been made available for purchase. (See Exhibit "3" for cost and ordering instructions.)

The success of the unclaimed property program is evident. Last year alone, almost $10 million dollars were restored to owners as a result of program effort.

* * * *

In addition to unclaimed property, we also receive Estates of Deceased Persons. These come to us under provision of the Probate Code. Microfilmed listings of the estates are also available for review or purchase. (See Exhibit "3" for cost). Unlike abandoned property accounts, which are held in perpetuity, these estates do permanently escheat after a period of time and are no longer available to claim after a specified date.

Estates with named heirs in the amount of $1,000 or greater are subject to judicial escheat. After we have held the money received on these estates for a period of five years, we send a list to the Attorney General's Office. Their office publishes the list, again verifies with us that there has been no activity on the account, then initiates a court order to affect permanent escheat. Five years from the date of this order we then complete the escheat action. Thus, on these estates the property is subject to claim for 10 years after receipt of funds by our office.

Estates with named heirs under $1,000 and all estates with no named heirs are subject to administrative escheat. The estates under $1,000 with known heirs escheat 10 years after we receive the money - the estates with no known heirs escheat 5 years after receipt of money.

We publish a legal notice listing the estates under $1,000 with known heirs in the San Francisco, Sacramento and Los Angeles areas.

The above escheated actions are reversible if it can be demonstrated that an inquiry or claim was initiated before the escheat date.

* * *

Older State Of California Unclaimed Property Policy

In addition to the unclaimed property the states also receive estates of deceased persons. Listings of the estates are also available for review or purchase. Unlike abandoned property accounts which are held in perpetuity these estates do permanently escheat after a period of time and are no longer available to claim after a specified date. In legal jargon, if an estate is subject to "escheat," it means that the state has the authority to take the money permanently if the rightful heirs don't claim it within a set number of years.

Contact your state office or any state office of unclaimed property. The unclaimed property office in your state may let you have access to this list.

Some state offices may not send you the list of names, or they may charge you a large fee. There's a way around this in most states, and that is to go to the unclaimed property office in person. A few states now require appointments, but be persistent and you can see the lists.

Different Types Of Intangible Unclaimed Property

Class Codes

CODE TYPE OF ORGANIZATION	CODE TYPE OF INTANGIBLE PROPERTY
Banking Organizations Financial Organizations Savings and Loans Business Associations ■ Title companies-Escrow ■ Escrow companies ■ Collection Agencies ■ Credit Bureaus Convalescent Homes Mortgage companies Equity & Mortgage	0. Demand Deposits 1. Savings Deposits and Interest 2. Money orders and Travelers checks 3. Drafts, Certified checks, Christmas Club Checks, Cashier Checks. 4. Contents of Safe Deposit Boxes and Safekeeping -Items 5. Trust Deposits (Escrow) 6. Liquidating Funds 7. Earnings due shareholders-Dividends 8. Shares of Stock 9. Miscellaneous Funds-Wages, Refunds, Accounts Payable, Collections, etc.)
Life Insurance companies	1. Matured or Terminated Policies. 2. Policy Holders Dividends. 3. Premium Refunds Returned 6. Liquidating Funds. 7. Earnings due Shareholders. 8. Unclaimed Shares Stock. 9. Miscellaneous Funds (Commissions, Wages, Accounts Payable, etc.)
Public Officer and Agencies Other Holders, Courts, etc.	9. All Intangible Personal Property
Utilities: ■ Telephone ■ Water ■ Electric	5. Trust Deposits (Escrow) 6. Liquidating Funds 7. Earnings due Shareholders 8. Shares of Stock

■ Natural Gas	9. Miscellaneous Funds-Wages, Refunds Accounts Payable, Collections, etc.)
Insurance Companies (Other than Life Insurance)	1. Terminated Policies 2. Policyholders Dividends 3. Premium Refund Returned 6. Liquidating Funds 7. Earnings Due Shareholders 8. Unclaimed Shares of Stock 9. Miscellaneous Funds-(Commissions, Wages, Accounts Payable, etc.)
Credit Unions Loan Companies Credit Associations	1. Savings Deposits and Interest 2. Money Orders and Travelers Checks 3. Drafts, Certified Checks, Christmas Club Checks, Cashier Checks 6. Liquidating Funds 9. Miscellaneous Funds

Persistence in going to the state office in person to get the unclaimed money list pays off. . A 14-year-old boy in Connecticut was having trouble getting the list from his state's office, so he went in person to the state office. He reviewed the list, jotted down 30 names, and began his search for the rightful owners. After finding the first few names on the list, he told me that he's now $16,212 richer— and he earned this money in just a few days.

You can run a small business finding people by the internet or by mail with very little money. In the next section I will give you the websites of the national unclaimed property database. You can use it but I advise you to get the list yourself. Your persistence will pay off when you get the list yourself.

National Unclaimed Property Databases

Below are the website addresses of the national websites that keep names and amounts of unclaimed fund owners in the United States and part of Canada. These data bases can help you find unclaimed property. For a detailed search go to each individual state website.

DO THIS FIRST:

1. Turn on a computer.
2. Go to the INTERNET.
3. Go to these WEBSITES.
4. On the search page type in your NAME.
5. The Database will tell you if you have lost or forgotten unclaimed MONEY.

1

National State Sponsored Database of Unclaimed Property . Listing of all 50 states and Canadian Provinces for locating unclaimed property records..
Web Site: http://www.missingmoney.com

2

National States' Unclaimed Property
National Association of Unclaimed Property Administrators. Search for unclaimed property nationwide. Check state offices in charge of reuniting property with its rightful owner.
Web Site: http://www.unclaimed.org

3

National Unclaimed Property Database to Search For Unclaimed Money. Search the database by all States.
Web Site: http://unclaimedmoney.org

No Internet

If you have no internet connection just use the mail or telephone to find out how much unclaimed money you have. Look up any state that you have lived in then write or call the unclaimed property office in that state.

The list that follows are the names and addresses of the state agencies to contact for unclaimed property. I have included all phone numbers and their internet sites that you need for finding unclaimed money and property.

The States Report

There is a reference program in addition to this book that will provide you with complete state list and state policy information. If you find this book helpful you should join the Money Finder Association. It is an excellent program. This reference program includes all 50 states and also includes District Of Columbia, Puerto Rico and other U.S. territories. It is an amazing reference book that will save years from your search of unclaimed property lists. The book will reference old 20 to 40 year old newspaper published lists that are only available in certain county newspapers. This reference book will give you this rare hard-to-find list information. The state reports book has sources of published list and state policies regarding unclaimed money. You need this book to make money with unclaimed property list. It is an excellent reference text that is a must for anyone making money from unclaimed property. The states report book is part of the 'Money finders association. The money finder's association includes expensive legal contracts that include the power of attorney clause.

Free With "The Money Finder Association."

1) **The Complete Manual To Finding Unclaimed Money,** which tells you exactly in precise detail how to set up your money finder's business so that you can start making up to $2,000 an hour. This manual will show you how:

- How you can recover the unclaimed money before it goes to the states and how to recover unclaimed money in distant countries.
- Advanced methods and sources of searching for people.
- How to set up your money finder business and design your own office for the lowest price.
- How to minimize costs and maximize efficiency.
- How to budget your business for maximum profits, including how to set up your accounting system and business records.
- How to assess your employee needs, including how to determine when it's the right time to hire.
- How to develop a professional company image.

2)   Save in legal fees. Save hundreds of dollars is what it cost me to get the finder's fee contract prepared. This alone makes your association membership worthwhile. You will receive a revised legal contract which includes a power of attorney contract written up by two attorneys in different states. This contract is to ensure that you get your money, and has already been used to recover thousands of dollars.

3)   Detailed "States" report. Which states are the easiest to make money in? That question is answered in a 50 plus page detailed report (included in your membership package) on the laws regarding unclaimed property in every state. We personally wrote and called every state in the U.S. to find out which states are most cooperative and which states to stay away from. And did you know your vacations to other states can be tax-deductible? It's true! If you make money by finding a person in another state, you may be able to write off a vacation trip to that state.

4)   Receive direct mail proven winners. These letters have helped the sender recover hundreds of thousands of dollars. These extremely well-written letters are sent out—with contracts enclosed —to potential claimants; they are designed to convince the claimant to send you back a signed contract. Many letters have been tested, but none has had as successful a return rate as these extremely luring letters.

Join The Money Finder's Association

Join the association and watch your financial dreams become a reality—you'll be amazed at the return on your investment! You could always use an association that will show you where to find money. If there is money in the streets of New York City, the heart of Minnesota or in the suburbs of Dallas we will show you how to get it. This association is an excellent investment. The legal contracts and the state reports on all 50 states and the direct mail proven winners is well worth at least $4,000 dollars alone. You will be getting $4,000 of tools you need for only $159 dollars plus $12 (shipping and handling). The small $159 + $12 (S&H) is worth every penny. Hurry because there is a limit to the amount of people that we allow in our "Money Finder Association." It is the best association you will every join in your life. Join today.

This association is an amazing bargain right now. Send $159 plus ($12 for shipping and handling) – a total of $171 to join the Money Finder Association.

David Bendah
914 E. 8th Street, Suite 110, Dept. B1
National City, CA 91950-2564
(619) 474-9200

If you would like more information on this program, please see the last chapter of this book or feel free to contact me at (619) 474-9200. I will be happy to discuss this program with you.   There is more information on joining the "Money Finder Association" in the last chapter of this book. The legal contracts and the state reports on all 50 states and the direct mail proven winners is well worth at least $4,000 dollars alone. You will be getting $4,000 of tools you need for only $171 dollars. Join this valuable "Money Finder Association" today.

State Offices Of Unclaimed Property

Alabama

Website Address
http://www.treasury.state.al.us
http://www.moneyquestalabama.com/

Mailing Address:
Office of State Treasurer
Unclaimed Property Division
PO Box 302520
Montgomery, AL 36130-2520

Street Address
RSA Union Building
100 North Union Street, Suite 636
Montgomery, AL 36104

Email: moneyquest@treasury.alabama.gov
Phone: (334) 242-9614 or
Toll Free: (888) 844-8400
Fax: (334) 242-9620

Alaska

Website Address
http://www.**unclaimedproperty.alaska.gov**
http://www.tax.alaska.gov/programs/

Mailing Address:
Alaska Department of Revenue
Treasury Division
Unclaimed Property Program
P O Box 110405
Juneau AK 99811-0405

Street Address: Physical / Overnight Delivery:
Alaska Department of Revenue
Treasury Division
Unclaimed Property Program
333 Willoughby Avenue

11th Floor State Office Building
Juneau AK 99801-1770

Email: ucproperty@alaska.gov
Telephone: Phone: (907) 465-3726
Fax: (907) 465-2394

Arizona

Website Address
http://www.**azunclaimed.gov**

Mailing Address:
Department of Revenue
Unclaimed Property Unit
PO Box 29026
Phoenix, Arizona
85038-9026

Street Address
Department of Revenue
Unclaimed Property Unit
1600 W Monroe
Phoenix, AZ 85007-2650

Email: unclaimedproperty@azdor.gov
Phone: (602) 364-0380
Toll Free: 1-877-492 -9957
Fax: (602) 542-2089

Arkansas

Website Address
http://arkansas.gov/auditor/unclprop
https://www.ark.org/auditor/unclprop/index.html

Mailing Address:
Arkansas Unclaimed Property
1401 West Capitol Avenue, Suite 325
Little Rock, AR 72201

Phone: (501) 682-6000
Fax: (501) 683-4285

California

Website Address
http://www.sco.ca.gov

Mailing Address:
Unclaimed Property Division
P.O. Box 942850,
Sacramento, CA 94250-5873

Street Address
Public Counter: Overnight Mail
Unclaimed Property Division
10600 White Rock Road, Suite 141,
Rancho Cordova, CA 95670

Phone: (916) 323-2827
Fax: (916) 323-2827
Toll Free: (800) 992-4647

Colorado

Website Address
http://www.**colorado.gov**/treasury

Mailing Address:
The Great Colorado Payback Office
1580 Logan St., Ste. 500
Denver, CO 80203

Phone: (303) 866-6070
Toll Free: (800) 825-2111
Fax: (303) 866-6154

Connecticut

Website Address
http://www.state.ct.us/ott
http://www.ctbiglist.com/

Mailing Address:

Office Of State Treasurer
Unclaimed Property
55 Elm Street

Hartford, CT 06106

Email: state.treasurer@ct.gov
Fax: (860) 702-3044
Toll Free: (800) 618-3404

Delaware

Website Address
http://revenue.delaware.gov/information

Mailing Address:
Delaware Division of Revenue
Bureau of Unclaimed Property
P.O. Box 8931
Wilmington, DE 19899

Email: Escheat.claimquestions@state.de.us
Phone: (302) 577-8782.
Fax: (302) 577-8656
Toll Free: 1-800-292-7826. (Delaware only)
Toll Free: 1-800-828-0632. (Outside Delaware)

Florida

Website Address
http://www.**fltreasurehunt.org**

Mailing Address:
Unclaimed Property
Post Office Box 8599,
Tallahassee, FL 32314-8599

Street Address
Florida Department of Financial Services ·
Bureau of Unclaimed Property
200 East Gaines Street,
Tallahassee, FL 32399-0358

Email:
FloridaUnclaimedProperty@MyFloridaCFO.com
Phone: (850)413-5555
Toll Free: (888) 258-2253
Fax: (850) 413-3017

Guam

Treasurer Of Guam

PO Box 884
Agana, GU 96910

Email: ypereira@mail.com
Phone: (671-475-1122
Fax: (671) 475-1243

Georgia

Website Address
http://etax.dor.ga.gov/ptd/ucp/index.aspx

Mailing Address:
Georgia Department of Revenue
Unclaimed Property Program
4245 International Parkway , Suite A
Hapeville, Georgia 30354

Email: ucpmail@dor.ga.gov
Phone: (404)968-0490
Fax: (404) 968-0772

Hawaii

Website Address
http://www.**unclaimedproperty.hawaii.gov**
http://pahoehoe.ehawaii.gov/lilo/app

Mailing Address:
State of Hawaii
Unclaimed Property Program
P.O. Box 150
Honolulu, Hawaii 96810

Street Address
No. 1 Capitol District Building
250 South Hotel Street, Room 304
Honolulu, Hawaii 96813

Phone: (808) 586-1589
Fax: (808) 586-1644
Toll Free: (800) 974-4000 (Hawaii only)
Toll Free: (800) 274-3141 (Kauai only)
Toll Free: (800) 984-2400 (Maui only)
Toll Free: (800) 468-4644 (Lanai & Molokai only)

Idaho

Website Address
http://www.sto.idaho.gov/UnclaimedProperty/
http://www.accessidaho.org/apps/tax/ucpsearch

Mailing Address:
Idaho State Tax Commission
Unclaimed Property
P.O. Box 83720
Boise, Idaho 83720-9101

Street Address
Idaho State Tax Commission
Unclaimed Property
304 N. 8th St., Suite 208
Boise, Idaho 83702

Email: UCPGeneralQuestions@sto.idaho.gov
Phone: (208) 332-2942
Toll Free: (877) 388-2942
Fax: (208) 332-2970

Illinois

Website Address
http://www.**treasurer.il.gov**
http://www.cashdash.net

Mailing Address:
Office of State Treasurer
Unclaimed Property Division
P.O. Box 19495
Springfield, IL 62794-9495

Email: info@cashdash.net
Phone: (217) 785-6998
Fax: (217) 557-5871

Indiana

Website Address
www.**indianaunclaimed.com**

Mailing Address:
Attorney General's Office
Unclaimed Property Division
PO Box 2504
Greenwood, IN 46142

Email: upd@atg.state.in.us
Toll Free: (866) 462-5246

Iowa

Website Address
https://www.greatiowatreasurehunt.com

Mailing Address:
Great Iowa Treasure Hunt
Lucas State Office Building
321 E. 12th St., 1st Floor.
Des Moines, IA 50319

Email: foundit@iowa.gov
Phone: (515) 281-5367
Fax: (515) 242-6962

Kansas

Website Address
http://www.**kansascash.com**

Property Search
See Website

Mailing Address:
Kansas State Treasurer
Unclaimed Property Division
900 SW Jackson, Suite 201
Topeka, KS 66612-0386

Email: Unclaimed@treasurer.ks.gov
Phone: (785) 296-4165
Fax: (785) 296-7950
Toll Free: (800) 432-0386 (Ask To Check Your Name)

Kentucky

Website Address
http://www.kentucky.gov
https://secure.kentucky.gov/treasury/unclaimedProperty/Default.aspx

Mailing Address:
Office of State Treasurer
1050 US Highway 127 South, Suite 100
Frankfort, Kentucky 40601

Phone: (502) 564-4722
Toll Free: (800) 465-4722
Fax: (502) 564-6545

Louisiana

Website Address
http://www.treasury.state.la.us

Mailing Address:
Unclaimed Property Division
P.O. Box 91010 301
Main Street 7th Floor
Baton Rouge, LA 70821

Street Address
Louisiana Department of the Treasury
Unclaimed Property Division
626 Main Street
Baton Rouge, LA 70801

Email:
http://www.treasury.state.la.us/HomePages/contactForm.aspx
Phone: (225) 219-9400
Fax: (225) 342-0046
Toll Free: (888) 925-4127

Maine

Website Address
http://www.**maine.gov**/treasurer/unclaimed_property

Mailing Address:
Unclaimed Property
39 State House Station,
Augusta, ME 04333-0039

Street Address
Unclaimed Property
3rd FL Cross Office Building, 111 Sewall St,
Augusta, ME 04330

Phone: 207-624-7470
Toll Free: (888) 283-2808 (Maine only)
Phone TTY: (207) 624-7630
Fax: (207) 287-2367

Maryland

Website Address
https://interactive.marylandtaxes.com/Individuals/Unclaim/default.aspx

Mailing Address:
State Office Bldg.
301 W. Preston Street,, Room 206
Baltimore, MD 21201-2384

Email: unclaim@comp.state.md.us
Phone: (410) 767-1700
Fax: (410) 333-7150
Toll Free: (800) 782-7383

Massachusetts

Website Address
http://abpweb.tre.state.ma.us/abp

Mailing Address:
Department of the State Treasurer
Commonwealth of Massachusetts
Abandoned Property Division
One Ashburton Place, 12th Floor
Boston, MA 02108-1608

Email: abp@tre.state.ma.us
Phone: (617) 367-0400
Fax: (617) 248-3944
Toll Free: 1-888-344-MASS (Massachusetts only)

Michigan

Website Address
http://www.michigan.gov/treasury

Mailing Address:
Michigan Department of Treasury
Unclaimed Property Division
P.O. Box 30756
Lansing, MI 48909

Phone: (517) 636-5320
Fax: (517) 322-5986

Minnesota

Website Address
http://www.commerce.state.mn.us
http://www.state.mn.us/portal/mn

Mailing Address:
Minnesota Department Of Commerce
Unclaimed Property Division
85 7th Place East, Suite 600
St. Paul, MN 55101-3165

Email: unclaimed.property@state.mn.us
Phone: (651) 296-2568
Fax: (651) 284-4108

Mississippi

Website Address
http://www.**treasury.state.ms.us/Unclaimed**

Mailing Address:
Unclaimed Property Division
Mississippi State Treasurer
PO Box 138
Jackson, MS 39205.

Phone: (601).359.3600
Fax: (601) 359.2001

Missouri

Website Address
http://www.**treasurer.mo.gov**

Mailing Address:
State Treasurer's Office
Unclaimed Property Division
PO Box 1004
Jefferson City, MO 65102-1004

Phone: (573) 751-0123
Fax: (573) 751-0343

Montana

Website Address
http://revenue.mt.gov/forbusinesses
http://mt.gov/revenue/programsandservices

Mailing Address:
Department Of Revenue
Unclaimed Property
PO Box 5805
Helena, MT 59604-5805

Street Address
Department Of Revenue
Unclaimed Property
2517 Airport Road
Helena, MT 59601-1237

Phone: (406) 444-6900
Phone TDD: (406) 444-2830 (Telephone Device for the Deaf)
Toll Free: (866) 859-2254
Fax: (406) 444-0722

Nebraska

Website Address
http://www.treasurer.state.ne.us

Mailing Address:
Unclaimed Property Division
PO Box 94788
Lincoln, NE 68509

Street Address
Office Of The State Treasurer
Unclaimed Property Division
809 P. Street
Lincoln, NE 68508

Email: nst.upclaims@nebraska.gov
Phone: (402) 471-5729
Fax: (402) 471-4390
Toll Free: (877) 572-9688
Toll Free: (800) 742-7474 (NE & IA only)

Nevada

Website Address
https://nevadatreasurer.gov/UnclaimedProperty.htm

Mailing Address:
Unclaimed Property Division
Office of the State Treasurer

Grant Sawyer Building
555 E. Washington Ave, Suite 4200
Las Vegas, Nevada 89101

Email:
unclaimedproperty@nevadatreasurer.gov
Phone: (702) 486-4140
Fax: (702) 486-4177
Toll Free: (800) 521-0019 (Nevada only)

New Hampshire

Website Address
www.**nh.gov**/treasury/Divisions/AP/APindex.htm

Mailing Address:
State of New Hampshire Treasury
Unclaimed Property Division
25 Capitol Street, Room 121
Concord, NH 03301

Email: treasury@treasury.state.nh.us
Phone: (603) 271-2621
Fax: (603) 271-3922

New Jersey

Website Address
http://www.unclaimedproperty.nj.gov/
http://www.state.nj.us/treasury/taxation/

Mailing Address:
Office Of The State Treasurer
Unclaimed Property
PO. Box 214
Trenton, NJ 08695-0214

Treasury Address
Department of the Treasury
PO. Box 002
Trenton, NJ 08625-0002

Email:
https://state.nj.us/treas/unclaimedproperty.shtml
Phone: (609) 292-9200
Fax: (609) 984-0593

New Mexico

Website Address
http://state.nm.us
https://ec3state.nm.us/ucp

Mailing Address:
Taxation & Revenue Department
Unclaimed Property Division
P.O. Box 25123
Santa Fe, NM 87504-5123

Email: uproperty@state.nm.us
Phone: (505) 476-1774

New York

Website Address
http://www.**osc.state.ny.us**

Mailing Address:
Office of the State Comptroller
Office of Unclaimed Funds
110 State Street
Albany, New York 12236

Email: NYSOUF@osc.state.ny.us
Fax: (518) 473-2177
Toll Free: (800) 221-9311

North Carolina

Website Address
https://www.nctreasurer.com/DstHome/AdminSe
rvices/UnclaimedProperty

Mailing Address:
Department of State Treasurer
Escheat & Unclaimed Property
325 N. Salisbury Street
Raleigh, NC 27603

Email: unclaimed.property@nctreasurer.com
Phone: (919)-508-1000
Fax: (919) 508-5167

North Dakota

Website Address
http://www.**land.nd.gov**/abp/abphome.htm

Mailing Address:
Unclaimed Property Division
North Dakota State Land Dept.
PO Box 5523
1707 N 9th St.
Bismarck, ND 58506-5523

Email: llfisher@nd.gov
Phone: (701)-328-2800
Fax: (701)-328-3650

Ohio

Website Address
http://www.**com.ohio.gov**/unfd

Mailing Address:
The Ohio Department of Commerce
Division of Unclaimed Funds
77 South High Street, 20th Floor
Columbus, Ohio 43215-6108

Email: unfd.claims@com.state.oh.us
Phone: (614) 466-4433
Fax: (614) 752-5078
Toll Free: (877) 644-6823

Oklahoma

Website Address
http://www.ok.gov/unclaimed

Mailing Address:
Oklahoma State Treasurer
Unclaimed Property Division
4545 N. Lincoln Blvd., Ste. 106
Oklahoma City , OK 73105-3413

Email: Unclaimed@treasurer.ok.gov
Phone: (405) 521-4273

Oregon

Website Address
http://www.oregon.gov/DSL/UP/index.shtml

Mailing Address:

Department of State Lands
Unclaimed Property Section
775 Summer St. NE Suite 100
Salem, OR 97301-1279

Email: claims@dsl.state.or.us
Phone: (503)-986-5200
Fax: (503)-378-4844

Pennsylvania

Website Address
http://www.**patreasury.org/Unclaimed**

Mailing Address:
Treasurer Department
Bureau Of Unclaimed Property
PO Box 1837
Harrisburg, PA 17105-1837

Street Address
Pennsylvania Treasury
129 Finance Building
Harrisburg, PA 17120

Email: tupmail@patreasury.org
Phone: (717) 787-2465
Fax: (717) 787-9079
Toll Free: (800) 222-2046

Puerto Rico

Website Address
http://www.ocif.gobierno.pr/unclaimedeng

Mailing Address:
Office Of The Commissioner Of Financial
Institutions
PO Box 11855
San Juan, PR 00910-3855

Email: comisionado@ocif.gobierno.pr
Phone: (787) 723-3131

Rhode Island

Website Address
http://www.**treasury.ri.gov**/unclaimedproperty

Mailing Address:
Office of the General Treasurer
Unclaimed Property Division
P.O. Box 1435
Providence, RI 02901

Email: ups@treasury.ri.gov

Phone: (401) 222-6505
Phone TDD: (401) 222-3399
Fax: (401) 274-3865

South Carolina

Website Address
http://treasurer.sc.gov/palm_payb_prog_uncla_p
rop
http://www.**state.sc.us**/treas/AS/Accounting/UP
P/as_upp_index.htm

Mailing Address:
State Treasurer's Office
Unclaimed Property Program
PO Box 11778
Columbia, SC 29211

Street Address
State Treasurer's Office
Unclaimed Property Program
Wade Hampton Building, Rm. 224
1200 Senate Street
Columbia, SC 29201

Email: payback@sto.sc.gov
Phone: (803) 737-4771
Fax: (803) 734-2668

South Dakota

Website Address
http://www.**sdtreasurer.gov**

Mailing Address:
Office Of The State Treasurer
Unclaimed Property
500 E. Capitol Ave.,
Pierre, SD 57501-5070

Phone: (605) 773-3379 (Unclaimed property)
Phone: (605) 773-3378 (State Treasurer)

Toll Free: (866) 357-2547 (South Dakota only)

Tennessee

Website Address
http://www.**tn.gov**/treasury/unclaim
http://treasury.state.tx.us/unclaim

Mailing Address:
Unclaimed Property Division
502 Deaderick St
Nashville, TN 37243-0203

Email: UCP.Information@tn.gov
Phone: (615) 741-6499

Texas

Website Address
http://www.window.state.tx.us/up

Mailing Address:
Texas Comptroller of Public Accounts
Unclaimed Property Division
Research and Correspondence Section
P.O. Box 12046
Austin, Texas 78711-2046

Email: unclaimed.property@cpa.state.tx.us
Toll Free: 1-800-**654-FIND (3463)**
Phone: (512) 463-3120
Note: there is a limit of three name searches
when calling by phone.

Fax: (512) 936-6224
Toll Free Fax: (888) 908-9991

Utah

Website Address
http://www.**up.utah.gov**

Mailing Address
State Treasurer's Office
Unclaimed Property Division
341 South Main Street, 5th Floor
Salt Lake City, UT 84111

Mailing Address:

Utah Unclaimed Property
PO Box 140530,
Salt Lake City, UT 84114-0530.

Email: ucprop@utah.gov
Phone: (801) 320-5360
Toll Free: (888) 217-1203
Fax: (801) 533-4096

Vermont

Website Address
http://www.vermonttreasurer.gov

Mailing Address:
State Treasurer's Office
Unclaimed Property Division
109 State Street, 4th Floor
Montpelier, VT 05609-6200

Email: unclaimed.property@state.vt.us
Phone: (802) 828-2301
Phone: (802) 828-2407 (Unclaimed Property Questions)
Fax: (802) 828-2772
Toll Free: (800) 642-3191 (Vermont only)
Toll Free TTY: (800) 253-0191

Virgin Islands

Us Virgin Islands Office Of The Lieutenant
Governor
Division Of Banking
18 Kongens Gade
St. Thomas, VA 00802

Phone: (340) 774-7166

Virginia

Website Address
http://www.trs.virginia.gov/Ucp
http://www.VaMoneySearch.org

Mailing Address:
Virginia Department of the Treasury
Division of Unclaimed Property
P.O. Box 2478
Richmond, VA 23218-2478

Street Address
Virginia Department of the Treasury •
101 North 14th Street •
Richmond, VA 23219 •
(804) 225-2142

Phone: (804) 225-2142
Toll Free: -(800) 468-1088

Washington

Website Address
http://ucp.dor.wa.gov

Mailing Address:
Department of Revenue
Unclaimed Property Section
PO Box 47477
Olympia, WA 98504-7477

Phone: (360) 705-6706
Fax: (360) 586-2163
Toll Free: (800) 435-2429

West Virginia

Website Address
http://www.**wvsto.com**/dept/UP/Pages/default.a
spx

Mailing Address:
West Virginia State Treasurer's Office
Unclaimed Property Division
One Players Club Drive
Charleston, West Virginia 25311

Phone: (304) 558-2937
Fax: (304) 558-4835
Toll Free: (800) 642-8687

Wisconsin

Website Address
http://www.**statetreasury.wisconsin.gov**
http://www.ost.state.wi.us/home/

Mailing Address:
Office Of The State Treasurer
Unclaimed Property Division
P.O. Box 2114.
Madison, WI 53701-2114.

Street Address
Wisconsin Office of the State Treasurer
P.O. Box 7871 •
Madison, Wisconsin 53707

Email: OSTUnclaimedProperty@wisconsin.gov
Phone: (608) 267-7977
Toll Free: (877) 699-9211
Fax: (608) 261-6799

Washington District Of Columbia

Website Address
http://cfo.dc.gov

Mailing Address:
Office of Finance and Treasury
Unclaimed Property Office
1350 Pennsylvania Avenue, NW, Suite 203
Washington, DC 20004

Email: dcunclaimed.property@dc.gov
Phone: (202) 442-8181
Fax: (202) 442-8180

Wyoming

Website Address
http://treasurer.state.wy.us/uphome.asp

Mailing Address:
Wyoming Unclaimed Property
2515 Warren Avenue, Suite 502
Cheyenne, WY 82002

Phone: (307) 777-5590
Fax: (307) 777-5430

Chapter 3

Business Basics

Now you are on your way to making big money by returning lost money to the rightful owners. Here is how the process works. first, you contact your local state office and get a list of unclaimed property owners if they offer a list. The state office can give you a list of all unclaimed owners or they can direct you to a newspaper publishing a list of current unclaimed property owners. Almost every state publishes the accounts in the largest circulation newspapers of every county either once or twice a year. The most popular month for the listings is in February. The lists are found in the Legal Notices section of the newspaper. This chapter contains one newspaper clipping of unclaimed owners.

Now that you have the list of names from your state office, I will help you out by giving you some business tips. The first question is: how much should you charge for your finder's fee?. The ball is in your court—you can charge whatever you think is fair, but what the states do have laws regarding how much money you can charge in finder fees. The states do limit finders from 5% to 25%. Check with each state for their rules and criteria for returning lost unclaimed property to the rightful owners.

After you find a particular individual you should contact him or her either by phone or mail. You would then explain to this person that they will receive a check for a sum of money if he or she signs and notarizes the contract you are sending them. Notarization is done by a public notary. All real estate offices can direct you to a public notary or you can look public notary in the yellow pages. After the person signs the contract, you will then send the information to the state and they will tell you what further information they need to process the claim. This is so easy. Do this and you'll have money in your pocket in a matter of weeks.

Some states won't release how much money is in the account until they know you have found the right person. What you tell the claimant is that you need a copy of their driver's license and/or social security number when they send the contract back to you so that initial verification can be made.

One State Requires:

- Social Security Number or Federal ID Number of the claimant(s)

- Address (Including City, State, and Zip code) of the claimant(s)

- Notarized claim form, if the property is a Safe Deposit Box, Stock, or worth in excess of $500.00

Gall, Brenda Humstone, Address Unknown

Gallegos, Luigi, 148-27 61st Rd., Flushing, NY

Garner, Charles E., Add. Ukn.

Gavin, Audrey c/o Philip Gavin, Esq., 104-26 Jamaica Avenue, Richmond Hill, NY 11418

Gene Frankel Theatre Workshop Inc. (The), Address Unknown

German, Emilio & Giovanna German, Wavecrest Drive, Mastic Beach, NY 11951

Gerodias, Maurine Assoc. Inc., Address Unknown

Giampontzef, Irene, 3 Box 268, Farmingdale, NJ 07727

Gibson, Mamie L., Address Ukn.

Gilbert, Timothy A., Add. Ukn.

Giordano, Linda A., 2044 21st Dr., Brooklyn, NY 11214

Gislason, Kristjan, 4218 Sonnierlok, Toledo, Ohio 43606

Gittens, Marjorie, 172-12 71st Ave., Flushing, NY 11365

Gladden, Earle, Address Ukn.

Glenmore Chrome Co., 157-16 Northern Blvd., Flushing, NY 11358

Gleitsman, Rael, P.O. Box 14, Foster Center, Rhode Island

Glenwood Fabrics, 80 Beckwith Ave., Patterson, NJ 07502

Global Aquatics Ltd., 1419 Neck Road, Brooklyn, NY 11229

Globe Motor Car Co., 1230 Bloomfield Ave., Fairfield. NJ 07006

Globus, Helen, Address Unknown

Goings, Alvin, Address Unknown

Gold Seal Vinemards, Add. Ukn.

Gold, Sonia, 2340 Linwood Ave., Fort Lee, NJ 07024

Golden, Riva L., Address Ukn.

Goldfarb, Morton M. D., Address Unknown

Gonzales, John, Address Unknown

Gonzalez, Antonio, Address Ukn.

Gordon, Dennis, 170 Varick St., New York, NY

Gordon, T. John, Address Ukn.

Goresiglio, Gertrude G., Address Unknown

Govatzidaki, Sofia, 33 Bayville Ave., Bayville, NY 11709

Granados, Pedro, 1443 Hildala Courtiepland, Cal. 91786

Great Adventure Inc., 320 E. 65th Street, New York, NY 10021

Great Eastern Linens, 25 Saddle River, Garfield, NJ 07026

Green, Anne E., 140-26 184 St., Springfield Gardens, NY

Greene, Jimmi, 90 Manor Dr., Great Neck, NY

Gropper, Fred, Address Unknown

Grosch, David L., 742 W. Bristol, Elkhart, Ind. 46514

Grossman, Nathan, 52 East 52nd St., Brooklyn, NY 11212

Grumapple Cafe Inc., 628 W. 52nd St., New York, NY 10019

Grune & Stratton, 111 Fifth Ave., New York, NY 10003

Guill, John, Address Unknown

Gutierrez, Jose F., Address Ukn.

Guzman, Carlos, Address Ukn.

H. F. D. Inc., Linden Plaza, 1111 W. St. Georges Ave., Linden, NJ 07036

Kristen, James, 893 Brooklyn Ave., Brooklyn, NY 11203

Krusher, Henry L. Foundation Inc., 25 W. 43rd St., NY 10036

Kunzig, Richard J., Add. Ukn.

Lack, Dorothy, Address Unknown

Ladies Aux of Prophet Elizah, American Orthodox Catholic Church-Bingo, 1610 Lexington Avenue, New York, NY

Lady Fair, 510 Franklin Avenue, Nutley, NJ 07110

Lady Vivian of The Village, 101 West 12th St., New York, NY

Laird, Bissell & Meeds Inc., Address Unknown

Lambray Maureen, Inc., Address Unknown

Larkin, Estelle E., 44 Rockelle St., Staten Island, New York

Laschener, Irving, 50 Brighton 1 Rd., Brooklyn, NY 11235

Laspada, E., Address Unknown

Laurel Lamp Mfg. Co., Address Unknown

Layanconpanion, Thomas, Address Unknown

Leavin, Gabrielle, Address Ukn.

Leddy, Mary B., Address Ukn.

Leeds, Grace L., Address Ukn.

Leiberman, John, Address Ukn.

Lerman, Rose, Address Unknown

Lesher, Maryon, Address Ukn.

Lessman, Lieschotte, Add. Ukn.

Levenson, Frances, 420 Central Park W., New York, NY 10025

Levesque, O'Rula, Address Ukn.

Lewie, Marjorie, 18-65 211th Ave., Bayside, NY 11360

Lezette, Richard, Address Ukn.

Liberty Travel, 135 West 41st, New York, NY

Lichter, Norman, Coin Process Center, 7425 Cirrack

Lilitizoh, Robert F., 250 W. 135th Street

Lin, Ryun Hee, c/o Mr. Hinder, 619 Sadler Street, Aberdeen, Maryland

Linen, Jahathan Scrantan, Address Unknown

Loews Clearing Corp., Hotels Tenant, Address Unknown

Lofton, Douglas, 757 Schnenk Avenue, Brooklyn, NY 11207

Locaripe, Donald, 1920 McGraw Avenue

Loveman, Mr. & Mrs., Add. Ukn.

Lumadue, Charles R., Add. Ukn.

Lurey Alpha Hairdressers, Inc., 490 Sixth Ave., New York, NY 10011

Lynch R. J. Co., 24 William Street, Staten Island, NY 10304

M.P. Card & Book Shops, Inc., Spruce St., Ramsey, NJ 07446

MacDonald, Lorraine M., Address Unknown

Mack, Adele F., Address Ukn.

Mac Kinnon, William, Add. Ukn.

Mahoney, J. & J. Address Ukn.

Mammon, Jack, 4206 12th Ave.

Mams, Hannah Shirley, 876 East 223rd Street, Bronx, NY

Mansley, D., Address Unknown

Manway, Damar, c/o Manway Construcion Co., 161-10 Jamaica Ave., Jam., NY 11432

Parish Securities Corp., Address Unknown

Parker, Edward O., 120-16 172nd Street, Jamaica, NY 11434

Parkes, Alice, 1429 Carroll Street, Brooklyn, NY 11213

Parotta, Joseph D., Address Ukn.

Paschetto, Robert W. / Cecilia, 130-07 59th Ave., Flushing, NY

Pascuiti, Pearl, 2166 Allan Ave., Yorktown Heights, NY 10598

Passalasqua, Deborah, Add. Ukn.

Patterson, Ethel, 200 Cozine St., Brooklyn, NY 11207

Patterson, Gussie A., 2160 Seward Avenue, Bronx, New York

Paulino, Romulo Miguel, Address Unknown

Pelletiere, Sal, Address Unknown

Penjola, C., Address Unknown

Peracasa, Veronica, Hotel Pierre, 5th Ave. & 61st St., New York, NY

Perez, Esther, 112-44 197th St., Hollis, NY 11412

Perez, Francisco, 89-15 Parsons Blvd., Jamaica, NY 11432

Pergament, Penny, Address Ukn.

Perkins, D. L., Address Unknown

Perlez, J., A.P.A., 13 East 10th St., NY

Permanent Mission of Guinea to U.N., United Nations, New York, NY

Perry, Harold C., Address Ukn.

Persepolis Chartering, Add. Ukn.

Pester, Goldberg & Schiff, Address Unknown

Phillips, Arthur L., Add. Ukn.

Phoenix Shipping Co. Inc., 105 Washington St., New York

Pickeus, Lon, Address Unknown

Pierce, Bruce, 701 Cleveland St., Brooklyn, NY 11208

Pierro, Gloria, 33-34th St., Brooklyn, NY

Pilgrim Baptist Cathedral (The), Address Unknown

Pine Rd. Estates Corp., Add. Ukn.

Piscapo, A. B., 16 Lake Gilead Rd., Carmel, NY 10512

Pitgairn, William S., Add. Ukn.

Piton, Jacqueline AnneMarie, 223-46 112th Rd., Queens Village, New York 11429

Pittman, David L., 1 Christopher St.

Pizzaro, Eugenia L., Add. Ukn.

Platt, Ronald L., Address Ukn.

Pleshette, Norman, Add. Ukn.

Ploss, Leon, Address Uknown

Pool, Priscilla, Address Unknown

Porcu, Joseph J., Address Ukn.

Porcu, Rose A., Address Ukn.

Pres, Karl Preuss, 283 Medford Ave., Patchogue, NY 11772

Priggen Photography Inc., Address Unknown

Promenade Cafe, Rock. Center, NY 10017

Prophet Elizah American Ort. Catholic Church Sp. Bingo, 1610 Lex. Ave., New York, NY

Protection Ins. Agcy Inc., Address Unknown

Puccino, Roslyn, 245-38 149th Ave., Rosedale, NY 11422

Pummer, Mendel, Address Ukn.

Quigley, Donald F., Add. Ukn.

New York newspaper listing of unclaimed property owners.

Tell the people that you contact, that your source (the state) will release an amount of money and you will tell them what it is once that verification is made. Some states won't allow you to share one-quarter with the property owner you've found. Some attorneys charge one third of the amount. Check with a lawyer if you are unsure of regulations in your state. I have included a guideline for drawing up the contract between you and the unclaimed property owner, but be sure you check with a lawyer first to make sure everything in your contract is legal—as you know each state is different.

Once you have the "unclaimed property names", the next step is contacting the person on your list. Here is a sample conversation for you to study In my experience of contacting unclaimed property owners, this is how a typical conversation would go:

Conversation

You: May I speak to Mr. John Doe?

John: Hello. This is he.

You: Hello, Mr. Doe. This is Tom Peters with People Finders here in San Diego.

John: What can I do for you?

You: We have come across $36,000 that we have assisted in obtaining for you.

John: Wait a minute, I don't have $36,000 coming to me.

You: Mr. Doe, haven't you heard of wealthy people leaving money behind to people that didn't even know them.

You: Well this could even be your own money that you forgot about.

John: Yes.

You: Well, Mr. Doe, this money is definitely yours; however, I can't tell you the source of this money at this point.

John: Are you telling me the truth? Is this some type of crank?

You: I assure you, Mr. Doe, that everything I am telling you is the complete truth.

John: I could sure use that money. What do I have to do to get it?

You: Mr. Doe, I will be sending you a form in the mail. All you have to do is sign the form and the money is yours.

John: That is all I have to do?

You: Yes, Mr. Doe. Is your correct address 1212 Folly Lane, San Diego, California, 92345?

John: No. It's 7865 Rockherst Street, San Diego, California, 92120.

You: All right. You'll find everything in the form exactly the way I explained it to you. If you have any questions, you're welcome to call me at 858-567-4564.

John: Okay.

You: Mr. Doe, it is very important that you send this form signed and dated back to me as quickly as possible. The sooner I get the form, the sooner you will have your money.

John: Thank you, and I'll be speaking to you soon. You: You're welcome. Goodbye.

The Contract

Below is a guideline for the contract between you (the Investigator) and the person whose property you've recovered (the Claimant):

Investigator Agreement/Contract

Claimant _____
Address _____
Reported _____
Social Security Number _____ — _____
Type of Account _____ Amount _____
Stock _____

I

This agreement is entered into by and between

_____

hereinafter referred to as "Claimant's and

_____

hereinafter referred to as Investigator.

II

The Investigator, through his/her efforts, has located claimant, who will be entitled to the below described assets.

_____

_____

III

Investigator and Claimant do hereby agree that in consideration of Investigator's efforts in locating Claimant and assisting in the actual recovery of the above described assets to Which Claimant is entitled, Claimant hereby assigns to the Investigator a set fee of $_____ for expenses and services rendered, providing Claimant recovers described assets.

IV

Investigator and Claimant agree that in the event Claimant is not entitled to assets described above and such assets are not recovered, there is no obligation on either party to the other.

This agreement is void unless executed by both parties.

Investigator_____
Phone_____   Address_____
_____
Date   Investigator's Signature

Claimant _____
Phone_____   Address_____
_____
Date   Claimant Signature

Sample Contract Instructions

In this sample contract, the reported line is to be filled in with the year that the bank or insurance company reported the money to the state. If you live in a state that doesn't release the information about the account, then you should leave off the type of account and amount of money. The state wouldn't expect you to know this if they haven't revealed this information. Even a person finding his own account wouldn't know what it was, if he just saw his name in the newspaper.

If the amounts of money aren't given to you, then you will also need to specify the percentage of the account that you will be receiving instead of listing the actual amount, since you don't know what it is. You will need to modify section three to specify the percentage of your share.

It would be a good idea to get the contract looked over by an attorney. Unclaimed property laws change from state to state, so it is important that you abide with the state laws that regulate unclaimed property in your state. The contract in this chapter contains a good guideline for you to follow.

Another regulation which changes is the need for a private investigator's license. There are some states that require certain types of license to recover unclaimed property for people.

When The Contract Is Returned To You

After you have received the contract signed and returned to you, continue with the next step. You would contact the state unclaimed property office and send them a copy of your signed contract as well as the identification that is needed to prove that the person you found is indeed the person that owns the unclaimed money

When they receive your paperwork, they will send you forms to fill out. After you fill out these forms, they in turn will send a check in the mail. Depending on the state, the check may be sent to you or to the claimant. Some states will send the check to you but in the claimant's name to make sure everybody gets their money. You will have to ask your state office how they write their checks. It is as easy as that.

Chapter 4

Tracking Down The Address

Now that you have the list of names of people that are owed money from the state, you must then find these missing people. The list you will receive from the state will give you the full name, address and type of account of the unclaimed property. You can now be a private investigator. It's not difficult to be an investigator, if you know what to do. In the next few chapters, I will tell you exactly how to find the person or persons you are searching for.

In most cases, these people are no longer living at the address you will receive from the state. But you never know where these people live. Send a letter to the address you have on record and see what happens. If someone is living at that address, contact these people and ask them for the whereabouts of the people you are searching for.

How do you find out who is living at that address? You can find the person through the post office, with telephone directories, city directories, plot maps, or the Department of Motor Vehicles (DMV) records or even the internet.. If you can't find the people you are searching for on the internet, you will have to use the other methods of searching for people. Use the internet first before using the other methods of finding people. Use the websites in the following section. Don't rely in the internet. It is so hard to find certain people on the internet. In many cases the internet is unreliable and old archaic methods, like visiting libraries or state offices are good for finding people.

Finding People On The Internet.

Go to the following websites to find people on the internet. Keep trying these free websites to find the address of the person you are looking for. After you have found the address write this person a letter with your commission agreement. You may also choose to call this person. You can use the internet to find this person's phone number in order to call this person over the phone. The websites are numbered from one to ten. Use any of these web sites in order to find a person with unclaimed property.

Ten Web Sites To Find People On The Internet

Number	Internet Web Site
1	www.zabasearch.com
2	www.Intelius.com

3	**www.publicrecordfinder.com**
4	**www.whitepages.com**
5	**www.facebook.com/find-friends**
6	**www.pipl.com**
7	**www.people.yahoo.com**
8	**www.usa-people-search.com**
9	**www.peoplefinders.com**
10	**www.whowhere.com**

How To Manually Obtain Address And Phone Numbers.

The United States Post Office

The United States Post Office delivers mail to every address in the United States. They know where everyone lives. You may be able to get the address you need through your local post office. There is a good chance the person you are looking for is no longer at the current address. This doesn't even present a problem if you handle it correctly.

1.) Send a letter to the last known address of the person you are searching for and write on the letter 'DO NOT FORWARD' and 'ADDRESS CORRECTION REQUESTED'. The cost for this service is fifty cents.

2.) Go to the United States Postal Service website: http://usps.whitepages.com/post_office. Do either a people search or a business search. You may be able to find your person through the USPS website.

3.) Look up the person you are searching for either through the white pages or a white page web site. The USPS web site is a white page website. The web site address is: http://usps.whitepages.com/post_office. If you have a partial address from the white pages that is missing a zip code go to the USPS website to find the zip code. The web site to find zip codes is http://zip4.usps.com/zip4/welcome.jsp. You will need the zip code to mail a letter to this person.

4.) You can send a registered letter to the person to get the letter mailed, but this method is expensive. A registered letter is recorded and tracked through it's time in the mail system. To deliver a registered letter a signature is required. The person you are looking for must sign the letter. Many legal paper and even contracts are sent registered. Items you send with Registered Mail are placed under tight security from the point of mailing to the point of delivery, and insured up to $25,000 against loss or damage. A registered letter will motivate the people at the post office to work on your case sooner.

5.) Got to the post office and ask for the current address of the person for which you are searching.

Directories

You will probably be able to find the person you are looking for by simply looking through the phone book. If you can't find the person you are looking for in your current phone book, look in older editions of that phone book. Older editions are available in public libraries or on the internet.   Librarians can tell you where you can find old phone books. You can call ATT to order telephone directories at 1-800-848-8000. The address for ATT is: AT&T, 208 S. Akard Street, Dallas, TX 75202. http://www.att.com.

Don't overlook calling up people with similar surnames of the person you are looking for. You may be surprised how many relatives this person may have in that town. Call up people with similar surnames and ask them first if the person you are looking for resides there. Then ask them if they know of the person you are looking for.

City directories might come in handy, too. They can be of great assistance to you; they can help you find out who is living at a given address. City directory companies find out "door to door" who lives at each address. You may find that their directories are more complete than the phone book directories because they even tell you where people with unlisted numbers live. These directories can be found on the internet or at most public libraries. You may want to look at old city directories. These are available on the internet or at the Library Of Congress, historical societies or some large public libraries. These books are available at a cost of about hundreds a year. If you claim to be with a library that leases the city directories, you can get free information about any address by calling the headquarters these city directories.

Real Estate Plot Maps

Real estate companies have to know who owns every piece of land in every part of this country. No matter what address you find, you will be able to look up the owner on a plot map. These maps are available from any real estate agent or the internet or at your local library. If you have a hard time getting these lists, they are available at no cost from your county assessor's office, or the county office for property taxes or property records. You can find their phone number in the front of the white pages.

Look up the address of the unclaimed owner that you received from the state. On the real estate lot maps you will see the name and address of the owner of the property. The person residing on the property may not necessarily be the owner. He could be renting the address from the owner. Contact the owner either by mail or just look up his phone number and call him. The owner if he is aware of the whereabouts of the person for whom you are searching, may give you the new address. This would be a good lead to follow.

With real estate plot maps you have the ability to look up the person by his address or by his name. Look up the person you are looking for in the town where the person last resided. By doing this, you may be able to find a piece of property that the person owns. If you do find that person, contact him by mail or phone or the internet.

The Departments Of Motor Vehicles

The Department of Motor Vehicles offices of some states have a free address verification service that you may use. If you contact them and give them the address, name and date of birth of the person you are looking for, they will tell you if they have the same address in their records. This service is mainly used by car rental agencies. If you want to use this service, use the DMV list I have provided for you in the next few chapters. Look up the correct state for the address of the unclaimed property owner.

Neighbors, Relatives & Friends

In the previous section I showed you how to find someone you are looking for at a particular address. If you are having a hard time locating a certain individual, you may want to ask the neighbors. They could tell you more in less time than you could find out yourself. There are some people who do very little else but watch their neighbors. These are the people you will want to contact. They love telling you everything they know if you approach them the right way. Contact them preferably by phone and ask them what they know about the person you are looking for. Let us review the methods in contacting neighbors and relatives.

1). You could use the internet websites to search for relatives or people with a similar last names.

2) You could use internet phone books, phone books and the US post office to look up relatives (people with similar last names).

3) You could use real estate plot maps to look up neighbors and landlords of neighbors, then contact them.

Typical Conversation

Here is how a typical conversation would be between you and one of the neighbors. Let's say the person you are looking for is John Peterson.

You: Hello, Mrs. Smith?

Smith: Yes, speaking.

You: Let me introduce myself. My name is John Doe and I'm with the Acme Financial Company. John Smith has money owed to him and I am trying to contact him. Could I ask you a few questions?

Smith: Sure.

You: How long have you known John Peterson?

Smith: I've known him ever since he moved into this building ... must be about six years.

You: Do you know where Mr. Peterson is employed?

Smith: Last I heard he was a high school teacher at Patrick Henry.

You: Do you know where Mr. Peterson's current address is right now?

Smith: He used to live across the street. He now lives on High Park Lane. Somewhere in the 3900 block.

You: Do you happen to have the exact address?

Smith: Hold on. Here it is. It's 3987 High Park Lane, Apt. 307.

You: One more question, Mrs. Smith. Mr. Peterson has left us 697-4865 as his phone number. Do you note the same phone number?

Smith: That's his old phone number; let me give you his new number. It's 467-9874.

You: I want to thank you for your help. You have been very helpful. Have a good day, Mrs. Smith.

Do you see how many leads Mrs. Smith has given you to the whereabouts of John Peterson? Not only will you know where he lives and works, but you will have his phone number. Using this technique will get you a great deal of information.

You may sense aggressiveness when you talk to some people. They may not have liked their old neighbor and would not want to help their old neighbor pass a credit application. If this is the case, tell the person the truth. You may be surprised how much people will help you for your sake and not for their neighbor's sake. If you still have a hard time getting any information from the neighbors, try the delivery man routine.

Go to the neighbor's door in person with a package, addressed to the person you are looking for, in your hands. Make sure the package is personally signed. Let us use John Peterson for this example. Go to the house where John last lived and try to deliver the package. If that person can't help you, go to all the neighbors and ask about John. Explain to the people living there it is an urgent delivery and you must find John. Ask them for a phone number or address. You will be surprised at how helpful neighbors can be. If they don't know very much, ask them for the name and address of a relative or a close friend with whom you could leave the package. One word of caution: do this stunt early or late in the day so that the neighbors are home.

Relatives And Friends

You will find that relatives and friends are more loyal than neighbors. It will be harder to get information from them. I have had success with the credit application story in getting information from relatives and friends. But they ask a lot of questions. You also stand the risk of them not trusting you if you lie to them. If you just want an address, appear at their doorstep with a package. Telling the truth sometimes works if they have a good relationship with the person you are looking for. You will have to use your intuition with friends and relatives for using the best technique. Relatives and good friends are one of the best sources of information you will get, so don't give up on them.

Chapter 5

Get The Government To Help You

The internet websites can sometimes find the person you are looking for. If you are having difficulties you may need to use manual methods to find that unclaimed money person. The government keeps files on everyone that lives in the country. They know where the person you are looking for lives. There is a wealth of information at your local county courthouse. You may be able to find the person you are looking for at the county courthouse. All of the information at the courthouse is supposed to be public information. There may be privacy rules, but you should try. Business registrations like the filing of fictitious names is public information. A fictitious name is a business name a person uses. You should be able to look up the address of a person or a company name.

Ask the clerk at the desk for a file on the person you are looking for or ask the court house clerk to help you search for a person. Look through the file and look to see what address was used. In some cases people use different addresses when they are served a citation other than the address on their driver's license.

There is always the possibility that the person you are looking for has passed away. In this case you would want to know that this person has indeed died. Obituary records are kept at the county clerk's office. If you use the county clerk's office, you must be sure that the person's last known address was in that county. Records are kept from county to county. County records are good.

Social Security Records

The Social Security department can practically reach everybody in the United States. These records can tell you anything you want to know about an individual. The only way you can get someone's records is if you knew someone who worked for the Social Security department. The department is always behind on its records about two to four months.

The Social Security department has one division that will help you out. This division will let you send a letter to any person. They will not give you the address of that person; they will just forward your letter. This comes in really handy so that you could contact a person who owns unclaimed money by mail. Include your phone number and address so that this person can contact you. Get the person excited about the money he will receive and be very honest with him. When you write to the Social Security department, try to include as much information as you can about the person you are looking for.

LETTER FORWARDING FROM SSA

We will attempt to forward a letter to a missing person under circumstances involving a matter of great importance, such as a death or serious illness in the missing person's immediate family, or a sizeable amount of money that is due the missing person. Also, the circumstances must concern a matter about which the missing person is unaware and would undoubtedly want to be informed. (Generally, when a son, daughter, brother, or sister wishes to establish contact, we write to the missing person, rather than forward a letter from the relative.) Because this service is not related in any way to a Social Security program, it's use must be limited so that it does not interfere with our regular program activities.

There is no charge for forwarding letters that have a humanitarian purpose. However, we must charge a $25 (effective July 1, 2001) fee to cover our costs when the letter is to inform the missing person of money or property due him or her. This fee is not refundable. The fee should be paid by a check that is made payable to the Social Security Administration.

We must read each letter we forward to ensure that it contains nothing that could prove embarrassing to the missing person if read by a third party. We do not believe that it would be proper to open a sealed letter; therefore, a letter that is sent to us for forwarding should be in a plain, unstamped, unsealed envelope showing only the missing person's name. Nothing of value should be enclosed.

To try to locate an address in our records, we need the missing person's Social Security number or identifying information to help us find the number. The identifying information needed is the person's date and place of birth, the father's name, and the mother's full birth name.

Usually, we forward a letter in care of the employer who most recently reported earnings for the missing person. We normally would have the current home address only if the person is receiving benefits. Therefore, we cannot assure that a letter will be delivered or that a reply will be received. Also, we cannot send a second letter.
Requests for letter forwarding should be sent to:

Social Security Administration
Letter Forwarding
P.O. Box 33022
Baltimore, MD 21290-3022

Social Security Prefixes

If you have the Social Security number of the person you are looking for, you may be able to use their prefix. By prefix I mean the first three numbers of a Social Security number. This prefix will show you what location this person is from. Sometimes people go back to the state they came from. If a person last resided in Kansas and his Social Security number is from New York, this person may be living in New York.

SSN	STATE
001-003	NEW HAMPSHIRE
004-007	MAINE
008-009	VERMONT
010-034	MASSACH USETTS
035-039	RHODE ISLAND
040-049	CONNECTICUT
050-134	NEW YORK

135-158	NEW JERSEY
159-211	PENNSYLVANIA
212-220	MARYLAND
221-222	DELAWARE
223-231	VIRGINIA
232-236	WEST VIRGINIA
232	NORTH CAROLINA
237-246	NORTH CAROLINA
247-251	SOUTH CAROLINA
252-260	GEORGIA
261-267	FLORIDA
268-302	OHIO
303-317	INDIANA
318-361	ILLINOIS
362-386	MICHIGAN
387-399	WISCONSIN
400-407	KENTUCKY
408-415	TENNESSEE
416-424	ALABAMA
425-428	MISSISSIPPI
429-432	ARKANSAS
433-439	LOUISIANA
440-448	OKLAHOMA
449-467	TEXAS
468-477	MINNESOTA
478-485	IOWA
486-500	MISSOURI
501-502	NORTH DAKOTA
503-504	SOUTH DAKOTA
505-508	NEBRASKA
509-515	KANSAS
516-517	MONTANA
518-519	IDAHO
520	WYOMING
521-524	COLORADO
525	NEW MEXICO
526-527	ARIZONA
528-529	UTAH
530	NEVADA
531-539	WASHINGTON
540-544	OREGON
545-573	CALIFORNIA
574	ALASKA
575-576	HAWAII
577-579	DISTRICT OF COLUMBIA
580	VIRGIN ISLANDS
580-584	PUERTO RICO
585	NEW MEXICO
586	GUAM

586	AMERICAN SAMOA
586	PHILIPPINE ISLANDS
587-588	MISSISSIPPI
589-595	FLORIDA
596-599	PUERTO RICO
600-601	ARIZONA
602-626	CALIFORNIA
627-645	TEXAS
646-647	UTAH
648-649	NEW MEXICO
650-653	COLORADO
654-658	SOUTH CAROLINA
659-665	LOUISIANA
667-675	GEORGIA
676-679	ARKANSAS
680	NEVADA
681-690	NORTH CAROLINA
691-699	VIRGINIA
700-728	RAILROAD BOARD – NUMBER ISSUANCE DISCONTINUED JULY/01/1963
729-733	ENUMERATION AT ENTRY
750-751	HAWAII
752-755	MISSISSIPPI
756-763	TENNESSEE
764-765	ARIZONA
766-772	FLORIDA

Strictly for information purposes.
Any number issued beginning with 000 will never be issued.

MILITARY LOCATORS

If you know that the person you want to reach is in the service — you are in luck. There are departments in all branches of the military that will locate a person in the service for you.

The following information is needed for all requests for all locator services:

The locator service is free to immediate family members and government officials. Other family members, civilian friends, businesses and others must pay $3.50. The check or money order must be made out to the U.S. Treasury. It is not refundable.

Give as much identifying information as possible about the person you wish to locate such as full name, rank, last duty assignment/last known military address, service number, and Social Security number.

There are four military locators that may include reserves and retired military of the same branches.

1. **Air Force**
2. **Army**
3. **Navy**
4. **Marine**
5. **Coast Guard**

The military may or may not be able to honor your request for military personnel search. Official requests are requests received from any government agency and the Department of Defense. All other requests are considered unofficial. All unofficial requests must be made in writing. Your address and phone number may be released to military members. .

AIR FORCE

For air force requests include:

- Full name to include a middle initial,
- Rank
- Social Security number
- Date of birth
- Any known assignment information (places/dates)

Your written request needs to include your name, address, and phone number. Put your written request in an unsealed envelope with a return address, proper postage affixed and the individual's (the person you're looking for) name in the addressee portion of the envelope. Place this envelope in a larger envelope with your check or money and mail to the locator address at:

HQ AFPC/DPDXIDL,
550 C St West Ste 50
Randolph AFB, TX 78150-4752

ARMY

The army has closed their World Wide locator to the public. To access the army locator an army knowledge on line account is needed.

Send your written requests to:

Commander
U.S. Army Enlisted Records & Evaluation Center
ATTN: Locator
8899 East 56th Street
Fort Benjamin Harrison, IN 46249-5301
1-866-771-6357

NAVY

Navy. The Navy World Wide Locator helps locate individuals on active duty and those who have been recently discharged (within one year). The Navy also has a current address for retired Navy service members. Retiree addresses and addresses for those who have recently separated, however, are protected under the provisions of the Privacy Act and cannot be released. In these cases, however, the locator can forward mail.

Give as much identifying information as possible about the person you wish to locate such as full name, rank (rate), last duty assignment/last known such as military address, service number, and Social Security number.
You can call the locator service toll free at 1-866-827-5672 or 1-901-874-3388, DSN 882-3388.

Mail your correspondence with your fee to:

Navy World Wide Locator
Navy Personnel Command
PERS 312E2
5720 Integrity Drive
Millington, TN 38055-3120

MARINE

The Marine Corps can provide the duty station for active duty personnel and reservists. For retired individuals, the locator service can provide the city and state, but not an address. The service will provide the service member's current rank and unit address; however, due to the locator's staffing, the office cannot forward mail except in special cases. Telephonic requests to 1-703-640-3942 / 3943 are free of charge to immediate family members and government officials calling on official business. In addition, telephonic service will be provided at no cost to any individual, business or organization, if the Marine locator decides the information would benefit the individual. Other requests cost $3.50, made payable by check or money order to the U.S. TREASURER.

Send written locator requests to:

Commandant of the Marine Corps
Headquarters, USMC
Code MMSB-10
Quantico, VA 22134-5030

COAST GUARD

Coast Guard. The Coast Guard World Wide Locator has duty stations for active duty personnel. They do not maintain listings for CG reserve or retired personnel. To locate an active duty Coast Guard member, you can send an email to: ARL-PF-CGPCCGlocator@uscg.mil. You can also write to:

Coast Guard Personnel Command (CGPC-adm-3)
2100 Second St, SW
Washington, DC 20593-0001
Telephone: (202) 267-0581

Military Service Records

National Archives and Records Administration

Cost:

Military personnel and health record information is usually **free** for veterans, next-of-kin, and authorized representatives. If your request involves a service fee, you will be notified as soon as possible.

NOTE: Some records (Navy and Marine Corps enlisted personnel pre-1939) are in the process of being accessioned into the National Archives' collection and are no longer considered part of the NPRC, but are now part of the new Archival Programs Division. Standard reproduction charges may apply for copies of these documents. The process for requesting these records remains the same for now.

Response Time:

They are responding to requests for replacement copies of separation documents only within 10 days about 90% of the time. For requests involving other types of information or documents from records that are on file, on average, in 3-4 weeks and may take up to six months when reconstruction due to missing or damaged reports.

Required Information:

Your request must contain certain basic information for us to locate your service records. This information includes:
- The veteran's complete name used while in service
- Service number
- Social security number
- Branch of service
- Dates of service
- Date and place of birth (especially if the service number is not known).
- If you suspect your records may have been involved in the 1973 fire, also include:
- Place of discharge
- Last unit of assignment
- Place of entry into the service, if known.
- All requests must be **signed** and **dated** by the veteran or next-of-kin.
- **If you are the next of kin of a deceased veteran**, you must provide proof of death of the veteran such as a copy of death certificate, letter from funeral home, or published obituary.

Where to send your request

You can mail or fax your **signed** and **dated** request to the National Archives's National Personnel Record Center (NPRC). Most, but not all records, are stored at the NPRC. **Be sure to use the address specified by eVetRecs or the instructions on the SF-180.** The locations of military service records for active and retired personnel are listed at **Location of Military Service Records**.

> **NPRC Fax Number :**
> **314-801-9195**
>
> **NPRC Mailing Address:**
> National Personnel Records Center
> Military Personnel Records
> 9700 Page Avenue
> St. Louis, MO 63132-5100
> **314-801-0800**

Please note that requests which are sent by Priority Mail, FedEx, UPS, or other "express" services will only arrive at the NPRC sooner. They will not be processed any faster than standard requests. See the section above on emergency requests and deadlines.

By Mail

Please address your stamped envelope to:

The National Archives and Records Administration
8601 Adelphi Road
College Park, MD 20740-6001

By Telephone

Call toll free at:

Toll Free: 1-866-272-6272 or
Toll Free: 1-86-NARA-NARA
Phone TDD: 301-837-0482 (College Park, MD)
Fax: 301-837-0483

Status of Orders

You can check the status of your reproduction order by **entering your order number online**.
http://www.archives.gov/order
- **Orders placed on NATF Forms 81 through 86** are generally completed in approximately 8 weeks from the time we receive them.
- **Orders placed on NATF Form 85**, for full pension files, generally take 12-16 weeks due to the large size of the files.
- You should receive a response to your **order for publications** within 3-4 weeks.

If you have not received a response to your order within the stated times, please send us an e-mail or call us:
- orderstatus@nara.gov
- Customer Service Center Telephone Number: 1-800-234-8861

Please provide the following information:

1. Your name and postal mailing address
2. The order number (preprinted on the NATF Forms 81 through 86), if applicable
3. A daytime phone number, if you wish to be called

Drivers Licenses & Automobile Records

Almost everyone over the age of eighteen years old has a driver's license. Drivers licenses records are public information in some cases. Many states do have restrictions on driving records. You can obtain certain records in certain states.   It is not difficult to get your own records but you would have to contact the DMV to see what the policy is for obtaining another person's home address. A list of every state's DMV website is included in the "State Information" chapter.

Driving Record Websites:

http://www.abika.com/Reports/VehicleDrivingRecords.htm
http://www.dmv.org/driving-records.php
Use other sources, if you are unable to find the person you are looking for with the website.

License Plate Search

http://www.dmv.org/driving-records.php

There is one company that can obtain driver's license information for you. It has large data bases that you can access through your computer. You can use this or you can use the department of motor vehicle lists I have provided a list for you in a later chapter with state agencies. Use other sources, if you are unable to find the person you are looking for with the website.

License Plates

It is always handy to be able to know who owns which car. In your attempt to locate an owner of unclaimed property you may be able to use license plate information. You may find a car at your subject's address that may be able to give you information. These are, however, circumstances where you would want to speak to an owner of a car. There are privacy laws. I have included state agencies to contact for car ownership information in a later chapter.

For Businesses And Individuals

1. Yellow Pages
2. Better Business Bureaus
3. Credit Bureaus

Other Methods Of Locating People

Credit Bureaus

Credit bureaus can help you to locate an individual. Many of their financial transactions are in their reports. In some cases you may not get an exact address but will be able to find out where they are located. Once you find out their approximate location finding their address is easy. Most credit bureaus are not a good resource of information. The three best ones are Equifax, Experian and TransUnion. Anyone can get information from these bureaus. You just have to be a business and pay their yearly fee.

Equifax	Experian	TransUnion
P.O. Box 740241	P.O. Box 2002	P.O. Box 1000
Atlanta, GA 30374	Allen, TX 75013	Chester, PA 19022
Toll Free: (800) 685-1111	Toll Free: 1-888-397-3742	800-888-4213
Toll Free Voice: 1-866-640-2273	Toll Free Voice: 1-800-493-1058	Toll Free Voice:1-800 916-8800
Web Site: http://www.equifax.com	http://www.experian.com	Web Site: http://www.transunion.com

Experian can reach 27 million business. Experian can also reach over 210 million consumers. Here is some of the services Experian Small Business Services can offer you.

Experian Small Business Services

1-888-808-8242   (Mailing lists, address verification, & market profile reports.
1-800-520-1221   (Business credit & business monitoring)
1-800-520-1221   (Business credit & monitoring)
Web Site: http://www.experian.com/small-business

Credit reports
- Offers 27 million active businesses

Mailing Lists
- Offers 210 million consumers
- Offers 110 million households
- Offers 14 million active U.S. businesses

Quality Sales Leads
- Real Estate Leads
- Sales Leads
- Business Leads
- Mortgage Leads
- Note Holder Leads
- Leads by Category

Consumer Credit Services
- Consumer Credit Reports
- Consumer Fraud Products
- Consumer Prospect Lists
- Screening Services

Direct Mail Marketing
- Direct Mail
- Marketing Leads
- Direct Mail Marketing
- Direct Mailing Lists
- Business Mailing Lists
- Mailing Lists
- Address Verification

Credit Card Companies

Credit card companies can help you find the person you are looking for. If you know the person you are looking for has a credit card and you know his credit card number, you will be able to get his current address. See how you would find an address. Let us say that you are looking for John Peterson and you have his credit card number, you could ask the credit card company for leads.

Operator: Acme Credit Department, may I help you?

You: I would like to inquire about statements.

Operator: What is the account number and name?

You: The name is John Peterson and the account number is 45-0098-0987. Can you tell me to what address you have been sending those statements?

Operator: We have been sending the statements to 1265 Tower Rd. San Diego, CA 92119.

Operator: You have an outstanding balance of $176.98.

You: I want to thank you for your help.

The Salvation Army

Many transients have been known to carry hundreds of thousands of dollars in their possessions. One transient that was found frozen to death in Montana had about $75,000 in bonds and securities in a plastic bag he carried with him. The person you are looking for might be a transient.

The Salvation Army operates many missions all over this country. If you have reason to believe that the person you are looking for is a transient, you may want to ask the Salvation Army for help. Remember that finding people is really not their specialty, though. They have four different offices. Contact the office that you would feel would help you the most.

Central USA:
(for states IL, IN, IA, KS, MI, MN, MO, NE, ND, SD and WI)
Salvation Army's Missing Person's Service
10 W. Algonquin Road
Des Plaines, IL 60016-6006
Web Site: www.usc.salvationarmy.org

Eastern USA
(for states CT, DE, ME, MA, NH, NJ, NY, OH, PA, VT and RI)
Salvation Army's Missing Person's Service
440 West Nyack Road West
Nyack, NY 10994-1739
Toll Free: 1 800 315-7699
Phone: (845) 620-7200
Fax: (845) 620-7755
Web Site: www.use.salvationarmy.org

Southern USA
(for states AL, AR, FL, GA, KY, LA, MD, MS,

NC, OK, SC, TN, TX, VA, DC and WV)
Salvation Army's Missing Person's Service
1424 NE Expressway
Atlanta, GA 30329-2088
Toll Free: 1 800 939-2769
Web Site: www.uss.salvationarmy.org

Western USA
(for states AK, AZ, CA, CO, HI, ID, MT, NY, NM, UT, WA and WY.)
Salvation Army's Missing Person's Service
2780 Lomita Blvd.
Torrance, CA 90505
Toll Free: 1 800 698-7728
Web Site: www.usw.salvationarmy.org

The Salvation Army National Headquarters
615 Slaters Lane
P.O. Box 269
Alexandria, VA 22313
Web Site: http://www.salvationarmy
.org

Cost of Search

There is a one-time non-refundable application fee of $25.00 per case to do a search. The nominal application fee required, in no way, covers the actual cost of processing a missing person's request. On average every inquiry costs The Salvation Army approximately $150.00 to $200.00 per case. They welcome your contribution to help offset the costs of this service."

Chapter 6

The Pensions And Other Money Could Be Yours.

You may own unclaimed money One out of ten people has lost money. You may be one of those people that have lost money or you could be an heir to a person who have left money after they have died. There could be a fortune waiting for you. Imagine being an heir to millions of dollars in unclaimed property.

People that die almost always leave some money behind. You may possibly be the heir to thousands and not even know it. You can receive your money by following these simple steps. Answer the following questions. You may have money waiting for you. You may be very surprised at how much money can be yours.

1. Have you been married or divorced?
2. Have you changed jobs?
3. Have you changed your name?
4. Have you moved in the past 15 years?
5. Are you retired?
6. Have you had a safe-deposit box?
7. Have you had a death in your family or someone related to you?
8. Have you bought stocks, bonds or any type of a security?
9. Have you worked for a city, state, county or federal government office?
10. Have you worked for the railroad?
11. Have you served with any division of the armed forces?

Getting Your Money

If you have answered yes to any one of these questions, you may have money waiting for you. This is the best way of insuring that you will have money coming to you.

Make a list of every relative you know that has died. If the relative was distant, you may be an heir but only if that relative had few direct descendants.

Write the Unclaimed or Treasury Office or phone them. Use the addresses in Chapter 2. Try to provide as much of this information as you can for the state office. Give them your name and address that would be applicable at the time an account in question account was opened. Also include your Social Security number.

Your chances are very good if you follow this step. Take the list of all your relatives that have died. Write the Unclaimed or Treasury Office or phone them. Use the addresses in Chapter 2. Try to provide as much of this information as you can for the state office. Give them the (your relative's) account owner's name (maiden name) and address and Social Security number that would be applicable at the time death had occurred. It is wise to include your relationship to the property owner, if that is applicable.

When the state office finds money, they will send you claim forms to fill out. After you fill Out the forms, the money is yours.

The deceased person may have had an insurance policy that you can't locate; to locate an insurance policy write to:

American Council of Life Insurers
101 Constitution Avenue, NW, Suite 700
Washington, DC 20001-2133
Phone: 202-624-2000
Toll Free: 1-877-674-4659
E-mail: WebAdmin@acli.com
Web Site: www.acli.com
Request a free policy search.

National Association of Insurance and Financial Advisors (NAIFA)
2901 Telestar Court, Falls
Church, VA 22042-1205
Toll Free: (877)-TO-NAIFA
Web Site: http://naifa.org

U.S. Office Of Personnel Management
Federal Employees Group Life Insurance
1900 E Street, NW
Washington, DC 20415
Phone: (202) 606-1800
Toll Free: (888) 767-6738
Web Site: http://www.opm.gov

Department Of Veterans Affairs
National Life Insurance Program
810 Vermont Ave. NW
Washington, DC 20420
Toll Free: (800) 827-1000
Web Site: www.va.gov

Pensions

You or the deceased person may have worked for a city, county or state government office. If so you may have earned a pension and not known about it. The next topic will help you get pension money.

Government Employee Retirement Pensions

If you have worked for a city, county or state government office, you may have earned a pension. Working on a part-time basis will not exclude you from earning your pension. If you would like to find out if you or someone else are owned a pension, write or phone the following government offices. Please include the name and address of where you were while employed by them as well as your location and dates of employment, Social Security number, and birth date. Here is the complete list of the offices.

PENSION BENEFIT GUARANTY CORPORATION

PBGC Pension Search Program
1200 K Street NW
Washington, D.C. 20005-4026.
Phone: (202) 326-4000
Web Site: http://www.pbgc.gov

U.S. OFFICE OF PERSONNEL MANAGEMENT

U.S. Office Of Personnel Management
Retirement Operations Center
1900 E Street, NW
Washington, DC 20415
Phone: (202) 606-1800
Web Site: http://www.opm.gov

INTERNAL REVENUE SERVICE

Internal Revenue Service
1111 Constitution Avenue, NW
Washington, DC 20224
Web Site: http://www.irs.gov
Toll Free: (800) 829-1040 (Tax Information)
Toll Free: (800) 829-0433 (Criminal Investigations)

DEPARTMENT OF JUSTICE

Department of Justice
950 Pennsylvania Ave, NW
Washington, DC 20530
Web Site: www.usdoj.gov
Phone: (202) 514-2000

DEPARTMENT OF LABOR

Department Of Labor
200 Constitution Ave., NW
Washington, DC 20210
Web Site: www.dol.gov
Toll Free: (866) 4-USA-DOL (866) 487-2365

RAILROAD RETIREMENT BOARD

Railroad Retirement Board
844 North Rush Street
Chicago, IL 60611
Web Site: www.rrb.gov
Toll Free: (877) 772-5772

State Government Pension Systems.

ALABAMA

Retirement Systems Of Alabama
201 South Union Street
Montgomery, Alabama 36104
Phone: (334).517.7000
Web Site: http://www.rsa-al.gov

ALASKA

Alaska Department Of Administration
Retirement & Benefits
6th Floor State Office Building,
PO Box 110203,
Juneau, AK 99811-0203
Phone: (907) 465-4460
Web Site: http://doa.alaska.gov/drb

ARIZONA

Arizona Department Of Administration
100 N. 15th Avenue
Phoenix, Arizona 85007
Phone: (602) 542.5482
Web Site: http://www.hr.az.gov

ARKANSAS

Arkansas Public Employees Retirement System
124 West Capitol, Suite 400
Little Rock, AR 72201 - 3704
Phone: (501) 682-7800

Web Site: http://www.apers.org

CALIFORNIA

CalPERS
Lincoln Plaza North
400 Q Street
Sacramento, CA 95811
Toll Free: 1-888-225-7377
Web Site: http://www.calpers.ca.gov

COLORADO

Colorado PERA
1301 Pennsylvania Street,
Denver, CO 80203
Fax: (303) 863-3727
Web Site: http://www.copera.org

CONNECTICUT

Connecticut Retirement Plans and Trust Funds
(CRPTF)
55 Elm Street
Hartford, CT 06106
Toll Free: (800) 618-3404
Web Site: http://www.state.ct.us

DELAWARE

Delaware Office of Pensions
McArdle Building
860 Silver Lake Blvd., Suite 1
Dover, Delaware 19904-2402
Phone: (302) 739-4208
Web Site: http://www.delawarepensions.com

FLORIDA

Division Of Retirement
1317 Winewood Blvd, Bldg 8
Tallahassee Fl 32399-1560
Phone: (850) 488-6491
Web Site: http://dms.myflorida.com

GEORGIA

Employees' Retirement System of Georgia
Two Northside 75
Atlanta, GA 30318
Phone: (404) 350-6300

Web Site: http://www.ers.ga.gov

HAWAII

State Of Hawaii Employment Retirement
Systems
City Financial Tower
201 Merchant Street, Suite 1400
Honolulu, HI 96813-2980
Phone: (808)586-1735
Web Site: http://www4.hawaii.gov/ers

IDAHO

Employment Retirement System Of Idaho
P.O. Box 83720
Boise, ID 83720-0078
Toll Free: 1-800-451-8228
Web Site: http://www.persi.state.id.us

ILLINOIS

State Employee Retirement System OF Illinois
2101 S. Veterans Parkway
Springfield, Illinois 62704
Phone: 217-785-7444
Web Site: http://www.state.il.us/srs

INDIANA

Indiana Public Employees Retirement Fund
143 W. Market Street
Indianapolis, IN 46204
Toll Free: 1-888-526-1687
Web Site: http://www.state.in.us/perf

IOWA

IPERS
P.O. Box 9117
Des Moines, IA 50306-9117
Phone: (515) 281-0020
Web Site: http://www.ipers.org

KANSAS

Kansas Public Employees Retirement System
611 S. Kansas Ave., Suite 100
Topeka, KS 66603-3869
Phone: (785) 296-6166
Web Site: http://www.kpers.org

KENTUCKY

Kentucky Retirement Systems
1260 Louisville Road,
Frankfort, KY 40601
Phone: (502) 696-8800
Web Site: http://kyret.ky.gov

LOUISANA

Louisiana (SERS)
8401 United Plaza Blvd.
Baton Rouge, LA 70809
Phone: (225) 922-0600
Web Site: http://www.lasersonline.org

MAINE

Maine Public Employees Retirement System's
(MainePERS)
46 State House Station
Augusta, ME 04333
Phone: 207-512-3100
Web Site: www.mainepers.org

MARYLAND

Maryland State Retirement Agency
120 East Baltimore Street
Baltimore, MD 21202
Phone: (410) 625-5555
Web Site: http://www.sra.state.md.us

MASSACHUSETTS

State Retirement Board
One Ashburton Place, 12th Floor
Boston MA, 02108
Phone: (617) 367-7770
Web Site: http://www.mass.gov

MICHIGAN

Office Of Retirement Services
PO Box 30171
Lansing, MI 48909-7671
Phone: (517) 322-5103
Web Site: http://www.michigan.gov

MINNESOTA

Public Employees Retirement Association Of
Minnesota
60 Empire Drive, Suite 200
St. Paul, MN 55103
Phone: (651) 296-7460
Web Site: http://www.mnpera.org

MISSISSIPPI

Mississippi.gov (PERS)
301 North Lamar, Suite 508
Jackson, MS 39201
Phone: (601) 359-3468
Web Site: http://www.mississippi.gov

MISSOURI

Missouri State Employees' Retirement System
(MOSERS),
907 Wildwood Drive
Jefferson City, MO 65109
Phone: (573) 632-6100
Web Site: https://www.mosers.org

MONTANA

Public Employee Retirement Administration
100 N Park Avenue Suite 200
PO Box 200131
Helena, MT 59620-0131
Phone: (406)444-3154
Web Site: http://mpera.mt.gov

NEBRASKA

Nebraska Public Employees Retirement
Systems (NPERS)
1221 N Street, Suite 325
P.O. Box 94816
Lincoln, NE 68509-4816
Phone: (402) 471-2053
Web Site: https://npers.ne.gov

NEVADA

Nevada (PERS)
693 W. Nye Lane,
Carson City, NV 89703
Phone: (775) 687-4200
Web Site: http://www.nvpers.org

NEW HAMPSHIRE

New Hampshire Retirement System
54 Regional Drive
Concord, NH 03301-8507
Phone: (603) 410-3500
Web Site: http://nhrs.org

NEW JERSEY

State of New Jersey Department of the Treasury
Division of Pensions and Benefits
PO Box 295
Trenton, NJ 08625-0295
Web Site:
http://www.state.nj.us/treasury/pensions

NEW MEXICO

Public Employees Retirement Association
33 Plaza La Prensa,
Santa Fe, NM 87507
Phone: (505) 476-9300
Web Site: http://www.pera.state.nm.us

NEW YORK

Office of the State Comptroller
110 State Street
Albany, NY 12236
Phone: (518) 474-7736
Web Site: http://www.osc.state.ny.us/pension

NORTH CAROLINA

Department of State Treasurer / Retirement
Systems Division
325 N. Salisbury Street
Raleigh, NC 27603
Web Site: http://www.nctreasurer.com

NORTH DAKOTA

North Dakota Public Employees Retirement
System
400 E Broadway Ave Suite 505
PO Box 1657
Bismarck ND 58502-1657
Phone: (701) 328-3900
Web Site: http://www.nd.gov/ndpers

OHIO

Ohio Public Employee Retirement System
277 East Town Street
Columbus, Ohio 43215-4642
Toll Free: (800) 222-PERS
Web Site: https://www.opers.org

OKLAHOMA

Oklahoma Public Employees Retirement System
5801 N. Broadway Extension, Suite 400
Oklahoma City, Oklahoma 73118-7484
Phone: (405) 858-6737
Web Site: http://www.opers.ok.gov

OREGON

Oregon (PERS)
11410 SW 68th Parkway
Tigard, OR 97223
Phone: 503-598-7377
Web Site: http://www.oregon.gov/PERS

PENNSYLVANIA

Pennsylvania (SERS)
30 North Third Street
Harrisburg PA 17101
Toll Free: (800) 633-5461
Web Site: http://www.sers.state.pa.us

PUERTO RICO

Government Development Bank for Puerto Rico
De Diego Ave. Stop 22
Santurce, P.R. 00907
Phone: (787) 722-2525
Web Site: http://www.gdb-pur.com

RHODE ISLAND

Employees' Retirement System of Rhode Island
(ERSRI)
40 Fountain Street, 1st Floor
Providence, RI 02903-1854
Phone: (401) 457-3900
Web Site: http://www.ersri.org

SOUTH CAROLINA

South Carolina Retirement Systems
Fontaine Business Center
202 Arbor Lake Drive
Columbia, SC 29223
Phone: (803) 737-6800
Web Site: http://www.retirement.sc.gov

SOUTH DAKOTA

South Dakota Retirement System
P.O. Box 1098
Pierre, South Dakota 57501-1098
Phone: (605) 773-3731
Web Site: http://www.sdrs.sd.gov

TENNESSEE

Tennessee Department of Human Resources
505 Deaderick Street
James K. Polk Building
Nashville, TN 37243-0635
Fax: (615) 401-7626
Web Site: http://tn.gov/dohr

TEXAS

Employees Retirement System of Texas
200 E 18th Street
Austin, TX 78701
Phone: (512) 867-7711
Web Site: http://www.ers.state.tx.us

UTAH

Utah Retirement Systems
560 East 200 South
Salt Lake City
Utah 84102-2099
Phone: (801) 366-7700
Web Site: http://www.urs.org

VERMONT

Office of the State Treasurer
109 State Street, 4th Floor
Montpelier, VT 05609-6200
Phone: (802) 828-2301
Web Site:
http://www.vermonttreasurer.gov/retirement

VIRGINIA

Virginia Retirement System
P.O. Box 2500
Richmond, VA 23218-2500
Toll Free: (888) VARETIR
Web Site: http://www.varetire.org

WASHINGTON

Washington State Department Of Retirement
Systems
6835 Capitol Boulevard
Tumwater, WA 98501
Phone: (360) 664-7000
Web Site: http://www.drs.wa.gov

WASHINGTON
DISTRICT OF COLUMBIA

DC Department of Human Resources
441 4th Street, NW, Suite 330S
Washington, DC 20001
Phone: (202) 442-9700
Web Site: http://dcop.dc.gov/dcop

WEST VIRGINIA

West Virginia Consolidated Public Retirement
Board
4101 MacCorkle Avenue, S.E.
Charleston, West Virginia 25304-1636
Phone: 304-558-3570
Web Site: http://www.wvretirement.com

WISCONSIN

Department of Employee Trust Funds
801 W. Badger Road
Madison, WI 53713-2526
Phone: (608) 266-3285
Web Site: http://etf.wi.gov

WYOMING

Wyoming Retirement System
6101 Yellowstone Road, Suite 500
Cheyenne, Wyoming 82002
Phone: (307) 777-7691
Web Site: http://retirement.state.wy.us

AMERICAN TERRITORIES

AMERICAN SAMOA

American Samoa Government Employees
Retirement Fund
Phone: (684) 633 5456
Web Site: http://asgerf.com

GUAM

Government of Guam Retirement Fund

424 Route 8, Maite
Guam 96910
Phone: (671) 475-8900
Web Site: http://www.ggrf.com

NORTHERN MARIANA ISLANDS

Northern Mariana Retirement Fund
P.O. Box 501247
Saipan, MP 96950
Phone: (670) 322-3863
Web Site: http://nmiretirement.com

How To Prevent Your Money From Being Lost

By now, you're probably worried that sometime in the future you'll forget about money that's yours or money due to you. To prevent your assets from being abandoned, lost or escheated, make sure you take the following precautions:

Insurance policies

1. Tell your attorney and your family about all insurance policies you have written for you and your family members.
2. Tell the beneficiaries of your policy and that they are the beneficiaries.
3. Keep a record of your policies and their policy numbers; then store these insurance policies in a safe place.

Safe-Deposit Boxes

1. Tell your family, attorney and accountant where your safe-deposit box is located.
2. Pay the box rental when payment is due so the bank does not close your safe-deposit box.

Bank accounts

Keep track of accounts opened by you, a friend or a relative for your child. These accounts are usually opened when a child is born, is christened, graduates, etc., and, after time, are easily lost track of. Make sure your savings account doesn't sit without activity for more than a year. Deposit some money, withdraw some money just make sure the account is 'active.' If you have a passbook account, have a bank teller enter your accrued interest.
For all CDs (certificates of deposit), note their maturity date on your calendar so you don't forget to claim them when due.

Stocks, Bonds, Interest, Dividends

1. Keep records of all stocks and bonds that you own.
2. Mark on your calendar the maturation dates of all your bonds.

3. If you can vote on issues facing stockholders, do so; vote your proxy card.
4. If you change brokers, check your holdings for errors.

The least you can do is to inform everyone you do financial business with if you move, change your name or job, your bank, if you retire, or have problems receiving your mail. To prevent loss, don't trust the postal service with your irreplaceable personal financial assets.

Chapter 7
International Unclaimed Money

People always lose money in bank accounts, corporate holdings and other financial instruments. Forgotten money is usually always sent to the government for safe-keeping. Each country has their own policies and laws concerning unclaimed property. Here is a list of countries in different parts of the world with their unclaimed property government agencies.

Canada

Bank Of Canada

Canadian unclaimed funds are held by the bank of Canada. Before the funds over $10 are sent to the Bank Of Canada they are published in Canada Gazette, which should be available at all public libraries.

You can contact that Bank Of Canada at:
Bank of Canada, Unclaimed Balances Services
234 Wellington,
Ottawa, ON, KIA OG9, CANADA
Toll Free: (888) 891-6398
Fax: (613) 782-7802
Web Site: http://ucbswww.bank-banque-canada.ca

Unclaimed Property Recovery In Canada
Web Site: http://www.cuar.ca

Canadian Bankruptcy Court Funds.
Web Site: https://strategis.ic.gc.ca/sc_mrksv/bankruptcy/ud/engdoc/intro.html

Ontario

Office of the Public Guardian and Trustee,
Suite 800, 595 Bay Street, 8th Floor,
Toronto, Ontario M5G 2M6. CANADA
Phone: (416) 314-2800 or
Fax: (416) 314-2781.

British Columbia

BC Unclaimed Property Society
Box 12136, Harbour Centre
555 West Hastings Street
Vancouver, BC V6B 4N6
Phone: 604.662.3518
Toll Free: 1.888.662.2877
Fax: 604.669.2079
Email: info@unclaimedpropertybc.ca
Web Site: http://www.unclaimedpropertybc.ca

British Columbia Unclaimed Property Society
http://www.bcunclaimedproperty.bc.ca

British Columbia Government
http://upo.fin.gov.bc.ca/ucp

Quebec

Revenu Québec
500, boulevard René-Lévesque Ouest, bureau 10.00
Montréal (Québec) H2Z 1W7
Toll Free: 1 866 840-6939
Phone - Hearing Impaired: (514) 873-4455
Toll Free - Hearing Impaired: 1 800 361-3795
Web Site: http://www.revenu.gouv.qc.ca/en/bnr

Quebec Public Curator ...
Unclaimed property administrator for the Province of Quebec
http://www.curateur.gouv.qc.ca/cura/en

Alberta

Tax and Revenue Administration
Alberta Finance and Enterprise
9811 - 109 Street
Edmonton, AB T5K 2L5
Phone: 780-427-3044
Fax: 780-422-3770
Email: unclaimed.property@gov.ab.ca
Web Site: http://www.finance.alberta.ca

Alberta Unclaimed Property
http://www.qp.gov.ab.ca

Australia

Australian Securities and Investments Commission,

Australian Securities and Investments Commission should be contacted regarding these funds
- Dormant Bank, Building Society or Credit Union Accounts
- Life Insurance unclaimed money
- Dissenting Shareholders

Contact: Australian Securities and Investments Commission,
National Office, Sydney, Level 18,
135 King St, Sydney, NSW 2001, AUSTRALIA
Phone: 9911 2000;
Web Site: **http://www.asic.gov.au.**
Web Site: **http://www.fido.asic.gov.au**

Australian Taxation Office

- Australian Taxation Office Lost Members Register should be contacted
- Superannuation when the member has not reached the eligibility age for a pension and who is not deceased

Wage Line,
Department of Employment Training and Industrial Relations,
PO Box 820,
Lutwyche Q 4030 or
State Awards contact / Magistrates Court/ Federal Awards contact
Unclaimed wages or salaries

Queensland

Trustee House
444 Queen Street
Brisbane QLD 4000,
AUSTRALIA

Australia **Queensland unclaimed Money**
http://www.pt.qld.gov.au/**Unclaimed-Money/Unclaimed-Money/**

New South Wales

Australia New South Wales Unclaimed Money
Web Site: http://www.**osr.nsw.gov.au**
Web Site: http://erevenue.nsw.gov.au/ucm/ucm_search.php

New Zealand

New Zealand Unclaimed Property
Unclaimed Money
New Zealand Inland Revenue
PO Box 38222

Wellington Mail Centre 5045
Web Site: http://www.ird.govt.nz/unclaimed-money

Europe

Sweden

Unclaimed Swedish Accounts
Web Site: http://www.wiesenthal.com/swiss/swedishquery.cfm

France

French Unclaimed Money
France - Association Française des Banques. Search for unclaimed monies held by banks in France. Information is available in French only.

Web Site: http://afb.fr

Switzerland

Swiss Bankers Association - Dormant Accounts
Web Site: http://www.dormantaccounts.ch

Frozen Swiss Bank Accounts
Web Site: http://www.wiesenthal.com/swiss/swissquery.cfm

Dormant accounts in Switzerland.
Web Site: http://www.swissbanking.org

United Kingdom

United Kingdom - My Lost Accounts ...
British banking and savings associations
Web Site: http://www.mylostaccount.org.uk

Holocaust Web Sites

New York Holocaust Web Site For Holocaust survivors and their heirs.
The New York State Holocaust Claims Processing Office provides information to Holocaust survivors and their heirs. This New York office attempts to recover assets deposited in European banks, monies never paid in connection with insurance policies issued by European insurers and lost or looted art for victims of the Holocaust.

The HCPO is processing claims for unpaid European insurance policies from before World War II and for deposits in Swiss banks both before and during the war. For further information, contact the HCPO directly at 800-695-3318 or at its Web site:
Web Site: http://www.claims.state.ny.us/.

International Commission on Holocaust Era Insurance Claims
Search for unpaid insurance policies issued to victims of the Holocaust.
Information is available in 23 languages.
Web Site: http://www.icheic.org.

Chapter 8
Contact The State Governments

All state governments have excellent resources to find people. Searching for a person is simple when a state government helps you find that person. Contact the state in which you are searching for a person. Contact an office in that state in order to find a person. The following lists are in alphabetical order for each state.

Alabama

Tourist Information

Alabama Tourism Department
401 Adams Avenue, Suite 126
PO Box 4927
Montgomery, AL 38103
Toll Free: 1-800-ALABAMA   (334) 242-4169
Web Site: http://www.alabama.travel

State Banking & Finance

State Banking Department
PO Box 4600
Montgomery, AL 36103-4600
Phone: 334-242-3452
Toll Free: 1-866-465-2279
Web Site: http://www.banking.alabama.gov

Driver Licensing & Vehicle Registration

Alabama Department of Public Safety
301 South Ripley St.
Montgomery, AL 36104
Phone: (334) 242-4371   General Information:
Phone: (334) 242-4400   Driver License:
Web Site:
http://dps.alabama.gov/DriverLicense

State Economic Development

Alabama Development Office
401 Adams Avenue
P.O. Box 304106
Montgomery, AL 36130-4106
Phone: 334-242-0400
Toll Free: 800-248-0033
Fax: 334-353-1330
Web Site: http://www.ado.alabama.gov

Alabama State Offices

Alabama Office of the Attorney General
500 Dexter Ave
Montgomery, AL 36130
334-242-7335
Toll free: 1-800-392-5658
Fax: 334-242-2433
Web Site: www.ago.state.al.us

Better Business Bureau

Better Business Bureau
1210 South 20th St.
Birmingham, AL 35205
Phone: (205) 558-2222
Toll Free: 1-800-824-5274 (AL)
E-mail: info@centralalabama.bbb.org
Web Site: http://www.bbb.org

State Government

Alabama
Web Site: http://www.alabama.gov

Alaska

Tourist Information

Alaska Travel Industry Association
2600 Cordova Street, Ste. 201
Anchorage, AK 99503
Email: feedback@alaskatia.org
Web Site: http://www.travelalaska.com

State Banking & Finance

Division of Banking and Securities
Department of Commerce, Community and
Economic Development
PO Box 110807
Juneau, AK 99811-0807
Phone: (907) 465-2521
Toll Free: 1-888-925-2521
Phone: TTY: (907) 465-5437
E-mail: dbsc@commerce.state.ak.us
Web Site:
www.commerce.state.ak.us/bsc/home.htm

Driver Licensing & Vehicle Registration

State of Alaska / Division of Motor Vehicles
1300 W Benson Boulevard, STE 900
Anchorage AK 99503-3696
Phone: 1-907-269-5551
Web Site: http://doa.alaska.gov/dmv

State Economic Development

Alaska Office Of Economic Development
P.O. Box 110803
Juneau, Alaska 99811-0803
Phone: 907 465-2506
Phone: 907 465-2563 Fax
Web Site: http://www.commerce.state.ak.us

Alaska State Offices

Alaska Office of the Attorney General

Consumer Protection Unit
PO Box 110300
Juneau, AK 99811-0300
907-465-2133
Toll free: 1-888-576-2529
Fax: 907-465-2075
Web Site: http://www.law.state.ak.us

Better Business Bureau

Better Business Bureau
341 W. Tudor Rd., Suite 209
Anchorage, AK 99503
Phone: 907-562-0704
E-mail: info@thebbb.org
Web Site: http://www.bbb.org

State Government

Alaska
Web Site: http://www.state.ak.us

Arizona

Tourist Information

Arizona Office of Tourism
1110 W. Washington Street, Suite 155
Phoenix, Arizona 85007
Phone: 602-364-3700
Fax: 602-364-3701
Toll-free: visitor information: 1-866-275-5816
Web Site: http://azot.gov

State Banking & Finance

Department of Financial Institutions
2910 North 44th St., Suite 310
Phoenix, AZ 85018
Phone: 602-771-2800
E-mail: consumeraffairs@azdfi.gov
Web Site: http://www.azdfi.gov

Driver Licensing & Vehicle Registration

Motor Vehicle Division
PO Box 2100
Phoenix AZ 85001-2100
Phone: (602) 255-0072 (Phoenix)
Phone: (520) 629-9808 (Tucson)

Web Site:
http://www.azdot.gov/mvd/driver/driverservices.asp

State Economic Development

Arizona Department of Commerce
1700 W. Washington, Suite 600
Phoenix, Arizona 85007
Phone: (602) 771-1100
E-mail: commerce@azcommerce.com
Web Site: http://www.azcommerce.com

Arizona State Offices

Arizona Office of the Attorney General

1275 West Washington St
Phoenix, AZ 85007
Phone: 602-542-5025
Phone: 602-542-5763 (Consumer Information and Complaints)
Toll free: 1-800-352-8431
Fax: 602-542-4085

Web Site: http://www.azag.gov

Better Business Bureau

Better Business Bureau
4428 N. 12th St.
Phoenix, AZ 85014-4585
Phone: 602-264-1721
E-mail: info@arizonabbb.org
Web Site: http://www.bbb.org

State Government

Arizona
Web Site: http://az.gov

Arkansas

Tourist Information

Arkansas Department Of Parks & Tourism
1 Capitol Mall - Little Rock, Arkansas 72201
Phone: (501) 682-7777 (V/TT)
Web Site: http://www.arkansas.com

State Banking & Finance

State Bank Department
400 Hardin Rd., Suite 100
Little Rock, AR 72211
Phone: 501-324-9019
E-mail: asbd@banking.state.ar.us
Web Site: http://www.accessarkansas.org/bank

Driver Licensing & Vehicle Registration

Department of Finance and Administration
1509 West 7th Street
Little Rock, AR 72201
Phone: (501)-324-9057
Fax: (501)-324-9070
Web Site: http://www.dfa.arkansas.gov

State Economic Development

Arkansas Economic Development Commission
900 West Capitol
Little Rock, Arkansas 72201
http://arkansasedc.com/900-w-capitol-little-rock-arkansas.aspxhttp://arkansasedc.com/900-w-capitol-little-rock-arkansas.aspx**Phone:** (501) 682-1121
Toll Free: 1-800-ARKANSAS
Fax: (501) 682-7394
E-mail: INFO@arkansasedc.com
Web Site: http://arkansasedc.com/

Arkansas State Offices

Arkansas Office of the Attorney General

Consumer Protection Division
323 Center St , Suite 200
Little Rock, AR 72201
Phone: 501-682-2007 (Office of the Attorney General Operator)
Phone: 501-682-2341 (Consumer Hotline)
Toll free: 1-800-482-8982
TTY: 1-800-482-8982 or 501-682-6073
Fax: 501-682-8118
E-mail: oag@arkansasag gov
Web Site: http://www.arkansasag.gov

Better Business Bureau

Better Business Bureau
12521 Kanis Rd.
Little Rock, AR 72211
Phone: 501-664-7274
E-mail: info@arkansas.org
Web Site: http://www.bbb.org

State Government

Arkansas
Web Site: http://portal.arkansas.gov

California

Tourist Information

California Tourism
P.O. Box 1499
Sacramento, CA 95812-1499
Phone: 1 (916) 444-4429.
Toll Free: (877) 225-4367.
E-mail: web@visitcalifornia.com
Web Site: http://www.visitcalifornia.com

State Banking & Finance

State Department of Financial Institutions
45 Fremont St., Suite 1700
San Francisco, CA 94105-2219
Phone: 415-263-8500
Phone: 916-322-0622
Toll Free: 1-800-622-0620 (CA)
E-mail: consumer@dfi.ca.gov
Web Site: http://www.dfi.ca.gov

Driver Licensing & Vehicle Registration

Department of Motor Vehicles
P. O. Box 942869
Sacramento, CA 94269-0001
Toll Free: 1-800-777-0133
Phone: Hearing Impaired: TTY 1-800-368-4327
Web Site: http://www.dmv.ca.gov

State Economic Development

Governor's Office Of Economic Development
1130 K Street
Sacramento CA, 95814
Phone: (916) 322-0694.

Toll Free: 1-877-345-GOED – 1-877-345-4633
Web Site:
http://www.business.ca.gov/Home.aspx

California State Offices

California Office of the Attorney General
Public Inquiry Unit
PO Box 944255
Sacramento, CA 94244-2550
Phone: 916-322-3360
Toll free: 1-800-952-5225
Toll free: 1-800-735-2929
Fax: 916-323-5341
E-mail: piu@doj ca gov
Web Site: http://www.caag.state.ca.us

Better Business Bureau

Better Business Bureau
3363 Linden Ave, Suite A
Long Beach, CA 90807
Phone: 562-216-9240
E-mail: info@labbb.org
Web Site: http://www.bbb.org

State Government

California
Web Site: http://www.ca.gov

Colorado

Tourist Information

Colorado Tourism Office
1625 Broadway, Suite 2700
Denver, CO 80202
Toll Free: 1.800 COLORADO
(1.800.265.6723)
Web Site: http://www.colorado.com

State Banking & Finance

Division of Banking
Department of Regulatory Agencies
1560 Broadway, Suite 975
Denver, CO 80202
Phone: 303-894-7575
E-mail: banking@dora.state.co.us

Web Site: http://www.dora.state.co.us/banking

Driver Licensing & Vehicle Registration

Motor Vehicles
1881 Pierce St.
Lakewood, Colorado 80214
Phone: (303) 205-5600
Web Site:
http://www.colorado.gov/revenue/dmv

State Economic Development

Colorado Office of Economic Development and
International Trade (OEDIT)
1625 Broadway, Ste. 2700
Denver, CO 80202
Phone: (303) 892-3840
Fax: (303) 892-3848
Web Site: http://www.colorado.gov

Colorado State Offices

Colorado Consumer Protection Division
1525 Sherman St., 7th Floor
Denver, CO 80203
Phone: 303-866-5079
Toll free: 1-800-222-4444
Fax: 303-866-4916
E-mail: stop.fraud@state.co.us

Web Site: http://www.ago.state.co.us

Better Business Bureau

Better Business Bureau
1020 Cherokee St.
Denver, CO 80204-4039
Phone: 303-758-2100
E-mail: info@denver.bbb.org
Web Site: http://www.bbb.org

State Government

Colorado
Web Site: http://www.colorado.gov

Connecticut

Tourist Information

Connecticut Commission on Culture & Tourism
One Constitution Plaza
2nd Floor
Hartford, CT 06103
Phone: (860) 256-2800
Fax: (860) 270-8077
Toll Free: (USA-Canada) 888-CTVisit, 888-288-4748
E-mail: ct.travelinfo@ct.gov
Web Site: http://www.ctbound.org

State Banking & Finance

Connecticut Department of Banking
Government Relations and Consumer Affairs
260 Constitution Plaza
Hartford, CT 06103
Phone: 860-240-8299
Toll Free: 1-800-831-7225
Web Site: http://www.state.ct.us/dob

Driver Licensing & Vehicle Registration

Department of Motor Vehicles
60 State Street
Wethersfield, CT 06161
Phone: 860-263-5700
Toll Free: 1-800-842-8222
Web Site:
http://www.ct.gov/dmv/site/default.asp

State Economic Development

Connecticut Economic Resource Center Inc.
805 Brook Street, Building 4,
Rocky Hill CT 06067
Toll Free: 1 (860)-571-7136
Web Site: http://www.cerc.com

Connecticut State Offices

Connecticut Dept. of Consumer
Protection
165 Capitol Ave.
Hartford, CT 06106-1630
Phone: 860-713-6050
Toll free: 1-800-842-2649
Toll free: 1-860-713-7240
Fax: 860-713-7239
E-mail: trade.practices@ct.gov

Web Site: http://www.ct.gov/dcp

Better Business Bureau

Better Business Bureau
94 S. Turnpike Rd.
Wallingford, CT 06492-4322
Phone: 203-269-2700
E-mail: info@ct.bbb.org
Web Site: http://www.bbb.org

State Government

Connecticut
Web Site: http://www.ct.gov

Delaware

Tourist Information

Delaware Tourism Office
99 Kings Highway
Dover, DE 19901
Toll Free: 1-866-284-7483
Web Site: http://www.visitdelaware.com

State Banking & Finance

Office of the State Bank Commissioner
555 East Loockerman St., Suite 210
Dover, DE 19901
Phone: 302-739-4235
Web Site: http://www.banking.delaware.gov

Driver Licensing & Vehicle Registration

Division of Motor Vehicles
2230 Hessler Boulevard
New Castle, Delaware 19720
Phone: (302).326.5000
Web Site: http://www.dmv.de.gov

State Economic Development

Delaware Economic Development Office
99 Kings Highway
Dover, DE 19901
Phone: (302) 739-4271 (Dover)
Phone: (302) 577-8477 (Wilmington)

Toll Free: 1-800-441-8846
Web Site: http://dedo.delaware.gov

Delaware State Offices

Delaware Office of Attorney General
Delaware Dept of Justice Consumer Protection
Division
Carvel State Office Building
820 North French St
Wilmington, DE 19801
Phone: 302-577-8600
Toll free: 1-800-220-5424
Fax: 302-577-6499
E-mail: consumer protection@state.de.us

Web Site:
http://www.attorneygeneral.delaware.gov

Better Business Bureau

Better Business Bureau
60 Reads Way
New Castle, DE 19720
Phone: 302-230-0108
E-mail: info@delaware.bbb.org
Web Site: http://www.bbb.org

State Government

Deleware
Web Site: http://www.delaware.gov

Florida

Tourist Information

Web Site: http://VisitFlorida.com
2540 W. Executive Center Circle Suite 200
Tallahassee,FL 32301
850-488-5607 or
Fax: 850-201-6906
Toll-Free: 1-866-972-5280 .
E-mail: kathyt@VISITFLORIDA.org
Web Site: http://www.visitflorida.com

State Banking & Finance

Office of Financial Regulation

Division of Financial Institutions
200 East Gaines St.
Tallahassee, FL 32399-0371
Phone: 850-410-9800
Toll Free: 1-800-848-3792 (FL)
E-mail: ofr@flofr.com
Web Site: http://www.flofr.com

Driver Licensing & Vehicle Registration

Department of Highway Safety and Motor
Vehicles
Neil Kirkman Building
2900 Apalachee Parkway
Tallahassee, FL 32399-0500
Phone: (850) 617-2000
E-Mail: publicrecords@flhsmv.gov
Web Site: http://www.flhsmv.gov

State Economic Development

Enterprise Florida
Atrium Building, Ste 201
325 John Knox Road
Tallahassee, FL 32303
Phone: (850) 298-6620
Fax: (850) 298-6659
Web Site: http://www.eflorida.com

Florida State Offices

Florida Dept. of Agriculture and
Consumer Services

Division of Consumer Services
Terry Lee Rhodes Building
2005 Apalachee Pkwy
Tallahassee, FL 32399-6500
Phone: 850-488-2221
Toll free: 1-800-435-7352
Toll free: 1-800-352-9832 (in Spanish)

Web Site: http://www.800helpfla.com

Better Business Bureau

Better Business Bureau
14750 NW 77 Ct., #317
Miami Lakes, FL 33016
Phone: 561-842-1918
Web Site: http://www.bbb.org

State Government

Florida
Web Site: http://www.myflorida.com

Georgia

Tourist Information

**Georgia Department of Economic
Development**
75 Fifth Street, N.W., Suite 1200
Atlanta, GA 30308
Toll Free: 1-800-VISIT GA (800.847.4842)
Phone: 404-962-4000
E-mail: travel@exploregeorgia.org
Web Site: http://www.exploregeorgia.org

State Banking & Finance

Department of Banking and Finance
2990 Brandywine Rd., Suite 200
Atlanta, GA 30341-5565
Phone: 770-986-1633
Toll Free: 1-888-986-1633 (GA)
Web Site: http://www.gadbf.org

Driver Licensing & Vehicle Registration

Department of Driver Services
2206 East View Parkway
Conyers, Georgia 30013
Phone: (678) 413-8400
Web Site: http://www.dds.ga.gov

State Economic Development

Georgia Department of Economic Development
75 Fifth Street, N.W., Suite 1200
Atlanta, GA 30308
Phone: (404)-962-4000
Web Site: http://www.georgia.org

Georgia State Offices

Georgia Governor's Office of Consumer Affairs
Two Martin Luther King Jr Dr , SE, Suite 356
Atlanta, GA 30334-4600
Phone: 404-651-8600

Toll free: 1-800-869-1123 (Outside Atlanta)
Fax: 404-651-9018
Web Site: http://consumer.georgia.gov

Better Business Bureau

Better Business Bureau
503 Oak Pl., Suite 590
Atlanta, GA 30349
Phone: 404-766-0875
E-mail: info@atlanta.bbb.org
Web Site: http://www.bbb.org

State Government

Georgia
Web Site: http://www.georgia.gov

Guam

Tourist Information

Guam Visitors Bureau
401 Pale San Vitores Road
Tumon, Guam 96913
Phone: (671) 646-5278/9
Fax: (671) 646-8861
Website: http://www.visitguam.org

State Economic Development

Guam Economic Development and Commerce
Authority
590 S. Marine Corps Dr., Suite 511
GITC Building
Tamuning, Guam 96913
Phone: (671) 647-4332
Fax: (671) 649-4146
E-mail: help@investguam.com
Web Site: http://www.investguam.com

State Government

Guam
Web Site: http://www.guam.gov/

Hawaii

Tourist Information

Hawaii Visitors and Convention Bureau
2270 Kalakaua Avenue, Suite 801
Honolulu, HI 96815
Toll Free: (U.S. and Canada): 1-800-GoHawaii
(1-800-464-2924)
E-mail: info@hvcb.org
Website: http://gohawaii.com

State Banking & Finance

Division of Financial Institutions
Department of Commerce and Consumer Affairs
PO Box 2054
Honolulu, HI 96805
Phone: 808-586-2820
Toll Free: 1-800-274-3141 (Kauai)
Toll Free: 984-2400, 6-2820# (Maui)
Toll Free: 974-4000, 6-2820# (HI)
Phone: TTY: (808)-586-2820
E-mail: dfi@dcca.hawaii.gov
Web Site: http://www.hawaii.gov/dcca/dfi

Driver Licensing & Vehicle Registration

Directory Of The Public Affairs Office
Aliiaimoku Building
869 Punchbowl Street
Honolulu, HI 96813
Phone: (808) 587-2160
Fax: (808) 587-2313
E-mail: dotpao@hawaii.gov
Web Site:
http://www.state.hi.us/dot/publicaffairs

State Economic Development

Hawaii Department of Business, Economic
Development, and Tourism
No. 1 Capitol District Building
250 S. Hotel Street
Honolulu, Hawaii 96813
Web Site: http://hawaii.gov/dbedt

Hawaii State Offices

Hawaii Dept. of Commerce and
Consumer Affairs

Office of Consumer Protection
235 South Beretania St , Room 801
Honolulu, HI 96813-2419

Phone: 808-586-2630
Phone: 808-587-3222
Fax: 808-586-2640

Web Site: http://www.hawaii.gov/dcca/ocp

Better Business Bureau

Better Business Bureau
1132 Bishop St., Suite 615
Honolulu, HI 96813-2822
Phone: 808-536-6956
E-mail: info@hawaii.bbb.org
Web Site: http://www.bbb.org

State Government

Hawaii
Web Site: http://www.ehawaii.gov

Idaho

Tourist Information

Idaho Division of Tourism Development
700 West State Street
P.O. Box 83720
Boise, ID 83720-0093
Phone: (208) 334-2470
Fax: (208) 334-2631
Website: http://www.visitidaho.org

State Banking & Finance

Department of Finance
Financial Institutions Bureau
PO Box 83720
Boise, ID 83720-0031
Phone: 208-332-8000
Toll Free: 1-888-346-3378 (ID)
E-mail: finance@finance.idaho.gob
Web Site: http://finance.idaho.gov

Driver Licensing & Vehicle Registration

Idaho Transportation Department
3311 W. State Street, PO Box 7129
Boise, ID 83707-1129
Phone: (208) 334-8000
Web Site: http://itd.idaho.gov

State Economic Development

Idaho Department of Commerce
700 W State Street
PO Box 83720
Boise, Idaho 83720-0093
Phone: (208) 334-2470
Fax: (208) 334-2631
Toll Free: (800) 842-5858
Web Site: http://commerce.idaho.gov

Idaho State Offices

Idaho Attorney General's Office

Consumer Protection Division
954 W Jefferson, 2nd Floor
PO Box 83720
Boise, ID 83720-0010
Phone: 208-334-2424
Toll free: 1-800-432-3545
Fax: 208-334-4151

Web Site: http://www2.state.id.us/ag

Better Business Bureau

Better Business Bureau
4355 Emerald St., Suite 290
Boise, ID 83706
Phone: 208-342-4649
E-mail: info@boise.bbb.org
Web Site: http://www.bbb.org

State Government

Idaho
Web Site: http://www.state.id.us

Illinois

Tourist Information

Illinois Office of Tourism - Chicago Office
100 W. Randolph St. 3-400
Chicago, IL 60601
Phone: 312-814-4733
Fax: 312-814-6175
Toll Free: 1-800-2CONNECT

Email: ceo.enjoyillinois@illinois.gov
Web Site: http://www.enjoyillinois.com

State Banking & Finance

Division of Banks and Real Estate
122 S. Michigan Ave., Suite 1900
Chicago, IL 60603
Phone: 312-793-3000
Toll Free: 1-877-793-3470
TTY: 312-793-0291
Web Site: http://www.idfpr.com

Driver Licensing & Vehicle Registration

Secretary Of State / Services For Motorists
213 State Capitol
Springfield, IL 62756
Toll Free: 1-800 252-8980
Web Site: http://www.sos.state.il.us/services

State Economic Development

Illinois Department of Commerce and Economic
Development
500 E Monroe
Springfield, IL 62701
Web Site:
http://www.commerce.state.il.us/dceo

Illinois State Offices

Illinois Office of the Attorney
General-Chicago

Consumer Fraud Bureau
100 West Randolph St , 12th Floor
Chicago, IL 60601
Phone: 312-814-3000
Toll free: 1-800-386-5438
Toll free: 1-800-964-3013
Fax: 312-814-2549
E-mail: ag_consumer@atg state il us

Web Site:
http://www.illinoisattorneygeneral.gov

Better Business Bureau

Better Business Bureau
330 North Wabash Ave., Suite 2006

Chicago, IL 60611-7621
Phone: 312-832-0500
E-mail: info@chicago.bbb.org
Web Site: http://www.bbb.org

State Government

Illinois
Web Site: http://www2.illinois.gov

Indiana

Tourist Information

Indiana Office of Tourism Development
One North Capitol, Suite 600
Indianapolis, IN 46204-2288
Phone: 1-800-677-9800
Fax: 317-233-6887
Web Site: http://www.in.gov/visitindiana/

State Banking & Finance

Department of Financial Institutions
30 S. Meridian St., Suite 300
Indianapolis, IN 46204
Phone: 317-232-3955
Toll Free: 1-800-382-4880 (IN)
Web Site: http://www.in.gov/dfi

Driver Licensing & Vehicle Registration

Indiana Bureau of Motor Vehicles
100 N. Senate Ave.
Indianapolis, IN 46204
Phone: (317)-233-6000
Toll Free: 1-888-myBMV411
Web Site: http://www.in.gov/bmv/

State Economic Development

Indiana Economic Development Corporation
One North Capitol, Suite 700
Indianapolis, IN 46204
Phone: 1 (317).232.8800
Fax: 1 (317).232.4146
Toll Free: 1-800-463.8081
Web Site: http://iedc.in.gov

Indiana State Offices

Indiana Office of Attorney
General

Consumer Protection Division
302 West Washington St , 5th floor
Indianapolis, IN 46204
Phone: 317-232-6330
Toll free: 1-800-382-5516 (Consumer Hotline)
Fax: 317-233-4393
Web Site: http://www.indianaconsumer.com

Better Business Bureau

Better Business Bureau
22 East Washington St., Suite 200
Indianapolis, IN 46204-3584
Phone: 317-488-2222
E-mail: info@indybbb.org
Web Site: http://www.indybbb.org

State Government

Indiana
Web Site: http://www.in.gov

Iowa

Tourist Information

Iowa Tourism Office
200 East Grand Avenue
Des Moines, IA 50309
Phone: 515.725.3084
Toll Free: 888.472.6035
E-mail: tourism@iowa.gov
Web Site: http://www.traveliowa.com

State Banking & Finance

Division of Banking
200 East Grand, Suite 300
Des Moines, IA 50309-1827
Phone: 515-281-4014
Web Site: http://www.idob.state.ia.us

Driver Licensing & Vehicle Registration

Iowa Motor Vehicle Division
6310 SE Convenience Blvd.

Ankeny, IA 50021
Toll Free: 800-532-1121 - Toll-Free in Iowa
Phone: 515-244-9124 - Local Des Moines
Phone: 515-244-8725 - Local Des Moines
Fax: 515-237-3152 - Local Des Moines
Web Site: http://www.iowadot.gov/mvd

State Economic Development

Iowa Department of Economic Development
200 East Grand Avenue
Des Moines, IA 50309 ~ USA
Phone: +1.(515).725.3000
Fax: +1.(515).725.3010
E-mail: info@iowa.gov

Iowa State Offices

Office of the Iowa Attorney General

Consumer Protection Division
1305 East Walnut St
Des Moines, IA 50319
Phone: 515-281-5926
Toll free: 1-888-777-4590
Fax: 515-281-6771
E-mail: consumer protection@ag state ia us

Web Site: http://www.IowaAttorneyGeneral.org

Better Business Bureau

Better Business Bureau
2435 Kimberly Rd., Suite 260 N
Bettendorf, IA 52722-4100
Phone: 563-355-6344
E-mail: info@dm.bbb.org
Web Site: http://www.desmoines.bbb.org

State Government

Iowa
Web Site: http://www.iowa.gov

Kansas

Tourist Information

Kansas Travel & Tourism Division
1000 S.W. Jackson Street

Suite 100
Topeka, Kansas 66612
Phone: (785) 296-2009
Fax: (785) 296-6988
TTY: (785) 296-3487
Website: http://www.travelks.com

State Banking & Finance

Office of the State Bank Commissioner
700 SW Jackson St., Suite 300
Topeka, KS 66603-3714
Phone: 785-296-2266
Toll Free: 1-877-387-8523 (Consumer Helpline)
Web Site: http://www.osbckansas.org

Driver Licensing & Vehicle Registration

Kansas Department Of Revenue
Docking State Office Building,
915 SW Harrison (10th & Harrison) Room 155
Topeka, Kansas
Phone: (785)-296-3909
Web Site:
http://www.ksrevenue.org/vehicle.htm

State Economic Development

Kansas Department of Commerce
1000 SW Jackson Street, Suite 100
Topeka, KS 66612-1354
Phone: (785) 296-3481
Fax: (785) 296-5055
TTY Service: (785) 296-3487
Web Site: http://www.thinkbigks.com

Kansas State Offices

Office of the Kansas Attorney

Consumer Protection & Antitrust
Division
120 SW 10th St , Suite 430
Topeka, KS 66612-1597
Phone: 785-296-3751 (Consumer Infoline)
Toll free: 1-800-432-2310
Fax: 785-291-3699
E-mail: cprotect@ksag org

Web Site: http://www.ksag.org

Better Business Bureau

Better Business Bureau
501 Southeast Jefferson, Suite 24
Topeka, KS 66607-1190
Phone: 785-232-0454
Web Site: http://www.bbb.org

State Government

Kansas
Web Site: http://www.kansas.gov

Kentucky

Tourist Information

Kentucky Department Of Travel
Capital Plaza Tower 22nd Floor, 500 Mero
Street
Frankfort, KY 40601
Toll Free: 1-800-225-8747
Web Site: http://www.kentuckytourism.com

State Banking & Finance

Department of Financial Institutions
1025 Capitol Center Dr., Suite 200
Frankfort, KY 40601
Phone: 502-573-3390
Toll Free: 1-800-223-2579
E-mail: kfi@ky.gov
Web Site: http://www.kfi.ky.gov

Driver Licensing & Vehicle Registration

Motor Vehicle Licensing
200 Mero Street
Frankfort, KY 40622
Phone: (502) 564-5301 (General Information)
Phone: (502) 564-2737 (Titles)
Email: KYTCMVLHelpDesk@Ky.gov
Web Site: http://www.kytc.state.ky.us/mvl

State Economic Development

Kentucky Cabinet for Economic Development
Old Capitol Annex
300 West Broadway
Frankfort, Kentucky 40601

Phone: 502-564-7140
Fax: 502-564-3256
Toll Free: 1-800-626-2930
Email: econdev@ky.gov
Web Site: http://www.thinkkentucky.com

Kentucky State Offices

Kentucky Office of the Attorney General

Consumer Protection Division
1024 Capital Center Dr
Frankfort, KY 40601
Phone: 502-696-5389
Toll free: 1-888-432-9257
Fax: 502-573-7151
E-mail: consumer protection@ag ky.gov
Web Site: http://www.ag.ky.gov/cp

Better Business Bureau

Better Business Bureau
1460 Newtown Pike
Lexington, KY 40511
Phone: 859-259-1008
E-mail: info@ky.bbb.org
Web Site: http://www.bbb.org

State Government

Kentucky
Web Site: http://kentucky.gov

Louisiana

Tourist Information

Louisiana Office Of Tourism
PO Box 94291
Baton Rouge, LA 70804
Toll Free: 1-800-99-GUMBO - 1-800-99-48626
Website: http://www.louisianatravel.com

State Banking & Finance

Office of Financial Institutions
PO Box 94095
Baton Rouge, LA 70804-9095
Phone: 225-925-4660
E-mail: ofila@ofi.louisiana.gov

Web Site: http://www.ofi.state.la.us

Driver Licensing & Vehicle Registration

Office of Motor Vehicles
7979 Independence Blvd.
Baton Rouge, LA 70806
Phone: (225) 925-6146
Web Site: http://omv.dps.state.la.us

State Economic Development

Louisiana Economic Development
1051 North Third Street
Baton Rouge, LA 70802-5239
Phone: 1 (225).342.3000
Toll Free: 1-800-450.8115 |
Web Site:
http://www.louisianaeconomicdevelopment.com

Louisiana State Offices

Louisiana Office of Attorney General

Consumer Protection Section
PO Box 94005
Baton Rouge, LA 70804-9005
Phone: 225-326-6465
Toll free: 1-800-351-4889
Fax: 225-326-6499
E-mail: ConsumerInfo@ag state la us

Web Site: http://www.ag.state.la.us

Better Business Bureau

Better Business Bureau
748 Main St.
Baton Rouge, LA 70802
Phone: 225-346-5222
E-mail: info@batonrouge.bbb.org
Web Site: http://www.bbb.org

State Government

Louisiana
Web Site: http://louisiana.gov

Maine

Tourist Information

Maine Office of Tourism
#59 State House Station
Augusta, ME 04333-0059
Toll Free: 1-888-624-6345
Web Site: http://www.visitmaine.com

State Banking & Finance

Bureau of Financial Instituions
36 State House Station
Augusta, ME 04333-0036
Phone: 207-624-8570
Toll Free: 1-800-965-5235
Phone: TTY: 207-624-8563
Web Site:
http://www.maine.gov/pfr/financialinstitutions

Driver Licensing & Vehicle Registration

Bureau of Motor Vehicles
29 State House Station
Augusta, Maine 04333-0029
Phone: 207-624-9000
Phone: TTY: 877-456-8195
Fax: 207-624-9013
Web Site: http://www.maine.gov/sos/bmv

State Economic Development

Maine Department of Community and Economic
Development
59 State House Station
Augusta, ME 04333-0059
Phone: (207) 624-9800
Toll Free: TTY 1-800-437-1220

Maine State Offices

Bureau of Consumer Credit Protection

35 State House Station
Augusta, ME 04333-0035
Phone: 207-624-8527
Toll free: 1-800-332-8529
Toll free: 1-888-577-6690
Fax: 207-582-7699

Web Site: http://www.credit.maine.gov

Better Business Bureau

Better Business Bureau
812 Stevens Ave.
Portland, ME 04103
Toll Free: 1-800-422-2811
E-mail: info@boston.bbb.org
Web Site: http://www.bbb.org

State Government

Maine
Web Site: http://www.maine.gov

Maryland

Tourist Information

Maryland Office of Tourism Development
401 East Pratt Street, 14th Floor
Baltimore, MD 21202
Toll Free: 1-866-639-3526
Web Site: info@visitmaryland.org

State Banking & Finance

Commisioner of Financial Regulation
500 North Calvert St., Suite 402
Baltimore, MD 21202
Phone: 410-230-6100
Toll Free: 1-888-784-0136 (MD)
Phone: TTY: 410-767-2117
E-mail: finreg@dllr.state.md.us
Web Site: www.dllr.state.md.us/finance

Driver Licensing & Vehicle Registration

Maryland Motor Vehicles
6601 Ritchie Highway, N.E.
Glen Burnie, MD 21062
Toll Free: 1-800-950-1MVA   (1-800-950-1682
Phone: 301-729-4550
Web Site: http://www.mva.maryland.gov

State Economic Development

The Department of Business and Economic
Development
World Trade Center
401 East Pratt Street

Baltimore, MD 21202
Phone: (410)-767-6300
Toll Free: 1 888-ChooseMD
Web Site: http://www.choosemaryland.org

Maryland State Offices

Maryland Office of Attorney General

Consumer Protection Division
200 Saint Paul Place
Baltimore, MD 21202-2021
Phone: 410-528-8662 (Consumer Complaints)
Phone: 410-576-6550 (Consumer Information)
Phone: 410-528-1840 (Health Advocacy unit)
Toll free: 1-888-743-0023
Toll free: 1-877-261-8807 (Health Advocacy unit)
TTY: 410-576-6372
Fax: 410-576-7040
E-mail: consumer@oag state md us
Web Site:
http://www.oag.state.md.us/consumer

Better Business Bureau

Better Business Bureau
1414 Key Hwy., Suite 100
Baltimore, MD 21230-5189
Phone: 410-347-3990
E-mail: info@greatermd.bbb.org
Web Site: http://www.bbb.org

State Government

Maryland
Web Site: http://www.maryland.gov

Massachusetts

Tourist Information

Massachusetts Office of Travel & Tourism
10 Park Plaza, Suite 4510
Boston, MA 02116 U.S.A.
Phone: (617) 973-8500
Toll-free: (800) 227-MASS (U.S. & Canada)
Fax: (617) 973-8525
Email: VacationInfo@state.ma.us
Web Site: http://www.massvacation.com/

State Banking & Finance

Division of Banks
One South Station, 3rd floor
Boston, MA 02110
Phone: 617-956-1500
Phone: 617-956-1501
Toll Free: 1-800-495-2265 (MA)
Phone: TTY: 617-956-1577
E-mail: dobconsumer.assistan@state.ma.us
Web Site: http://www.mass.gov/dob

Driver Licensing & Vehicle Registration

Mass DOT - RMV Division
Section 5
P O BOX 55897
Boston, MA 02205
Phone: (617)-351-4500
Toll Free: 1-800-858-3926
Web Site: http://www.massdot.state.ma.us/rmv

State Economic Development

Executive Office of Housing and Economic Development
One Ashburton Place, Room 2101
Boston, MA 02108
Phone: (617) 788-3610
Fax: (617) 788-3605
Web Site: http://www.mass.gov

Massachusetts State Offices

Massachusetts Office of the Attorney General

Consumer Complaints and Information
1 Ashburton Place
Boston, MA 02108
Phone: 617-727-8400 (Consumer Hotline)
Phone: 617-727-4765
Fax: 617-727-3265
E-mail: emailcomplaints@state ma us
Web Site: http://www.mass.gov/ago

Better Business Bureau

Better Business Bureau
340 Main St., Suite 802
Worcester, MA 01608

Phone: 508-755-2548
E-mail: info@cne.bbb.org
Web Site: http://www.bbb.org

State Government

Massachusetts
Web Site: http://www.mass.gov

Michigan

Tourist Information

Travel Michigan/MEDC
300 N Washington Square
Lansing, Michigan 48913
Toll Free: 888-784-7328
Web Site: http://www.michigan.org

State Banking & Finance

Office of Financial and Insurance Regulation
PO Box 30220
Lansing, MI 48909-7720
Phone: 517-373-0220
Toll Free: 1-877-999-6442
E-mail: ofis-fin-info@michigan.gov
Web Site: http://www.michigan.gov/ofir

Driver Licensing & Vehicle Registration

Michigan Department of State
Driver & Vehicle Services
Lansing, MI 48918
Phone: (517) 373-2520
Toll Free: (888) SOS-MICH; (888) 767-6424
Web Site: http://www.michigan.gov/sos

State Economic Development

Michigan Economic Development Corporation
300 N. Washington Sq.,
Lansing, MI 48913
Toll Free: 1-888-522-0103
E-mail: MEDCservices@michigan.org
Web Site: http://www.michiganadvantage.org

Michigan State Offices

Michigan Office of Attorney

General
Consumer Protection Division
PO Box 30213
Lansing, MI 48909
Phone: 517-373-1140
Toll free: 1-877-765-8388
Fax: 517-241-3771
Web Site: http://www.michigan.gov/ag

Better Business Bureau

Better Business Bureau
40 Pearl NW, Suite 354
Grand Rapids, MI 49503
Phone: 616-774-8236
E-mail: bbbinfo@iserv.net
Web Site: http://www.bbb.org

State Government

Michigan
Web Site: http://www.michigan.gov

Minnesota

Tourist Information

Explore Minnesota Tourism
121 7th Place E
Metro Square, Suite 100
St. Paul, MN 55101
Phone: 651/296-5029
Toll Free: 1-888-TOURISM (868-7476);
E-mail: explore@state.mn.us
Web Site: http://www.exploreminnesota.com

State Banking & Finance

Financial Examinations Division
Department of Commerce
85 Seventh Pl. East, Suite 500
St. Paul, MN 55101
Phone: 651-296-2135
Phone: TTY: 651-296-2860
Web Site:
http://http://www.commerce.state.mn.us/www.commerce.state.mn.us

Driver Licensing & Vehicle Registration

Driver and Vehicle Services
Town Square Building
445 Minnesota Street, Suite 190
Saint Paul, MN 55101-5190
Phone: (651)-297-3298 (Driver Licenses)
Phone: (651)-296-2940 (Driver Records)
Phone: (651)-297-2126 (Motor Vehicles)
Phone: (651)-296-2940 (Vehicle Records)
Email: DVS.motor.vehicles@state.mn.us_
(Motor Vehicles)
Email: DVS.driverslicense@state.mn.us
(Driver License)
Web Site: http://www.dps.state.mn.us/dvs

State Economic Development

Positively Minnesota
1st National Bank Building
332 Minnesota Street, Suite E-200
Saint Paul, MN, 55101-1351
Phone: (651)-259-7114
Toll Free: 1-800-657-3858
Web Site: http://www.positivelyminnesota.com

Minnesota State Offices

Minnesota Office of the Attorney General
Consumer Services Division
1400 Bremer Tower
445 Minnesota St.
St. Paul, MN 55101
Phone: 651-296-3353
Toll free: 1-800-657-3787
TTY: 651-297-7206 or 1-800-366-4812
Fax: 651-282-2155
Web Site: http://www.ag.state.mn.us

Better Business Bureau

Better Business Bureau
2706 Gannon Rd.
St. Paul, MN 55116-2600
Phone: 651-699-1111
E-mail: ask@thefirst.bbb.org
Web Site: http://www.bbb.org

State Government

Minnesota
Web Site: http://www.state.mn.us

Mississippi

Tourist Information

Division of Tourism Development
Post Office Box 849
Jackson, MS 39205
Phone: 601.359.3297 ()
Phone: 601.359.5757 (Fax)
Toll Free: 1.866.SEE.MISS (733.6477)
E-mail: tourdiv@mississippi.org
Web Site: http://www.visitmississippi.org

State Banking & Finance

Department of Banking and Consumer Finance
901 Woolfolk Building, Suite A
501 N. West St.
Jackson, MS 39201
Phone: 601-359-1031
Toll Free: 1-800-844-2499 (MS)
E-mail: webmaster@dbcf.state.ms.us
Web Site: http://www.dbcf.state.ms.us

Driver Licensing & Vehicle Registration

Mississippi Department of Public Safety
Headquarters
1900 East Woodrow Wilson Drive
Jackson, MS 39216
Phone: (601) 987-1212
Web Site: http://www.dps.state.ms.us/dps

State Economic Development

Mississippi Development Authority
501 North West Street
Jackson, Mississippi 39201
Phone: (601) 359.3449
Fax: (601) 359.2832
Web Site: http://www.mississippi.org

Mississippi State Offices

Mississippi Attorney General's Office
PO Box 22947
Jackson, MS 39225-2947
Phone: 601-359-4230
Toll free: 1-800-281-4418
Fax: 601-359-4231

Web Site: http://www.ago.state.ms.us

Better Business Bureau

Better Business Bureau
601 Renaissance Way, Suite A
Ridgeland, MS 39157
Phone: 601-707-0960
E-mail: info@ms.bbb.org
Web Site: http://www.bbb.org

State Government

Mississippi
Web Site: http://www.mississippi.gov

Missouri

Tourist Information

Missouri Division of Tourism
P.O. Box 1055
Jefferson City, MO 65102
Phone: 573-751-4133
Fax: 573-751-5160
Toll Free: 800-519-2100.
E-mail: tourism@ded.mo.gov
Web Site: http://www.visitmo.com/

State Banking & Finance

Department of Finance
PO Box 716
301 W. High St., Room 630
Jefferson City, MO 65102
Phone: 573-751-3242
E-mail: finance@dof.mo.gov
Web Site: http://www.missouri-finance.org

Driver Licensing & Vehicle Registration

Department Of Revenue
Harry S Truman State Office Building
301 West High Street Jefferson City, MO 65101
Phone: (573) 526-3669 (Driver License)
Phone: (573)-526-2407) Motor Vehicle
Email: dormail@dor.mo.gov
Web Site: http://dor.mo.gov

State Economic Development

Missouri Department of Economic Development
301 W. High Street
P.O. Box 1157
Jefferson City, Missouri 65102
Phone: 573-751-4962
Fax: 573-526-7700
E-mail: ecodev@ded.mo.gov
Web Site: http://www.ded.mo.gov

Missouri State Offices

Missouri Attorney General's
Office
Consumer Protection Unit
PO Box 899
Jefferson City, MO 65102
Phone: 573-751-3321
Toll free: 1-800-392-8222 (Hotline)
Fax: 573-751-7948
E-mail: consumer@ago.mo.gov
Web Site: http://www.ago.mo.gov

Better Business Bureau

Better Business Bureau
8080 Ward Pkwy., Suite 401
Kansas City, MO 64114
Phone: 816-421-7800
E-mail: info@kansascity.bbb.org
Web Site: http://www.bbb.org

State Government

Missouri
Web Site: http://www.missouri.gov

Montana

Tourist Information

Travel Montana, Department Of Commerce
301 S Park Avenue
PO Box 20053
Helena, MT 59601
Toll Free: 1-800 VISITMT - 1-800 847-4868
Web Site: http://www.visitmt.com

State Banking & Finance

Division of Banking & Financial Institutions
301 South Park, Suite 316
PO Box 200546
Helena, MT 59620-0546
Phone: 406-841-2920
Toll Free: 1-800-914-8423
Phone: TTY: 406-444-1421
Web Site: http://www.banking.mt.gov

Driver Licensing & Vehicle Registration

Department of Justice
P.O. Box 201401
Helena, MT 59620-1401
Phone: (406) 444-2026
Fax: (406) 444-3549
E-mail: contactdoj@mt.gov
Web Site: http://doj.mt.gov/driving/default.asp

State Economic Development

Montana Governor's Office of Economic
Development
P.O. Box 200801
Helena, MT 59620-0801
Phone: (406) 444-5634
E-mail: business@mt.gov
Web Site: http://business.mt.gov

Montana State Offices

Montana Office of Consumer
Protection
2225 11th Ave.
PO Box 200151
Helena, MT 59620-0151
Phone: 406-444-4500
Toll free: 1-800-481-6896
Fax: 406-444-9680
E-mail: contactocp@mt.gov
Web Site: http://www.doj.mt.gov/consumer

Better Business Bureau

See another state

State Government

Montana
Web Site: http://www.mo.gov

Nebraska

Tourist Information

Nebraska Department of Economic
Development, Division of Travel and Tourism
301 Centennial Mall South
PO Box 94666
Lincoln, NE 68509-4666
Toll Free: 1-877-NEBRASKA - 1-877-632-72752
Web Site: http://www.visitnebraska.gov

State Banking & Finance

Nebraska
Department of Banking & Finance
PO Box 95006
Lincoln, NE 68509-5006
Phone: 402-471-2171
Toll Free: 1-877-471-3445
Web Site: http://www.ndbf.org

Driver Licensing & Vehicle Registration

Nebraska State Office Building
Driver Licensing Services
301 Centennial Mall South
P.O. Box 94726
Lincoln, Nebraska 68509-4726
Phone: (402) 471-3861
Fax: (402) 471-4020
Web Site: http://www.dmv.state.ne.us

State Economic Development

Nebraska Department of Economic
Development
301 Centennial Mall South
P.O. Box 94666
Lincoln, NE 68509-4666
Fax: (402) 471-3778
Toll Free: (800) 426-6505
Web Site: http://www.neded.org

Nebraska State Offices

Nebraska Office of the Attorney
General
Consumer Protection Division

2115 State Capitol
PO Box 98920
Lincoln, NE 68509
Phone: 402-471-2682
Toll free: 1-800-727-6432
Toll free: 1-888-850-7555 (In Spanish)
Fax: 402-471-0006
Web Site: http://www.ago.ne.gov

Better Business Bureau

Better Business Bureau
11811 P St.
Omaha, NE 68137
Phone: 402-391-7612
Toll Free: 1-800-649-6814 (Outside Omaha)
E-mail: info@bbbnebraska.org
Web Site: http://www.bbb.org

State Government

Nebraska
Web Site: http://www.nebraska.gov

Nevada

Tourist Information

Nevada Commission on Tourism
401 North Carson Street
Carson City, NV 89701
Phone: (775) 687-4322
Fax: 775 687-6779
Toll Free: 1-800-NEVADA-8
Web Site: http://travelnevada.com

State Banking & Finance

Financial Institutions Division
Department of Business & Industry
PO Box 3239
Carson City, NV 89702
Phone: 702-486-4120
Toll Free: 1-866-858-8951 (NV)
E-mail: FIDMaster@fid.state.nv.us
Web Site: http://www.fid.state.nv.us

Driver Licensing & Vehicle Registration

Nevada Department of Motor Vehicles

555 Wright Way
Carson City, NV 89711
Fax: (775) 684-4992
Toll Free: 486-4DMV (702) 486-4368 Las
Vegas Area
Toll Free: 684-4DMV (775) 684-4368
Reno/Sparks/Carson City
Web Site: http://www.dmvstat.com

State Economic Development

Nevada Commission on Economic Development
808 West Nye Lane
Carson City, Nevada 89703
Phone: (775) 687-9900
Fax: (775) 687-9924
Toll Free: (800) 336-1600
Web Site: http://www.diversifynevada.com

Nevada State Offices

Nevada Consumer Affairs
Division
4600 Kietzke Ln., Building B, Suite 113
Reno, NV 89502
Phone: 775-688-1800
Toll free: 1-800-326-5202 (NV)
TTY: 702-486-7901
Fax: 775-688-1803
E-mail: renocad@fyiconsumer.org
Web Site: http://www.fightfraud.nv.gov

Better Business Bureau

Better Business Bureau
6040 S. Jones Blvd.
Las Vegas, NV 89118
Phone: 702-320-4500
Web Site: http://www.bbb.org

State Government

Nevada
Web Site: http://www.nv.gov

New Hampshire

Tourist Information

NH Department of Resources and Economic

Development
Division of Travel and Tourism Development
P.O. Box 1856, 172 Pembroke Road
Concord, NH 03302-1856
Phone: (603) 271-2665
Fax: (603) 271-6870
Web Site: http://www.visitnh.gov/

State Banking & Finance

State Banking Department
53 Regional Dr., Suite 200
Concord, NH 03301
Phone: 603-271-3561
Toll Free: 1-800-437-5991
Toll Free: TTY: 1-800-735-2964 (Toll Free)
E-mail: NHBD@Banking.State.NH.US
Web Site: http://www.nh.gov/banking

Driver Licensing & Vehicle Registration

Department of Safety
Division of Motor Vehicles
23 Hazen Drive
Concord NH 03305
Phone: (603)271-2371
Email: NH.OnlineDL@dos.nh.gov
Web Site:
http://www.nh.gov/safety/divisions/dmv

State Economic Development

New Hampshire Department of Resources and
Economic Development
172 Pembroke Road
P.O. Box 1856 Concord, NH 03302-1856
Phone: (603)271-2411
Fax: (603)271-2629
E-mail: info@nheconomy.com
Web Site: http://www.dred.state.nh.us

New Hampshire State Offices

New Hampshire Office of the Attorney General
Consumer Protection and Antitrust Bureau
33 Capitol St.
Concord, NH 03301
Phone: 603-271-3641
Toll free: 1-888-468-4454
Toll free: 1-800-735-2964
Fax: 603-223-6202

Web Site: http://www.doj.nh.gov/consumer

Better Business Bureau

Better Business Bureau
25 Hall St., Suite 102
Concord, NH 03301
Phone: 603-224-1991
E-mail: info@bbbnh.org
Web Site: http://www.bbb.org

State Government

New Hampshire
Web Site: http://www.nh.gov

New Jersey

Tourist Information

Department of State, Division of Travel and
Tourism
P.O. BOX 460
Trenton, NJ 08625
Phone: (609) 292-2470
Toll Free: 1-800-VISITNJ - 1-800-847-4865
Web Site: http://www.visitnj.org/

State Banking & Finance

Department of Banking and Insurance
PO Box 471
Trenton, NJ 08625
Phone: 609-292-7272
Toll Free: 1-800-446-7467
Web Site: http://www.njdobi.org/

Driver Licensing & Vehicle Registration

New Jersey Motor Vehicle Commission
P.O. Box 160
Trenton, NJ 08666
Phone: (609) 292-6500 out-of-state
Phone: (609) 292-5120 TTY
Toll Free: (888) 486-3339 toll-free in NJ
Web Site: http://www.state.nj.us/mvc

State Economic Development

New Jersey Economic Development Authority

36 West State Street
Trenton, NJ 08625
Phone: (609) 292-1800
E-mail: njeda@njeda.com
Web Site: http://www.njeda.com

New Jersey State Offices

New Jersey Dept. of Law and Public Safety
Division of Consumer Affairs
PO Box 45025
Newark, NJ 07101
Phone: 973-504-6200
Toll free: 1-800-242-5846 (NJ)
TTY: 973-504-6588
Fax: 973-648-3538
E-mail: askconsumeraffairs@lps.state.nj.us
Web Site: http://www.njconsumeraffairs.gov

Better Business Bureau

Better Business Bureau
1700 Whitehorse-Hamilton Square Rd.
Suite D-5
Trenton, NJ 08690-3596
Phone: 609-588-0808
E-mail: info@trenton.bbb.org
Web Site: http://www.newjersey.bbb.org

State Government

New Jersey
Web Site: http://www.state.nj.us

New Mexico

Tourist Information

New Mexico Tourism Department
491 Old Santa Fe Trail
Santa Fe, New Mexico 87501
Phone: (505).827.7400
Email: enchantment@newmexico.org
Web Site: http://www.newmexico.org

State Banking & Finance

Financial Institutions Division
Regulation and Licensing Department
2550 Cerrillos Rd., 3rd Floor

Santa Fe, NM 87505
Phone: 505-476-4885
Web Site: http://www.rld.state.nm.us/FID/

Driver Licensing & Vehicle Registration

New Mexico Taxation And Revenue Department
1100 South St. Francis Drive
Santa Fe, NM 87504-0630
Phone: (505) 827-0700
Web Site: http://www.tax.newmexico.gov

State Economic Development

New Mexico Partnership
117 Gold Avenue, SW
Albuquerque, New Mexico 87102
Phone: (505) 247-8500
Toll Free: (888) 715-5293
Web Site: http://www.edd.state.nm.us/

New Mexico State Offices

Office of Attorney General
Consumer Protection Division
PO Drawer 1508
Santa Fe, NM 87504-1508
Phone: 505-827-6060
Toll free: 1-800-678-1508
Fax: 505-827-5826
Web Site: http://www.nmag.gov

Better Business Bureau

Better Business Bureau
2625 Pennsylvania NE, Suite 2050
Albuquerque, NM 87110-3658
Phone: 505-346-0110
E-mail: info@bbbsw.org
Web Site: http://www.bbb.org

State Government

New Mexico
Web Site: http://www.newmexico.gov

New York

Tourist Information

New York State Division Of Tourism
30 South Pearl Street
Albany, NY 12245
Phone: 1(518) 474-4116
Toll Free: 1-800-CALL-NYS – 1-800- 225-5697
Web Site: https://www.iloveny.com

State Banking & Finance

Banking Department
Consumer Help Unit
One State St.
New York, NY 10004-1417
Phone: 212-709-3530
Toll Free: 1-877-226-5697 (NY)
E-mail: consumer@banking.state.ny.us
Web Site: http://www.banking.state.ny.us

Driver Licensing & Vehicle Registration

New York Department Of Motor Vehicles
6 Empire State Plaza
Albany, NY 12228
Phone: 1-212-645-5550 (In New York)
Phone: 1-718-966-6155 (In New York)
Phone: 1-518-473-5595 (Outside New York)
Web Site: http://www.nydmv.state.ny.us

State Economic Development

Empire State Development
633 Third Avenue
New York City, New York 10017
Toll Free: 1 800 STATE-NY - 1 800 782-8369
Web Site: http://www.empire.state.ny.us

New York State Offices

New York Bureau of Consumer
Frauds and Protection
State Capitol
Albany, NY 12224-0341
Phone: 518-474-5481
Phone: 518-474-7330
Toll free: 1-800-771-7755
Toll free: 1-800-788-9898
Fax: 518-474-3618

Web Site: http://www.oag.state.ny.us

Better Business Bureau

Better Business Bureau
55 St. Paul St.
Rochester, NY 14604
Phone: 585-423-6341
E-mail: geninquiries@upstatenybbb.org
Web Site: http://www.bbb.org

State Government

New York
Web Site: http://www.ny.gov

North Carolina

Tourist Information

North Carolina Department of Commerce,
Division of Tourism, Film and Sports
Development
4332 Mail Service Center
Raleigh NC 27699-4332
Toll Free: 1-800-VISITNC - 1-800-847-4862
Phone: (919) 733-8372
Fax: (919) 715-3097
Website: http://www.visitnc.com

State Banking & Finance

Commissioner of Banks
4309 Mail Service Center
Raleigh, NC 27699-4309
Phone: 919-733-3016
Toll Free: 1-888-384-3811
Web Site: http://www.nccob.org

Driver Licensing & Vehicle Registration

Division of Motor Vehicles
3148 Mail Service Center
Raleigh, NC 27699-3148
Phone: (919)-715-7000
Web Site: http://www.ncdot.org/DMV

State Economic Development

North Carolina Department of Commerce
301 North Wilmington Street
Raleigh, North Carolina 27601-1058
Phone: (919) 733-4151

Phone: (919) 807-4280
Toll Free: (800) 228-8443
Web Site: http://www.nccommerce.com

North Carolina State Offices

North Carolina Office of the Attorney General

Consumer Protection Division
9001 Mail Service Center
Raleigh, NC 27699-9001
Phone: 919-716-6000
Toll free: 1-877-566-7226
Fax: 919-716-6050
Web Site: http://www.ncdoj.gov

Better Business Bureau

Better Business Bureau
3608 W. Friendly Ave.
Greensboro, NC 27410-4895
Phone: 336-852-4240
E-mail: info@greensboro.bbb.org
Web Site: http://www.bbb.org

State Government

North Carolina
Web Site: http://www.ncgov.com

North Dakota

Tourist Information

North Dakota Tourism Division
Century Center
1600 E. Century Ave. Suite 2 PO Box 2057
Bismarck, N.D. 58502-2057
Phone: 701-328-2525
Fax: 701-328-4878
Toll Free: 800-435-5663
Web Site: http://www.ndtourism.com

State Banking & Finance

Department of Financial Institutions
2000 Schafer St., Suite G
Bismarck, ND 58501-1204
Phone: 701-328-9933
Phone: TTY: 1-800-366-6888 (ND)

E-mail: dfi@nd.gov
Web Site: http://www.nd.gov/dfi

Driver Licensing & Vehicle Registration

Department Of Transportation
608 East Boulevard Avenue .
Bismarck, ND 58505-0700
Phone: (701) 328-2500
Web Site: http://www.dot.nd.gov/public

State Economic Development

North Dakota Division of Economic
Development and Finance
Economic Development & Finance Division
P.O. Box 2057
Bismarck, North Dakota 58502-2057
Phone: 701-328-5300
Fax: 701-328-5320
Email: plucy@nd.gov
Web Site: http://www.business.nd.gov

North Dakota State Offices

North Dakota Office of the
Attorney General

Consumer Protection and Antitrust
Division
4205 State St
PO Box 1054
Bismarck, ND 58502-1054
Phone: 701-328-3404
Toll free: 1-800-472-2600
Toll free: 1-800-366-6888
Fax: 701-328-5568
E-mail: ndag@nd gov

Web Site: http://www.ag.nd.gov

Better Business Bureau

See other state

State Government

North Dakota
Web Site: http://www.nd.gov

Ohio

Tourist Information

Ohio Division of Travel and Tourism
P.O. Box 1001
Columbus, OH 43216-1001
Toll Free: 1-800-BUCKEYE - 1-800-282-5393
Web Site: http://consumer.discoverohio.com

State Banking & Finance

Division of Financial Institutions
Department of Commerce
77 South High St., 21st Floor
Columbus, OH 43215-6120
Phone: 614-728-8400
Toll Free: 1-866-278-0003
Phone: TTY: 1-800-750-0750
E-mail: webdfi@dfi.com.state.oh.us
Web Site: http://www.com.ohio.gov/fiin

Driver Licensing & Vehicle Registration

Ohio Bureau of Motor Vehicles
1970 West Broad Street
Columbus, Ohio 43223-1101
Web Site: http://bmv.ohio.gov

State Economic Development

Ohio Means Business
41 South High Street
Columbus, Ohio 43215
Phone: (614) 857-0900 ext. 231
Toll Free: (800) 848-1300
E-mail: mmcquade@ohiomeansbusiness.com
Web Site: http://www.ohiomeansbusiness.com
Web Site: http://development.ohio.gov

Ohio State Offices

Ohio Attorney General's Office

Consumer Protection Section
30 East Broad St , 14h Floor
Columbus, OH 43215-3400
Phone: 614-466-4320
Toll free: 1-800-282-0515
Fax: 614-728-7583

Web Site: http://www.ohioattorneygeneral.gov
Web Site: http://www.speakoutohio.gov

Better Business Bureau

Better Business Bureau
7 West 7th St., Suite. 1600
Cincinnati, OH 45202
Phone: 513-421-3015
E-mail: info@cincinnati.bbb.org
Web Site: http://www.bbb.org

State Government

Ohio
Web Site: http://www.ohio.gov

Oklahoma

Tourist Information

Oklahoma Tourism & Recreation Department
120 N Robinson, 6th Floor
PO Box 52002
Oklahoma City, OK 73152-2002
Toll Free: 1-800-652-6552
E-mail: info@travelok.com
Web Site: http://www.travelok.com

State Banking & Finance

State Banking Department
2900 North Lincoln Blvd.
Oklahoma City, OK 73105
Phone: 405-521-2782
Web Site: http://www.osbd.state.ok.us

Driver Licensing & Vehicle Registration

Oklahoma Department of Public Safety
P.O. Box 11415
Oklahoma City, Oklahoma 73136
Phone: (405) 425-2424
Web Site: http://www.dps.state.ok.us/dls

State Economic Development

Oklahoma Department of Commerce
900 North Stiles Ave.
Oklahoma City, OK 73104

Phone: 405-815-6552
Toll Free: 800-879-6552
Web Site: http://www.okcommerce.gov

Oklahoma State Offices

Oklahoma Attorney General
Consumer Protection Unit
313 NE 21st St
Oklahoma City, OK 73105
Phone: 405-521-3921
Fax: 405-522-0085
Web Site: http://www.oag.ok.gov

Better Business Bureau

Better Business Bureau
17 S, Dewey St.
Oklahoma City, OK 73102-2400
Phone: 405-239-6081
E-mail: info@oklahomacity.bbb.org
Web Site: http://www.bbb.org

State Government

Oklahoma
Web Site: http://www.state.ok.us

Oregon

Tourist Information

Travel Oregon
670 Hawthorne SE, Suite 240
Salem, OR 97301
Toll Free: 1 800-547-7842
Web Site: http://www.traveloregon.com

State Banking & Finance

Department of Consumer & Business Services
Division of Finance and Corporate Securities
PO Box 14480
Salem, OR 97309-0405
Phone: 503-378-4140
Toll Free: 1-866-814-9710
Email: dcbs.dfcsmail@state.or.us
Email: dfcs.oregon.gov

Driver Licensing & Vehicle Registration

Oregon Department Of Transportation
1905 Lana Ave NE
Salem, OR 97314
Phone: (503) 945-5000   Salem Metro Area
Phone: (503) 299-9999   Portland Metro Area
Web Site: http://www.oregon.gov/ODOT/DMV

State Economic Development

Business Oregon
775 Summer St. NE, Suite 200
Salem, OR 97301-1280
Phone: 503-986-0123
Toll Free: 866-467-3466
Web Site: http://www.oregon4biz.com

Oregon State Offices

Department of Justice
Financial Fraud/Consumer Protection Section
1162 Court St , NE
Salem, OR 97301-4096
Phone: 503-378-4320 (Salem)
Phone: 503-229-5576 (Portland)
Phone: 503-947-4333
Toll free: 1-877-877-9392
Toll free: 1-800-735-2900
Fax: 503-378-5017
E-mail: consumer hotline@doj state.or.us
Web Site: http://www.doj.state.or.us

Better Business Bureau

Better Business Bureau
4004 SW Kruse Way Pl., Suite 375
Lake Oswego, OR 97035
503-212-3022
E-mail: info@thebbb.org
Web Site: http://www.bbb.org

State Government

Oregon
Web Site: http://oregon.gov

Pennsylvania

Tourist Information

Pennsylvania Tourism Office
Department of Community and Economic Development
4th Floor, Commonwealth Keystone Building
400 North Street
Harrisburg, PA 17120-0225
Phone: (717)-787-5453
Fax: 717-787-0687
Toll Free: 800-VISIT-PA – 1-800-847-4872
Toll Free: 800-237-4363 (Office)

State Banking & Finance

Department of Banking
17 N. Second St., Suite 1300
Harrisburg, PA 17101-2290
717-787-2665
Toll Free: 1-800-722-2657
Phone: TTY: 1-800-679-5070
E-mail: ra-pabanking@state.pa.us
Web Site: http://www.banking.state.pa.us

Driver Licensing & Vehicle Registration

Pennsylvania Department Of Transportation
1101 South Front Street
Harrisburg, PA 17104
Phone: 1-717-412-5300   Out-of-State
Toll Free: 1-800-932-4600   In-State
Web Site: http://www.dmv.state.pa.us

State Economic Development

Pennsylvania Department of Community & Economic Development
Commonwealth Keystone Building
400 North Street, 4th Floor
Harrisburg, PA 17120-0225
Toll Free: 866-GO-NEWPA (866-466-3972)
Web Site: http://www.newpa.com

Pennsylvania State Offices

Pennsylvania Office of the Attorney General
Office of the Consumer Advocate
555 Walnut St
5th Floor, Forum Place
Harrisburg, PA 17101-1923
Phone: 717-783-5048 (Utilities Only)
Toll free: 1-800-684-6560
Fax: 717-783-7152

E-mail: consumer@paoca org
Web Site: http://www.oca.state.pa.us

Better Business Bureau

Better Business Bureau
1880 John F. Kennedy Blvd., Suite 1330
Philadelphia, PA 19103
Phone: (215)-985-9313
E-mail: info@mybbb.org
Web Site: http://www.bbb.org

State Government

Pennsylvania
Web Site: http://pa.gov

Puerto Rico

Tourist Information

Puerto Rico Tourism Company
PRTC La Princesa Bldg. #2
Paseo La Princesa
Old San Juan, P.R. 00902
Toll Free: 1-800-866-7827
Web Site: http://www.gotopuertorico.com

State Banking & Finance

Office of the Commissioner of Financial Institutions
PO Box 11855
San Juan, PR 00910-3855
Phone: (787) 723-3131
Web Site: http://www.cif.gov.pr

Driver Licensing & Vehicle Registration

Motor Vehicle & Driver Services
Phone: (787)-977-2200 (área metro)
Toll Free: 1-800-981-3021 (libre de cargos)
Email: webmaster@act.dtop.gov.pr
Web Site: http://www.dtop.gov.pr/disco

State Economic Development

Puerto Rico Industrial Development Company
#355 FD Roosevelt Avenue Suite 404
Hato Rey, Puerto Rico 00918

Phone: (787)-764-1175
Phone: (787)-758-4747
Fax: (787)-764-1415
Web Site: http://www.pridco.com

Puerto Rico State Offices

Puerto Rico Dept. de Asuntos Del Consumidor
Apartado 41059, Minillas Station
Santurce, PR 00940
Phone: 787-722-7555
Fax: 787-726-0077

Web Site: http://www.daco.gobierno.pr

Better Business Bureau

Better Business Bureau
530 Avenida De La Constitucion #206
San Jan, PR 00901
Phone: 787-289-8710
E-mail: info@wpbbb.com
Web Site: http//www.bbb.org

State Government

Puerto Rico
Web Site: http://www2.pr.gov

Rhode Island

Tourist Information

Rhode Island Tourism Division
315 Iron Horse Way, Suite 101
Providence, RI 02908
Fax: 401-273-8270
Toll Free: 1-800-250-7384
Web Site: http://www.visitrhodeisland.com/

State Banking & Finance

Division of Banking
Department of Business Regulation
1511 Pontiac Ave.
Cranston, RI 02920
Phone: 401-462-9503 (Banking)
E-mail: bankinquiry@dbr.state.ri.us
Web Site: http://www.dbr.state.ri.us

Driver Licensing & Vehicle Registration

Department Of Motor Vehicles
73 Valley Road
Middletown, RI 02840
Phone: (401) 462-4DMV (401) 462-4368
Web Site: http://www.dmv.ri.gov

State Economic Development

Rhode Island Economic Development
Corporation
315 Iron Horse Way, Suite 101
Providence, Rhode Island 02908
Phone: (401) 278-9100
Fax: (401) 273-8270
Web Site: http://www.riedc.com

Rhode Island State Offices

Rhode Island Dept. of Attorney General

Consumer Protection Unit
150 South Main St
Providence, RI 02903
Phone: 401-274-4400
Phone: 401-453-0410
Fax: 401-222-5110
E-mail: contactus@riag ri gov

Web Site: http://www.riag.state.ri.us

Better Business Bureau

Better Business Bureau
475 Tiogue Ave.
Coventry , RI 02816
Toll Free: 1-800-422-2811
E-mail: info@boston.bbb.org
Web Site: http://www.bbb.org

State Government

Rhode Island
Web Site: http://www.ri.gov

South Carolina

Tourist Information

SC Department of Parks, Recreation and Tourism
1205 Pendleton St
Columbia, SC 29201
Phone: 1 (803) 734-1700 (Information)
Phone: 1 (803) 734-0156 (State Parks)
Toll Free: 1-866-224-9339
Web Site:
http://www.discoversouthcarolina.com

State Banking & Finance

Office of the Commissioner of Banking
State Board of Financial Institutions
1205 Pendleton St., Suite 305
Columbia, SC 29201
Phone: 803-734-2001
Web Site: http://banking.sc.gov

Driver Licensing & Vehicle Registration

Department Of Motor Vehicles
10311 Wilson Boulevard - Building C
Blythewood, South Carolina 29016
Phone: (803) 896-5000
Toll Free: (800) 442-1DMV (1368)
E-mail: help@scdmvonline.com
Web Site: http://www.scdmvonline.com

State Economic Development

South Carolina Economic Development
1201 Main Street, Suite 1600
Columbia, SC 29201-3200
Phone: (803) 737-0400
Toll Free: (800) 868-7232
Web Site: http://sccommerce.com

South Carolina State Offices

South Carolina Dept. of Consumer Affairs
3600 Forest Dr , 3rd floor
PO Box 5757
Columbia, SC 29250-5757
Phone: 803-734-4200
Toll free: 1-800-922-1594
Toll free: 1-877-734-4215
Fax: 803-734-4286
E-mail: scdca@scconsumer gov
Web Site: http://www.scconsumer.gov

Better Business Bureau

Better Business Bureau
408 N. Church St., Suite C
Greenville, SC 29601-2164
Phone: 864-242-5052
E-mail: info@greenville.bbb.org
Web Site: http://www.bbb.org

State Government

South Carolina
Web Site: http://www.sc.gov

South Dakota

Tourist Information

Department of Tourism and State Development
Office of Tourism
Capitol Lake Plaza
711 East Wells Avenue
c/o 500 East Capitol Avenue
Pierre, SD 57501-5070
Phone: 1 (605) 773-3301
Fax: 1 (605) 773-3256
Toll Free: 1-800-S-DAKOTA - (1-800-732-5682)
E-mail: sdinfo@state.sd.us
Web Site: http://www.travelsd.com/

State Banking & Finance

Division of Banking
217 1/2 W. Missouri Ave.
Pierre, SD 57501-4590
Phone: 605-773-3421
E-mail: drr.banking.info@state.sd.us
Web Site: http://www.state.sd.us/banking

Driver Licensing & Vehicle Registration

Department of Public Safety
118 West Capitol Avenue
Pierre, South Dakota 57501
Phone: (605).773.3178
Fax: (605).773.3018
Toll Free: 1.800.952.3696
Web Site: http://dps.sd.gov

State Economic Development

South Dakota Governor's Office of Economic Development
711 E Wells Ave
Pierre, SD 57501
Toll Free: 800-872-6190
E-mail: goedinfo@state.sd.us
Web Site: http://www.sdreadytowork.com

South Dakota State Offices

South Dakota Office of the
Attorney General

Consumer Affairs
1302 E Hwy 14, Suite 3
Pierre, SD 57501-8503
Phone: 605-773-4400
Toll free: 1-800-300-1986
TTY: 605-773-6585
Fax: 605-773-7163
E-mail: consumerhelp@state sd us

Web Site: http://www.state.sd.us/atg

Better Business Bureau

Better Business Bureau
300 N. Phillips Ave., #202
Sioux Falls, SD 57104
Phone: 605-271-2066
E-mail: info@bbbsouthdakota.org
Web Site: http://www.bbb.org

State Government

South Dakota
Web Site: http://www.sd.gov

Tennessee

Tourist Information

State of Tennessee's Department of Tourist Development
Wm. Snodgrass/Tennessee Tower
312 Rosa L. Parks Avenue, 25th Floor
Nashville, TN 37243

Phone: (615) 741-2159
Toll Free: 1-800-462-8366 or email us at
E-mail: info@tnvacation.com
Web Site: http://www.tnvacation.com
Web Site: http://www.tnvacation.com

State Banking & Finance

Department of Financial Institutions
Consumer Resources Division
414 Union St., Suite 1000
Nashville, TN 37219
Phone: 615-253-2023
Toll Free: 1-800-778-4215
E-mail: TDFI.ConsumerResources@state.tn.us
Web Site: http://www.tennessee.gov/tdfi

Driver Licensing & Vehicle Registration

Tennessee Department of Safety
PO BOX 945
Nashville, TN 37202
Phone: (615) 253-5221
Toll Free: 1-866-849-3548 (Toll Free)
Fax: (615) 253-2092
E-mail: Safety@tn.gov
Web Site:
https://www.tennesseeanytime.org/tndlr

State Economic Development

Tennessee Department of Economic & Community Development
312 Rosa L. Parks Ave., Eleventh Floor
Nashville, TN 37243
Phone: (615) 741-3282
Fax: (615) 741-5829
Toll Free: (877) 768-6374
Web Site: http://tennessee.gov/ecd

Tennessee State Offices

Tennessee Division of Consumer Affairs
500 James Robertson Pkwy , 5th Floor
Nashville, TN 37243-0600
Phone: 615-741-4737
Toll free: 1-800-342-8385
Fax: 615-532-4994
E-mail: consumer affairs@tn gov
Web Site: http://www.tn.gov/consumer

Better Business Bureau

Better Business Bureau
201 Fourth Ave North, Suite 100
Nashville, TN 37219
Phone: 615-242-4222
E-mail: bbbnash@aol.com
Web Site: http://www.bbb.org

State Government

Tennessee
Web Site: http://tennessee.gov

Texas

Tourist Information

Texas Tourism
PO Box 12428
Austin, TX 78711
Toll Free: 1-800-452-9292
Web Site: http://www.traveltex.com

State Banking & Finance

Department of Banking
2601 North Lamar Blvd., Suite 201
Austin, TX 78705
Phone: 512-475-1300
Toll Free: 1-877-276-5554 (Consumer Hotline)
E-mail:
consumer.complaints@banking.state.tx.us
Web Site: http://www.banking.state.tx.us

Driver Licensing & Vehicle Registration

Texas Department of Public Safety
5805 North Lamar Blvd.
Austin, Texas 78752-4422
Web Site: http://www.txdps.state.tx.us

State Economic Development

Texas Economic Development and Tourism
P.O. Box 12428
Austin, Texas 78711
Phone: (512) 463-2000
Fax: (512) 463-1849
Web Site:

http://www.governor.state.tx.us/ecodevo

Texas State Offices

Texas Office of the Attorney General
Consumer Protection Dept
PO Box 12548
Austin, TX 78711-2548
Phone: 512-463-2100
Toll free: 1-800-621-0508
Fax: 512-473-8301
Web Site: http://www.oag.state.tx.us

Better Business Bureau

Better Business Bureau
1601 Elm St., Suite 3838
Dallas, TX 75201-3093
Phone: 214-220-2000
E-mail: info@dallas.bbb.org
Web Site: http://www.bbb.org

State Government

Texas
Web Site: http://www.texas.gov

Utah

Tourist Information

Utah Office Of Tourism,
Council Hall/Capitol Hill
300 N State Street
Salt Lake City, UT 84114
Toll Free: (800) 200-1160
Web Site: http://www.utah.com

State Banking & Finance

Department of Financial Institutions
PO Box 146800
Salt Lake City, UT 84114-6800
Phone: 801-538-8830
Web Site: http://www.dfi.utah.gov

Driver Licensing & Vehicle Registration

Utah Department of Transportation
4501 South 2700 West

P.O. Box 141265
Salt Lake City, UT 84114-1265
Phone: 801-965-4000
E-mail: srwebmail@utah.gov
Web Site: http://www.udot.utah.gov

State Economic Development

Utah Governor's Office of Economic
Development
324 South State Street, Suite 500
Salt Lake City, UT 84111
Phone: 1: 801-538-8700
Fax: 801-538-8888
Toll Free: 877-488-3233
Web Site: http://goed.utah.gov
Web Site: http://business.utah.gov

Utah State Offices

Utah Dept. of Commerce
Division of Consumer Protection
160 East 300 South
PO Box 146704
Salt Lake City, UT 84114-6704
Phone: 801-530-6601
Fax: 801-530-6001
E-mail: consumerprotection@utah.gov
Web Site:
http://www.consumerprotection.utah.gov

Better Business Bureau

Better Business Bureau
5673 S. Redwood Rd, Suite 22
Salt Lake City, UT 84123-5322
Phone: 801-892-6009
E-mail: info@utah.bbb.org
Web Site: http://www.bbb.org

State Government

Utah
Web Site: http://www.utah.gov

Vermont

Tourist Information

Vermont Dept. of Tourism and Marketing

One National Life Drive, 6th Floor
Montpelier, VT 05620-0501
Phone: 1-802-828-3237
Toll Free: 1-800-VERMONT
E-mail: info@VermontVacation.com
Web Site: http://www.1-800-vermont.com

State Banking & Finance

Department of Banking, Insurance, Securities
and Health Care Administration
89 Main St., Drawer 20
Montpelier, VT 05620-3101
Phone: 802-828-3301
Phone: 802-828-3307 (Banking)
E-mail: bankdiv@bishca.state.vt.us
Web Site: http://www.bishca.state.vt.us

Driver Licensing & Vehicle Registration

Vermont Department of Motor Vehicles
120 State Street
Montpelier, VT 05603-0001
Phone: 802-828-2000
E-mail: CommissionersOffice@state.vt.us
Web Site: http://dmv.vermont.gov/licenses

State Economic Development

Vermont Department of Economic Development
1 National Life Drive
Montpelier, VT 05620-0501
Phone: 802 828 3080
Fax: 802 828 3258
E-mail: info@thinkvermont.com
Web Site: http://www.thinkvermont.com

Vermont State Offices

Vermont Office of the Attorney General
Consumer Assistance Program
206 Morrill Hall, UVM
Burlington, VT 05405
Phone: 802-656-3183
Toll free: 1-800-649-2424
Fax: 802-656-1423
E-mail: consumercomplaint@atg.state vt us
Web Site: http://www.atg.state.vt.us

Better Business Bureau

See other state.

State Government

Vermont
Web Site: http://www.vermont.gov

Virgin Islands

Tourist Information

USVI Division Of Tourism
PO Box 6400
St Thomas, VI 00804
Toll Free: 1 (800)372-USVI - 1 800-372-8784
E-mail: LosAngeles@usvitourism.vi
Web Site: http://www.usvitourism.vi

State Banking & Finance

Division of Banking and Insurance
Office of the Lt. Governor
#18 Kongens Gade
St. Thomas, VI 00802
Phone: 340-774-7166
Web Site: http://www.ltg.gov.vi

Driver Licensing & Vehicle Registration

State Economic Development

U.S. Virgin Islands Economic Development
Authority
1050 Norre Gade # 5,
Government Development Bank Bldg.
P.O. Box 305038,
St. Thomas, USVI 00803
Phone: (340) 714-1700
Web Site: http://www.usvieda.org

Virgin Islands State Offices

Virgin Islands Dept. of Licensing and Consumer
Affairs
3000 Golden Rock Shopping Center, Suite 9
Christiansted, VI 00820-4311
Phone: 340-773-2226
Fax: 340-778-8250
Web Site: http://www.dlca.gov.vi

Better Business Bureau

See other state.

State Government

U.S. Virgin Islands
Web Site: http://ltg.gov.vi

Virginia

Tourist Information

Virginia Tourism Corporation
901 E. Byrd St.
Richmond, VA 23219
Phone: 1 (800) VISIT VA – 1 (800-847-4882)
E-mail: VAinfo@helloinc.com
Web Site: http://www.virginia.org

State Banking & Finance

Bureau of Financial Institutions
PO Box 640
Richmond, VA 23218
804-371-9657
804-371-9705
Toll Free: 1-800-552-7945 (VA)
Phone: TTY: 804-371-9206
E-mail: bfiquestions@scc.virginia.gov
Web Site: http://www.scc.virginia.gov

Driver Licensing & Vehicle Registration

Virginia Department of Motor Vehicles
P.O. Box 27412
Richmond, VA 23269
Phone: (804) 497-7100
Toll Free: 1-888-337-4782
Web Site: http://www.dmv.state.va.us/

State Economic Development

Virginia Economic Development Partnership
901 East Byrd Street
P.O. Box 798
Richmond, VA 23218-0798
Phone: (804) 545-5600 (General)
Phone: (804) 545-5700 (Domestic)

Phone: (804) 545-5750 (International)
Web Site: http://www.yesvirginia.org

Virginia State Offices

Dept. of Agriculture and
Consumer Services
PO Box 1163
Richmond, VA 23218
Phone: 804-786-2042
Toll free: 1-800-552-9963 (VA)
Toll free: 1-800-828-1120
Fax: 804-225-2666
E-mail: webmaster.vdacs@vdacs.virginia.gov
Web Site: http://www.vdacs.virginia.gov

Better Business Bureau

Better Business Bureau
720 Moorefield Park Dr., Suite 300
Richmond, VA 23236
Phone: 804-648-0016
E-mail: info@richmond.bbb.org
Web Site: http://www.bbb.org

State Government

Virginia
Web Site: http://www.virginia.gov

Washington

Tourist Information

Washington State Tourism Office
128 10th Avenue, SW
PO Box 42525
Olympia, CA 98504
Toll Free: 1-800-544-1800
E-mail: tourism@cted.wa.gov
Web Site: http://www.experiencewa.com

State Banking & Finance

Department of Financial Institutions
PO Box 41200
Olympia, WA 98504-1200
Phone: 360-902-8700
Toll Free: 1-877-RING-DFI
Phone: TTY: 360-664-8126

Web Site: http://www.dfi.wa.gov

Driver Licensing & Vehicle Registration

Department of Licensing
PO Box 9030
Olympia, WA 98507-9030
Phone: (360) 902-3900
Phone: (360) 902-3770   Vehicle & Boat
Registration
Web Site: http://www.dol.wa.gov

State Economic Development

Washington Economic Development Finance
Authority
1000 Second Avenue, Suite 2700
Seattle, WA 98104-1046
Rodney G. Wendt
Executive Director
Phone: (206) 587-5634
Fax: (206) 587-5113
Mobile: (206) 579-0782
E-mail: info@wedfa.org
Web Site: http://wedfa.org

Washington State Offices

Seattle Consumer Resource Center
Office of the Attorney General
800 Fifth Ave., Suite 2000
Seattle, WA 98104
206-464-6684
Toll free: 1-800-551-4636
Toll free: 1-800-833-6384
Fax: 206-389-2801
Web Site: http://www.atg.wa.gov

Better Business Bureau

Better Business Bureau
152 S. Jefferson, Suite 200
Spokane, WA 99201
Phone: 509-455-4200
E-mail: info@spokane.bbb.org
Web Site: http://www.bbb.org

State Government

Washington
Web Site: http://access.wa.gov

Washington District Of Columbia

Tourist Information

Destination DC
901 7th Street NW, 4th Floor, Washington, DC
20001-3719
Toll Free: 800-422-8644 Toll Free
Conventions: 800-635-MEET
Phone: 202.789.7000 FAX 202.789.7037
Web Site: http://washington.org

State Banking & Finance

Department of Insurance, Securities and
Banking
ATTN: Consumer Protection Advocate
810 First, NE, Suite 701
Washington, DC 20002
Phone: 202-727-8000
Phone: 202-442-7843
E-mail: disb@dc.gov
Web Site: http://www.disb.dc.gov

Driver Licensing & Vehicle Registration

District Of Columbia DMV
Georgetown Service Center
Georgetown Park Mall- Lower Level
3222 M Street, NW
Washington, DC 20007
Phone: (202) 737-4404
Web Site: http://dmv.dc.gov/serv/dlicense.shtm

State Economic Development

Office of the Deputy Mayor for Planning and Economic Development
John A. Wilson Building
1350 Pennsylvania Avenue, NW, Suite 317
Washington, DC 20004
Phone: (202) 727-6365
Web Site: http://dcbiz.dc.gov/dmped

District Of Columbia State Offices

District of Columbia Office of the
Attorney General

Office of Consumer Protection
441 4th St , NW
Suite 600, South
Washington, DC 20001
Phone: 202-727-3400
Fax: 202-478-9296

Web Site: http://www.oag.dc.gov

Better Business Bureau

Better Business Bureau
1411 K St., NW, 10th Floor
Washington, DC 20005-3404
Phone: 202-393-8000
E-mail: info@mybbb.org
Web Site: http://www.bbb.org

State Government

DC
Web Site: http://dc.gov

West Virginia

Tourist Information

West Virginia Division Of Tourism
90 MacCorkie Avenue, SW
South Charleston, WV 25303
Toll Free: 1-800-CALL-WVA - 1-800-225-5982
Web Site: http://wvtourism.com

State Banking & Finance

Division of Banking
One Players Club Dr., Suite 300
Charleston, WV 25311
Phone: 304-558-2294
Toll Free: 1-800-642-9056 (WV)
Web Site: http://www.wvdob.org

Driver Licensing & Vehicle Registration

West Virginia Department Of Transportation
1900 Kanawha Blvd E
Charleston, WV 25305
Phone: (304)558-2723
Toll-Free: 1-800-642-9066

Fax: (304)558-1987
E-mail: dot.dmvcommissioner@wv.gov
Web Site: http://www.transportation.wv.gov

State Economic Development

West Virginia Economic Development Authority
Greenway Building, Northgate Business Park
160 Association Drive
Charleston, WV 25311-1217
Telephone: (304) 558-3650
Fax: (304) 558-0206
Web Site: http://www.wveda.org

West Virginia State Offices

Office of the Attorney General
Consumer Protection Division
PO Box 1789
Charleston, WV 25326-1789
Phone: 304-558-8986
Toll free: 1-800-368-8808
Fax: 304-558-0184
E-mail: consumer@wvago.gov
Web Site: http://www.wvago.gov

Better Business Bureau

Better Business Bureau
910 Quarrier St., Suite 405-406
Charleston, WV 25301
Phone: 304-345-7503
E-mail: info@cantonbbb.org
Web Site: http://www.bbb.org

State Government

West Virginia
Web Site: http://www.wv.gov

Wisconsin

Tourist Information

Wisconsin Department of Tourism
201 West Washington Avenue
PO Box 8690
Madison WI 53708-8690
Phone: 1-(608)-266-2161
Toll Free: 1-800-432-8747

E-mail: tourinfo@travelwisconsin.com
Web Site: http://www.travelwisconsin.com

State Banking & Finance

Department of Financial Institutions
Division Of Banking
PO Box 7846
Madison, WI 53707-7846
608-261-7577
Toll Free: 1-800-452-3328 (WI)
Phone: TTY: 608-266-8818
E-mail: askthesecretary@dfi.state.wi.us
Web Site: http://www.wdfi.org

Driver Licensing & Vehicle Registration

Wisconsin Department of Transportation
Hill Farms State Transportation Building
4802 Sheboygan Avenue
P.O. Box 7999
Madison, WI 53707-7999
Phone: (608) 266-2353 Driver Licenses
Phone: (608) 266-3666 Vehicle Records
Web Site: http://www.dot.wisconsin.gov

State Economic Development

WI Department of Commerce
Central Building Location:
201 W. Washington Ave.
Madison, WI 53703
Phone: (608) 266-1018
Web Site: http://www.commerce.state.wi.us

Wisconsin State Offices

Dept. of Agriculture, Trade and
Consumer Protection
PO Box 8911
2811 Agriculture Dr.
Madison, WI 53708-8911
Phone: 608-224-4976
Toll free: 1-800-422-7128
TTY: 608-224-5058
Fax: 608-224-4939
E-mail: hotline@datcp.state.wi.us
Web Site: http://www.datcp.state.wi.us

Better Business Bureau

Better Business Bureau
10101 W. Greeenfield Ave., Suite 125
West Allis, WI 53214
Phone: 414-847-6000
E-mail: info@wisconsin.bbb.org
Web Site: http://www.bbb.org

State Government

Wisconsin
Web Site: http://www.wisconsin.gov

Wyoming

Tourist Information

Wyoming Travel & Tourism
1520 Etchepare Circle
Cheyenne, WY 82007
Phone: : 1-307-777-7777
Fax: 1-307-777-2877
E-mail: info@visitwyo.gov
Toll Free: 1-800-225-5996
Web Site: http://www.wyomingtourism.org

State Banking & Finance

Division of Banking
122 West 25th St.
Herschler Bldg., 3rd Floor, East
Cheyenne, WY 82002
Phone: 307-777-7797
Web Site: http://audit.state.wy.us/banking

Driver Licensing & Vehicle Registration

Wyoming Department Of Transportation
5300 Bishop Blvd.
Cheyenne, WY 82009-3340
Phone: (307) 777-4375
Web Site: http://www.dot.state.wy.us/wydot

State Economic Development

Wyoming Business Council
214 West 15th St.
Cheyenne, WY 82002-0240
Phone: 307-777-2800
Fax: (307)-777-2838
Toll Free: 800-262-3425
E-mail: info@wyomingbusiness.org
Web Site: http://www.wyomingbusiness.org

Wyoming State Offices

Office of the Attorney General
Consumer Protection Unit
123 State Capitol, 200 W. 24th St.
Cheyenne, WY 82002
Phone: 307-777-7874
Toll free: 1-800-438-5799
Fax: 307-777-7956
Web Site: http://attorneygeneral.state.wy.us

Better Business Bureau

See other state.

State Government

Wyoming
Web Site: http://www.wyoming.gov

U.S. Territories

Midway Islands
Web Site: http://www.fws.gov/midway

American Samoa
Web Site: http://americansamoa.gov

Federated States Of Micronesia
Web Site: http://www.fsmgov.org

Chapter 9

National Birth, Death, Marriage And Divorce Records.

Centers for Disease Control And Prevention.

The Centers For Disease Control And Prevention has detailed national and international information on birth, death, marriage and divorce records for American citizens and naturalized American residents.

Contact

Centers for Disease Control and Prevention
1600 Clifton Rd. Atlanta, GA 30333, USA

Toll Free: 800-CDC-INFO (800-232-4636) TTY: (888)
Phone: 232-6348, 24 Hours/Every Day –
Email: cdcinfo@cdc.gov
Website: http://www.cdc.gov/nchs/w2w.htm

Instruction Section

The following "Instruction section" includes instructions for purchasing all birth, death, marriage and death certificates and records.

Certificates

All birth records, death records, marriage records and divorce records are available as certificates or printed reports.

Locating Records Not Listed In Each State Section.

Each state section describes the dates that records are available. Many records that are kept in archives are still available for earlier dates then the dates described in this book. Contact the state to located birth, death, marriage or divorce records that are available at an earlier date then the date listed in this chapter's state sections. States like Wisconsin have records dating back to 1836. New Hampshire has records since 1640 with marriage and divorce records since 1808. Some states provide printed records as opposed to certificates. In many state sections a double date is shown with back slash like 1923/1892. This pudnctuation indicates that records are available since 1923 but a good selection of additional records are available from 1892 from that state.

Certified Copies Of Birth, Death, Marriage and Divorce Records.

Contact state office for price quotes of certified copies of certificates. In many cases certification is available from the county where the event took place.

Information To Include With Birth Or Death Request

1. Type or print all names and addresses.
2. Full name of person whose record is being requested.
3. Sex of person.
4. Parent's names, including maiden name of mother.
5. Month, day, and year of birth or death.
6. Place of birth or death (city or town, county, and State and name of hospital if known).
7. Purpose for which copy is needed.
8. Relationship to person whose record is being requested.
9. States do require a copy of a government photo ID of applicant.

Information To Include With Marriage Or Divorce Request

1. Type or print all names and addresses.
2. Full name of bride/wife or groom/husband.
3. Month, day and year of marriage or annulment/divorce.
4. Place of marriage or divorce or annulment (city, town, county and state).
5. For divorce records (Type of final decree)
6. Purpose for which copy is needed
7. Relationship to persons whose record is being requested.
8. **States do require a copy of a government photo ID of applicant.**

Alabama

Address
Alabama Center For Health Statistics
Alabama Department Of Public Health
PO Box 5625
Montgomery, AL 36103-5625
Phone: (334) 206-5418
Web Site: http://adph.org.vitalrecords

Cost & Availability Of Certificates/Records

Money orders made payable to "Center For Health Statistics".

- **Birth: $15.00 Records since 1908**
- **Death: $15.00 Records since 1908**
- **Marriage: $15.00 Records since 1936. Cost varies for some records only with Probate Court.**
- **Divorce: $15.00 Records since 1950. Cost varies for all records prior to 1950 and some records after 1950; Contact the Clerk Of Circuit Court in county for these records**

Remarks: Additional copies ordered at the same time, $6.00 each. Earlier years are available. See instruction section for purchasing all certificates and records.

Alaska

Address
Bureau Of Vital Statistics
Department Of Health And Social Services
5441 Commercial Boulevard
Juneau, AK 99801
Phone: (907) 465-3391
Web Site: http://www.hss.state.ak.us/dph/bvs/

Cost & Availability Of Certificates/Records

Money orders made payable to "Bureau Of Vital Statistics".

- **Birth: $25.00 Records since 1890's**
- **Death: $25.00 Records since 1890's**
- **Marriage: $25.00 Records since 1890's.**
- **Divorce: $25.00 Records since 1950. Cost varies for some records only with Clerk Of Superior Court is event county.**

Remarks: Additional copies ordered at the same time, $20.00 each. All requests must include a copy of a picture ID of the applicant. Earlier years are available. See instruction section for purchasing all certificates and records.

Gifts: Alaska fancy artistic heirloom birth certificates $50.00. Alaska fancy artistic heirloom marriage certificate $55.00. Family and friends may order gift certificates.

American Samoa

Address
American Samoa Government Governor's Office.
Registrar Of Vital Records Office
Pago Pago, AS 96799
Phone: (684) 633-1406. (Verify current fees)
Phone: (684) 633-4606 (Office)

Cost & Availability Of Certificates/Records

Money orders made payable to "ASG

Treasurer".

- **Birth: $5.00**
- **Death: $5.00**
- **Marriage: $5.00**
- **Marriage License: $10.00**
- **Divorce: $5.00**

Remarks: Additional copies ordered at the same time, $20.00 each. All requests must include personal identification. Earlier years are available. See instruction section for purchasing all certificates and records.

Arizona

Address
Office Of Vital Records
Arizona Department Of Health Services
PO Box 3887
Phoenix, AZ 85030-3887
Phone: (602) 364-1300
Web Site: http://www.azdhs.gov

Cost & Availability Of Certificates/Records

Money orders made payable to "Office Of Vital Records".

- **Birth: Cost varies Records since 1909.**
- **Death: Cost varies Records since 1909.**
- **Marriage: Cost varies Records since 1909. See Clerk Of Superior Court in event county.**
- **Divorce: Cost varies Records since 1909. See Clerk Of Superior Court in event county.**

Remarks: All requests must include a copy of picture identification or have their request notarized. Earlier years are available. See instruction section for purchasing all certificates and records.

Arkansas

Address

Vital Records H-44
4815 West Markham
Little Rock, AR 72205
Phone: (501) 661-2336
Web Site: http://healthyarkansas.com

Cost & Availability Of Certificates/Records

Money orders made payable to "Arkansas Department Of Health".

- **Birth: $12.00   Records since 1914/1881**
- **Death: $10.00   Records since 1914/1881**
- **Marriage: $10.00   Records since 1917. Cost varies for some records only with County Clerk.**
- **Divorce: $10.00   Records since 1923. Cost varies for some records only with Chancery Clerk.**

Remarks: Additional copies ordered at the same time, $8.00 each for birth and death and $10.00 each for marriage and divorce. Earlier years are available. See instruction section for purchasing all certificates and records.

California

Address
Office Of Vital Records
CA Department Of Public Health, MS: 5103
PO Box 997410
Sacramento, CA 95899-7410
Phone: (916) 445-2684
Web Site:
http://www.cdph.ca.gov/certlie/birthdeathmar/Pages/default.aspx
Other website address for marriage and divorce.

Cost & Availability Of Certificates/Records

Money orders made payable to "Office Of Vital Records.

- **Birth: $14.00   Records since 1905**
- **Death: $12.00   Records since 1905**
- **Marriage: $14.00   Records since 1949. Cost varies for some records**

only with County recorder.
- **Divorce: $13.00   Records since 1962. Cost varies for some records only with Clerk Of Superior Court.**

Remarks: Some years have been omitted. Additional years are available.   Contact California for additional information. Earlier years are available. See instruction section for purchasing all certificates and records.

Canal Zone

Address
Vital Records Section Passport Services
U.S. Department Of State
111 19th Street, NW, Suite 510
Washington, DC 20522-1705
Phone: (202) 955-0307

Cost & Availability Of Certificates/Records

Money orders made payable to "U.S. Department Of State".

- **Birth: $30.00   Records since 1904**
- **Death: $30.00   Records since 1904**
- **Marriage: $30.00   Records since 1904-1979**

Remarks: Additional copies ordered at the same time, $20.00 each. Earlier years are available. See instruction section for purchasing all certificates and records.

Colorado

Address
Vital Records Section
CO Department Of Public Health And Environment
4300 Cherry Creek Drive South
Denver, CO 80246-1530
Phone: (303) 692-2200
Web Site:
http://cdphe.state.co.us/certs/index.html

Cost & Availability Of Certificates/Records

Money orders made payable to "Vital Records

Section".

Birth: $17.75   Records since 1910
Death: $17.00   Records since 1900
Marriage: $17.00   Fee is for verification.
Certified copies not available from State.
Cost varies for some records only available
from County Clerk.
Divorce: $17.00   Fee is for verification.
Certified copies not available from State.
Cost varies for some records only available
from Clerk Of District Court.

Remarks: Additional copies of records ordered at the same time are $10.00 each.   Requests for birth and death must include a copy of requester's identification. Earlier years are available. See instruction section for purchasing all certificates and records.

Connecticut

Address
Department Of Public Health
410 Capitol Ave, MS #11 VRS
Hartford, CT 06134
Phone: (806) 509-7897
Web Site: http://www.et.gov/dph

Cost & Availability Of Certificates/Records

Money orders made payable to "Treasurer, State Of Connecticut".

- **Birth: $30.00   Records since 1890's**
- **Death: $20.00   Records since 1890's**
- **Marriage: $20.00   Records since 1890's**
- **Divorce/Dissolution Of Marriage: Contact Clerk of the Superior Court.**

Remarks: Birth certificate requests must include a copy of a picture ID of the applicant. Earlier years are available. Civil unions recorded as well. See instruction section for purchasing all certificates and records.

Delaware

Address

Office Of Vital Statistics
Division Of Public Health
417 Federal Street
Dover, DE 19901
Phone: (302) 744-4549
Web Site:
http://www.dhss.delaware.gov/dhss/dph/ss/vitalstats.html

Cost & Availability Of Certificates/Records

Money orders made payable to "Office Of Vital Statistics".

- **Birth: $25.00   Records since 1938.**
- **Death: $25.00   Records since 1938.**
- **Marriage: $25.00   Records since 1969.**
- **Divorce: $25.00   Records since 1935.**

Remarks: Write Archives Hall Of Records, Dover, DE 19901 for earlier years of birth records. All requests must include a copy of a picture ID of the applicant. Earlier years are available. See instruction section for purchasing all certificates and records.

Florida

Address
Department Of Health
Bureau Of Vital Statistics
1217 Pearl Street
Jacksonville, FL 32202
Phone: (904) 359-6900
Web Site:
http://www.doh.stat.fl.us/planning_eval/vital_statistics/birth_death.htm

Cost & Availability Of Certificates/Records

Money orders made payable to "Bureau Of Vital Statistics".

- **Birth: $9.00   Records since 1917/1865 -**
- **Death: $5.00   Records since 1917/1865**
- **Marriage: $5.00   Records since 1927**
- **Divorce: $5.00   Records since 1927**

Remarks: Search fee of $9.00 (includes one copy) for births and $5.00 (includes one copy) for deaths records and $2.00 up to a maximum of $50.00 for each additional date searched if the exact date of birth or death or marriage or divorce is not known. Additional copies ordered at the same time are $4.00 each. Earlier years are available. See instruction section for purchasing all certificates and records.

Georgia

Address
Vital Records
Department Of Community Health
2600 Skyland Drive, NE
Atlanta, GA 30319-3640
Web Site:
http://www.state.ga.us/programs/vitalrecords

Cost & Availability Of Certificates//Records

Money orders made payable to "Vital Records".

- **Birth: $25.00 Records since 1919**
- **Death: $25.00 Records since 1919**
- **Marriage: $10.00 Records since 1952. Cost varies for some records only available from County Probate Judges.**
- **Divorce: $2.00 per certification and $.50 per page Records since 1952.**

Remarks: Additional copies of records ordered at the same time are $5.00 each. All requests must include a copy of photo ID. State office does not record marriages after 1997. Earlier years are available. See instruction section for purchasing all certificates and records.

Guam

Address
Office Of Vital Statistics
PO Box 2816
Hagatna, Guam 96932
Phone: (671) 735-7292

Cost & Availability Of Certificates/Records

Money orders made payable to "Treasurer Of Guam".

- **Birth: $5.00 Records since 1901**
- **Death: $5.00 Records since 1901**
- **Marriage: $5.00 Records since 1901**
- **Divorce: Cost varies Contact Clerk, Superior Court Of Guam, Guam Judicial Center, 120 West O'Brian Drive, Hagatna, Guam, 96910. Records since 1901.**

Remarks:
Additional copies of records ordered at the same time are $5.00 each. All requests must include a copy of photo ID. Earlier years are available. See instruction section for purchasing all certificates and records.

Hawaii

Address
State Department Of Health
Office Of Health Status Monitoring
Issurance/Vital Statistics Section
PO Box 3378
Honolulu, HI 96801
Phone: (808) 586-4533
Web Site: http://hawaii.gov/health/vital-records/vital-records

Cost & Availability Of Certificates/Records

Money orders made payable to "State Department Of Health".

- **Birth: $10.00 Records since 1951/1853**
- **Death: $10.00 Records since 1951/1853**
- **Marriage: $10.00 Records since 1951/1853**
- **Divorce: $10.00 Records since 1951/1853. Records from 2003 to present available from County Circuit Court. Cost varies for other records only available from County Circuit Court.**

Remarks: Additional copies of records ordered at the same time are $4.00 each. All requests must include a copy of photo ID. Earlier years are available. See instruction section for purchasing all certificates and records.

Idaho

Address
Vital Records Unit
Bureau Of Vital Records and Health Statistics
PO Box 83720
Boise, ID 83720-0036
Phone: (208) 334-5988
Web Site: http://healthandwelfare.idaho.gov

Cost & Availability Of Certificates/Records

Money orders made payable to "Idaho Vital Records".

- **Birth: $13.00(Computer Generated)/$18.00(Photostatic) Records since 1911**
- **Death: $14.00(Computer Generated)/$19.00(Photostatic) Records since 1911**
- **Marriage: $13.00(Computer Generated)/$18.00(Photostatic) Records since 1947. Cost varies for some records available from County recorder.**
- **Divorce: $13.00(Computer Generated)/$18.00(Photostatic) Records since 1947. Cost varies for some records available from Clerk Of The Court.**

Remarks: For records from 1907-1911 write the county recorder in that county.
All requests must include a copy of both sides of a government photo ID with signature or have their request notarized. Earlier years are available. See instruction section for purchasing all certificates and records.

Illinois

Address

Division Of Vital Records
Illinois Department Of Public Health
925 E Ridgely Avenue
Springfield, IL 62702
Phone: (217) 782-6553
http://www.idph.state.il.us

Cost & Availability Of Certificates/Records

Money orders made payable to "Illinois Department Of Public Health".

- **Birth: $10.00 Records since 1916 -**
- **Death: $10.00 Records since 1916**
- **Marriage: $5.00 Records since 1962**
- **Divorce: $5.00 Records since 1962**

Remarks: $15.00 for certified birth records. $17.00 for certified death records. Additional copies of records ordered at the same time are $2.00 each. Earlier years are available. See instruction section for purchasing all certificates and records.

Indiana

Address
Vital Records
Indiana State Department Of Health
PO Box 7125
Indianapolis, IN 46206-7125
Phone: (317) 233-2700
Web Site: http://www.in.gov/isdh/index.htm

Cost & Availability Of Certificates/Records

Money orders made payable to "Indiana State Department Of Health".

- **Birth: $10.00 Records since 1907**
- **Death: $8.00 Records since 1900**
- **Marriage: Cost varies Records since 1958. Cost varies for some records only available from Clerk Of Circuit Court or Clerk Of Superior Court of the county where event took place.**
- **Divorce: Cost varies Brief statistical record since 1906. Contact county clerk in county where divorce was granted.**

Remarks: Additional copies of records ordered at the same time are $4.00 each. Earlier years are available. See instruction section for purchasing all certificates and records.

Iowa

Address
Iowa Department Of Public Health
Bureau Of Vital Records
Lucas Office Building, 1st Floor
321 East 12th Street
Des Moines, IA 50319-0075
Phone: (515) 281-4944
Web Site: http://www.idph.state.ia.us

Cost & Availability Of Certificates/Records

Money orders made payable to "Iowa Department Of Public Health".

- **Birth: $15.00 Records since 1880**
- **Death: $15.00 Records since 1880**
- **Marriage: $15.00 Records since 1880**
- **Divorce: $6.00 Records since 1906**

Remarks: All requests must include a copy of government issued photo ID and applicant's notarized signature. Certified copies of divorce records not available from State Health Department. Earlier years are available. See instruction section for purchasing all certificates and records.

Kansas

Address
Office Of Vital Statistics
Curtis State Office Building
1000 SW Jackson Street, Suite 120
Topeka, KS 66612-2221
Phone: (785) 296-1400
Web Site: http://www.kdheks.gov/vital

Cost & Availability Of Certificates/Records

Money orders made payable to "Vital Statistics".

- **Birth: $15.00 Records since 1911**

- **Death: $15.00 Records since 1911**
- **Marriage: $15.00 Records since 1913. Cost varies for some records available from District Judge.**
- **Divorce: $15.00 Records since 1951. Cost varies for some records available from Clerk Of District Court.**

Remarks:
Additional copies of the same records ordered at the same time are $15.00 each for birth and death records and $7.00 each for marriage and divorce records. All requests must include a copy of photo ID and a handwritten signature with request. Earlier years are available. See instruction section for purchasing all certificates and records.

Kentucky

Address
Office Of Vital Statistics
Department For Public Health
Cabinet For Health And Family Services
275 East Main Street 1E-A
Frankfort, KY 40621-0001
Phone: (502) 564-4212
Web Site: http://chfs.ky.gov/dph/vital

Cost & Availability Of Certificates/Records

Money orders made payable to "Kentucky State Treasurer".

- **Birth: $10.00 Records since 1911**
- **Death: $6.00 Records since 1911**
- **Marriage: $6.00 Records since 1958. Cost varies for some records available from Clerk Of County Court.**
- **Divorce: $6.00 Records since 1958. Cost varies for some records available from Circuit Court.**

Remarks: Earlier years are available. See instruction section for purchasing all certificates and records.

Louisiana

Address
Office Of Public Health
Vital Records Registry
PO Box 60630
New Orleans, LA 70160
Web Site:
http://www.dhh.louisiana.gov/offices/?ID=252.

Cost & Availability Of Certificates/Records

- **Birth: $15.50(long form) / $9.50(short form) Records kept 100 years past the date of birth.**
- **Death: $7.50 Records kept 50 years beyond the date of death.**
- **Marriage: $5.50 Records kept 50 years beyond the date of marriage.**
- **Divorce: Cost varies. Certified copies are issued by Clerk Of The Court.**

Remarks: Earlier years are available. Older records are available through the Louisiana State Archives, PO Box 94125, Baton Rouge, LA 70804. Certified copies of marriage and divorce records are issued by the Clerk of Court in the parish where the marriage license or divorce certificate was issued. See instruction section for purchasing all certificates and records.

Maine

Address
Vital Records
Maine Department Of Health And Human Services
244 Water Street, #11
Augusta, ME 04333-0011
Phone: (207) 287-3181
Web Site: http://www.state.me.us

Cost & Availability Of Certificates/Records

Money orders made payable to "Treasurer, State Of Maine".

- **Birth: $10.00(Non-certified), $15.00(Certified) Records since 1923/1892**
- **Death: $10.00(Non-certified),**

- **$15.00(Certified) Records since 1923/1892**
- **Marriage: $5.00 Records since 1927**
- **Divorce: $5.00 Records since 1927. Cost varies for some records available from Clerk Of District Court.**

Remarks: Additional copies of records ordered at the same time are $6.00 each. Earlier years are available. See instruction section for purchasing all certificates and records.

Maryland

Address
Division Of Public Records
Department Of Health And Mental Hygene
6550 Reisterstown Road
PO Box 68760
Baltimore, MD 21215-0020
Phone: (410) 764-3038
Web Site: http://www.vsa.state.md.us

Cost & Availability Of Certificates/Records

Money orders made payable to "Division Of Vital Records".

- **Birth: $12.00 Records since 1898/1875**
- **Death: $12.00 Records since 1898/1875**
- **Marriage: $12.00 Records since 1990**
- **Divorce: $12.00 Records since 1992**

Remarks: For genealogical studies and early records, you must apply through the Maryland State Archives, 350 Rowe Blvd., Annapolis, MD 21401. (410) 260-6400. See instruction section for purchasing all certificates and records.

Gifts: Fancy commemorative birth certificates for $30.

Massachusetts

Address
Registry Of Vital Records And Statistics

150 Mount Vernon Street, 1st Floor
Dorchester, MA 02125-3105
Phone: (617) 740-2600
Web Site:
http://state.ma.us/dph/bhsrc/rvr/vrcopies.htm

Cost & Availability Of Certificates/Records

Money orders made payable to "Commonwealth Of Massachusetts".

- **Birth: $18.00 (In person). $28.00 (By mail). $3.00 (State archives) Records since 1916.**
- **Death: $18.00 (In person). $28.00 (By mail). $3.00 (State archives) Records since 1916**
- **Marriage: $18.00 (In person). $28.00 (By mail). $3.00 (State archives) Records since 1916**
- **Divorce: No Fee Records since 1952 – Cost varies for other records available from the Registrar of Probate Court in county where divorce was granted.**

Remarks: For earlier records then 1916 write to the Massachusetts Archives at Columbia Point, 220 Morrissey Boulevard, Boston, MA 02125. (617) 727-2816. Certified copies are not available from state office. See instruction section for purchasing all certificates and records.

Michigan

Address
Vital Records Request
PO Box 30721
Lansing, MI 48909
Phone: (517) 335-8666
Phone: (517) 335-8656 (verify fees)
Web Site: http://www.michigan.gov/mdch

Cost & Availability Of Certificates/Records

Money orders made payable to "State Of Michigan".

- **Birth: $26.00 $7.00 (For seniors**

requesting their own birth records). Records since 1906/1867
- **Death: $26.00 Records since 1897/1867**
- **Marriage: $26.00 Records since 1926/1867. Cost varies for some records available from the County Clerk.**
- **Divorce: $26.00 Records since 1924/1867. Cost varies for some records available from the County Clerk.**

Remarks: Additional copies of records ordered at the same time are $12.00 each. Earlier years are available. See instruction section for purchasing all certificates and records.

Minnesota

Address
Office Of The State Registrar
MN Department Of Health
PO Box 64882
St. Paul, MN 55164
Phone: (651) 201-5970
Web Site: http://www.health.state.mn.us

Cost & Availability Of Certificates/Records

Money orders made payable to "Minnesota Department Of Health".

- **Birth: $26.00 Records since 1900**
- **Death: $13.00 Records since 1908**
- **Marriage: $9.00 Contact Local Register in county where license was issued.** Additional copies of marriage records ordered at the same time are $2.00 each.
- **Divorce: $10.00 Contact Court Administrator in county where license was issued.**

Remarks: Earlier years are available from the Local Registrar in county where event took place. See instruction section for purchasing all certificates and records.

Mississippi

Address
Mississippi Vital Records
State Department Of Health
PO Box 1700
Jackson, MS 39215-1700
Phone: (601) 576-7981 (Current Fees)
Phone: (601) 576-7450 (Recorded Message)
Web Site: http://www.msdh.state.ms.us

Cost & Availability Of Certificates/Records

Money orders made payable to "Mississippi State Department Of Health".

- **Birth: $15.00 Records since 1912**
- **Death: $15.00 Records since 1912**
- **Marriage: $15.00 Records since 1926-1938, 1942-Present. Cost varies for some records with Circuit Clerk.**
- **Divorce: Cost varies Records since 1926. Index search at $15 for each 5 year increment. Certified copies not available from State Office. Cost varies for some records with Chancery Clerk.**

Remarks: Additional copies of records ordered at the same time are $5.00 each.
All requests must include a copy of photo ID. Earlier years are available. See instruction section for purchasing all certificates and records.

Missouri

Address
Missouri Department Of Health And Senior Services
Bureau Of Vital Records
930 Wildwood
PO Box 570
Jefferson City, MO 65102-0570
Phone: (573) 751-6387
Web Site: http://dhss.mo.gov

Cost & Availability Of Certificates/Records

Money orders made payable to "Missouri

Department Of Health And Senior Services". Include legal size self-addressed stamped envelope.

- **Birth: $15.00 Records since 1910**
- **Death: $13.00 Records since 1910**
- **Marriage: Cost varies Records since 1910. Contact Recorder Of Deeds in the county where the license was issued.**
- **Divorce: Cost varies Records since 1910. Contact Clerk Of Circuit Court in county where divorce was granted.**

Remarks: Certified copies are available from local county health department. If event occurred before 1910 contact local city or county health department. Additional copies of the same death records ordered at the same time are $10.00 each. Earlier years are available. See instruction section for purchasing all certificates and records.

Montana

Address
Office Of Vital Statistics
MT Dept Of Public Health And Human Services
111 N Sanders, Room 209
PO Box 4210
Helena, MT 59604
Toll Free: 1-888-877-1946
Web Site: http://www.dphhs.state.mt.us

Cost & Availability Of Certificates/Records

Money orders made payable to "Montana Vital Records".

- **Birth: $12.00 Records since 1907.**
- **Death: $12.00 Records since 1907.**
- **Marriage: $10.00 (Fee for search and verification of facts of marriage). Records since 1943. Apply to Clerk Of District Court where marriage license was purchased.**
- **Divorce: $10.00 (Fee for search and verification of facts of divorce). Records since 1943. Apply to Clerk Of District Court where divorce was**

granted.

Remarks: Additional copies of records ordered at the same time are $5.00 each. Earlier years are available. See instruction section for purchasing all certificates and records.

Nebraska

Address
Vital Records
1033 O Street, Suite 130
PO Box 95065
Lincoln, NE 68509-5065
Phone: (402) 471-2871
Web Site: http://www.hhss.ne.gov/vitalrecords

Cost & Availability Of Certificates/Records

Money orders made payable to "Vital Records".

- **Birth: $12.00   Records since 1904**
- **Death: $11.00   Records since 1904**
- **Marriage: $11.00   Records since 1909. Cost varies for some records available from County Court.**
- **Divorce: $11.00   Records since 1909. Cost varies for some records available from Clerk Of District Court.**

Remarks: Write state office for earlier records. See instruction section for purchasing all certificates and records.

Nevada

Address
Office Of Vital Records and Statistics
Capitol Complex
410 Technology Way, Suite 104
Carson City, NV 89706
Phone: (775) 684-4280
Web Site: http://health.nv.gov/VS.htm

Cost & Availability Of Certificates/Records

Money orders made payable to "Office Of Vital Records and Statistics".

- **Birth: $13.00   Records since 1911**

- **Death: $10.00   Records since 1911**
- **Marriage: Cost varies   Records since 1968. Cost varies for some records available from County Recorder.**
- **Divorce: Cost varies   Records since 1968. Cost varies for some records available from County Clerk.**

Remarks: Certified copies not available from the State Health Department. For earlier records then 1911 write County Recorder in county where event took place. See instruction section for purchasing all certificates and records.

New Hampshire

Address
Division Of Vital Records Administration
Archives Building
71 South Fruit Street
Concord, NH 03301-2410
Phone: (603) 271-4654
Web Site: http://www.sos.nh.gov/vitalrecords

Cost & Availability Of Certificates/Records

Money orders made payable to "Treasurer, State Of New Hampshire".

- **Birth: $15.00   Records since 1640**
- **Death: $15.00   Records since 1640**
- **Marriage: $15.00   Records since 1808. Cost varies for some records available from Town Clerk.**
- **Divorce: $15.00   Records since 1808. Cost varies for some records available from Clerk Of The Superior Court.**

Remarks: Recent records, birth since 1988, death since 1990 and marriage since 1989 may be obtained from any city or town running Vital Records Automated Software called.NHVRIN. Additional copies of records ordered at the same time are $10.00 each.
Earlier years are available. See instruction section for purchasing all certificates and records.

New Jersey

Address
New Jersey State Archives
225 West State Street
PO Box 370
Trenton, NJ 08625-0370
Phone: (609) 292-6260
Toll Free: 1-866-649-8726
Web Site: http://www.state.nj.us/health/vital

For Divorce Records
Clerk Of The Superior Court
Superior Court Of New Jersey
Public Information Center
171 Jersey Street
PO Box 967
Trenton, NJ 08625-0967

Cost & Availability Of Certificates/Records

Money orders made payable to "New Jersey General Treasury".

- **Birth: $25.00   Records since 1901/1848**
- **Death: $25.00   Records since 1901/1848**
- **Marriage: $10.00   Records since 1901/1848**
- **Divorce: $10.00 (Certified Blue Seal Copy) Records since 1901/1848 – Contact the Clerk Of The Superior Court.**

Remarks: New Jersey State archives searches vital records from 1900 to 1848. Additional copies of records ordered at the same time are $2.00 each. Earlier years are available. See instruction section for purchasing all certificates and records.

New Mexico

Address
NM Vital Records
PO Box 26110
Santa Fe, NM 87502
Toll Free: 1-866-534-0051

Web Site: http://www.VitalRecordsNM.org

Cost & Availability Of Certificates/Records

Money orders made payable to "NM Vital Records".

- **Birth: $10.00   Records since 1920/1880**
- **Death: $5.00   Records since 1920/1880**
- **Marriage: Cost varies   Contact County Clerk where license was issued.**
- **Divorce: Cost varies   Contact Clerk Of The Court where divorce was granted.**

Remarks: Earlier years are available. See instruction section for purchasing all certificates and records.

New York

Address
Certification Unit
Vital Records Section, 2nd Floor
800 North Pearl Street
Menands, NY 12204
Phone: (518) 474-3075
Web Site: http://www.health.state.ny.us

Cost & Availability Of Certificates/Records

Money orders made payable to "New York State Department Of Health".

- **Birth: $30.00   Records since 1881**
- **Death: $30.00   Records since 1881**
- **Marriage: $30.00/$10.00   Records since 1880. Some records available for $10 that date from 1907-1880 and certain city records cost only $10.**
- **Divorce: $30.00   Records since 1963. Cost varies for some records available from County Clerk.**

Remarks: For records from 1880 to 1907 and records issued before 1914 in certain cities and other records issued in certain cities contact Registrar of Vital Statistics, Health Center Building, Yonkers, NY 10701. Earlier years are available. See instruction section for purchasing all certificates and records.

New York City

Address
Office Of Vital Records
NYC Department Of Health And Mental Hygiene
125 Worth St., CN4, Rm. 133
New York, NY 10013-4090
Phone: (212) 788-4520
Web Site:
http://www.nyc.gov/html/records/html/vitalrecords/home.shtml

Cost & Availability Of Certificates/Records

- **Birth: $15.00   Records since 1910.**
- **Death: $15.00   Records since 1949 for those occurring in certain cities.**
- **Marriage: $10.00   Records since 1996. Contact City Clerk's Office in correct city. 1 (212) 669-8090 – Marriage records by phone.**
- **Divorce: Go to New York State page.**

Remarks: For birth records prior to 1910 and death records prior to 1949 write: Archives Division, Department Of Records and Information Service, 31 Chambers Street, New York, NY 10007. Earlier years are available. See instruction section for purchasing all certificates and records.

North Carolina

Address
NC Vital Records
1903 Mail Service Center
Raleigh, NC 27699-1903
Phone: (919) 733-3000
Web Site: http://www.vitalrecords.nc.gov

Cost & Availability Of Certificates/Records

Money orders made payable to "NC Vital Records".

- **Birth: $24.00   Records since 1913**
- **Death: $24.00   Records since 1930**
- **Marriage: $24.00   Records since 1962. Contact either Registrar Of Deeds or NC State Office Of Vital Statistics.**
- **Divorce: $24.00   Records since 1958. Contact either Registrar Of Deeds or NC State Office Of Vital Statistics.**

Remarks: For marriage records before 1962 and for divorce records before 1958 contact Registrar Of Deeds. Register Of Deeds can provide copies of birth and death records upon request. Earlier years are available. See instruction section for purchasing all certificates and records.

North Dakota

Address
ND Dept. Of Health
Division Of Vital Records
600 East Boulevard Avenue, Dept 301
Bismarck, ND 58505-0200
Phone: (701) 328-2360
Web Site: http://www.ndhealth.gov/vital

Cost & Availability Of Certificates/Records

Money orders made payable to "ND Department Of Health".

- **Birth: $7.00   Records since 1921/1870-1920 (incomplete records).**
- **Death: $5.00   Records since 1921/(incomplete records).**
- **Marriage: Cost varies   Contact http://www.ndhealth.gov/vital/marriage.htm**
- **Divorce: Cost varies   Contact http://www.ndhealth.gov/vital/divorce.htm**

Remarks: Additional copies of birth records are $4.00 each and death records are $2.00 each if ordered at the same time. Copies processed 5-7 days after order. Earlier years are available. See instruction section for purchasing all certificates and records.

Northern Mariana Islands

Address

Cost & Availability Of Certificates/Records
Vital Statistics Office
Division Of Public Health
PO Box 500409
Saipan, MP 96950
Phone: (670) 236-8717 (Verify Fees)
Phone: (670) 236-8700 (Fax)
Email: dphstat1@pticom.com

Money orders made payable to "CNMI Treasurer".

- **Birth: $20.00 Records since 1946 (1946-1950 Incomplete)**
- **Death: $15.00 Records since 1946 (1946-1950 Incomplete)**
- **Marriage: $10.00**
- **Divorce: $.50 per page for Divorce Decree plus $2.50 for certification. Records since 1960**

Remarks: Earlier years are available. See instruction section for purchasing all certificates and records.

Ohio

Address
Vital Statistics
Ohio Department Of Health
246 North High Street, 1st Floor
Columbus, OH 43216
Phone: (614) 466-2531
Web Site:
http://okh.ohio.gov/vitalstatistics/vitalstats.aspx

Cost & Availability Of Certificates/Records

Money orders made payable to "Treasury, State Of Ohio".

- **Birth: $21.50 Records since 1908.**
- **Death: $21.50 Records since 1954.**

Death records from 1908-1954 can be obtained from: Ohio Historical Society, Archives Library Division, 1982 Velma Avenue, Columbus, OH 43211-2497.

- **Marriage: Cost varies Records since 1949. Contact probate judge in county where license was granted.**
- **Divorce: Cost varies Records since 1949. Contact Clerk Of Court Of Common Pleas.**

Remarks: Certified copies of marriage and divorce records not available from State Health department. A searchable index of years 1913 to 1944 is available for the internet website: http://www.ohiohistory.org. Earlier years are also available. See instruction section for purchasing all certificates and records.

Oklahoma

Address
Vital Records Service
State Department Of Health
1000 Northeast 10th Street
Oklahoma City, OK 73117
Phone: (405) 271-4040
Web Site: http://vr.health.ok.gov

Cost & Availability Of Certificates/Records

Money orders made payable to "Vital Records Service".

- **Birth: $15.00 Records since 1908**
- **Death: $15.00 Records since 1908**
- **Marriage: Cost varies Records since 1908**
- **Divorce: Cost varies Records since 1908**

Remarks: Earlier years are available.

Gifts: $35.00 for one commemorative heirloom fancy certificates with one certified copy. See instruction section for purchasing all certificates and records.

Oregon

Address
Oregon Vital Records
PO Box 14050
Portland, OR 97293-0050
Phone: (971) 673-1190
Web Site: http://www.ohd.hr.state.or.us

Older Oregon Records – 1845-1953
Birth Records: 1845-1903.
Death Records: 1862-1955.
Marriage Records: Prior 1906.
Oregon State Archives
800 Summer Street, NE
Salem, OR 97310
Phone: 1 (503) 373-0701
Fax: 1 (503) 373-0953
Web Site:
http://arcweb.sos.state.or.us/reference.html

Cost & Availability Of Certificates/Records: 1903 – Present.

Money orders made payable to "DHS/Vital Records".

- **Birth: $20.00 Records since 1903/1845.**
- **Death: $20.00 Records since 1903/1862.**
- **Marriage: $20.00 Records since 1910. Cost varies for some records available from County Clerk.**
- **Divorce: $20.00 Records since 1925. Cost varies for some records available from County Circuit Court Clerk.**

Remarks: Additional copies of records ordered at the same time are $15.00 each. Earlier years are available. See instruction section for purchasing all certificates and records.

Gifts: $45.00 for one commemorative heirloom fancy birth certificate.

Pennsylvania

Address
Division Of Vital Records
ATTN: Birth Unit/Death Unit
101 Mercer Street, Room 401
PO Box 1528
New Castle, PA 16103
Phone: (724) 656-3100
Web Site:
http://www.health.state.pa.us/vitalrecords

Cost & Availability Of Certificates/Records

- **Birth: $10.00 Records since 1906**
- **Death: $9.00 Records since 1906**
- **Marriage: Cost varies Records since 1906. Contact Marriage License Clerks, County Court House in event county.**
- **Divorce: Cost varies Records since 1906. Contact Prothonotary, Court House in county seat.**

Remarks: All requests must include a copy of government photo ID with a signature of the applicant. Birth or Death Records prior to 1906 available from county courthouse. Earlier years are available. See instruction section for purchasing all certificates and records.

Puerto Rico

Address
Department Of Health
Demographic Registry
PO Box 11854
Ferandez Juncos Station
San Juan, PR 00910
Phone: (787) 767-9120
Web Site:
http://www.prfaa.com/servvices.asp?id=44

Cost & Availability Of Certificates/Records

Money orders made payable to "Secretary Of The Treasury".

- **Birth: $5.00 Records since 1931**
- **Death: $5.00 Records since 1931**
- **Marriage: $5.00 Records since 1931**
- **Divorce: $2.00 Records since 1931.**

Contact Superior Court where the divorce was granted.

Remarks: Additional copies of records ordered at the same time are $4.00 each.
Earlier years are available from local Registrar (Registrador Demografico). See instruction section for purchasing all certificates and records.

Rhode Island

Address
RI Department Of Health
Office Of Vital Records, Room 101
3 Capitol Hill
Providence, RI 02908-5097
Phone: (401) 222-2811 (Current Fees)
Phone: (401) 222-5960 (Health hotline)
Web Site:
http://www.health.ri.gov/chic/vital/clers.php

Older Records
Rhode Island State Archives
337 Westminster Street
Providence, RI 02903

Cost & Availability Of Certificates/Records

Money orders made payable to "Rhode Island General Treasurer".

- **Birth: $20.00 Records kept 100 years.**
- **Death: $20.00 Records kept 50 years.**
- **Marriage: $20.00 Records kept 100 years.**
- **Divorce: $3.00 Contact Clerk Of Family Court, 1 Dorrance Plaza, Providence, RI 02903.**

Remarks: Additional copies of records ordered at the same time are $15.00 each. Earlier years are available. See instruction section for purchasing all certificates and records.

South Carolina

Address

Office Of Vital Records, SCDHEC
2600 Bull Street
Columbia, SC 29201
Phone: (803) 898-3630 (verify current fees)
Web Site: http://www.scdhec.net/vr

Cost & Availability Of Certificates/Records

Money orders made payable to "SCDHEC".

- **Birth: $12.00 Records since 1915/1877**
- **Death: $12.00 Records since 1915/1822**
- **Marriage: $5.00 Records since 1950. Records prior to 1950 contact probate judge where the marriage was issued.**
- **Divorce: $5.00 Records since 1962. Records since 1940 available from Clerk of Court.**

Remarks:
Additional copies of birth records ordered at the same time are $3.00 each. All requests must include a copy of photo ID. Earlier years are available. See instruction section for purchasing all certificates and records.

South Dakota

Address
Vital Records
State Department Of Health
207 E Missouri Ave, Ste 1-A
Pierre, SD 57501
Phone: (605) 773-4961
Web Site: http://vitalrecords.sd.gov

Cost & Availability Of Certificates/Records

Money orders made payable to "South Dakota Department Of Health".

- **Birth: $15.00 Records since 1905**
- **Death: $15.00 Records since 1905**
- **Marriage: $15.00 Records since 1905. Also available from County Register Of Deeds.**
- **Divorce: $15.00 Records since 1905. Also available from Clerk Of Courts.**

Remarks: Earlier years are available. See instruction section for purchasing all certificates and records.

Tennessee

Address
Tennessee Vital Records, 1st Floor
Central Services Building
4215th Avenue, North
Nashville, TN 37243
Phone: (615) 741-1763 (verify current fees)
Web Site: http://health.state.tn.us/vr/

Older Records
- Birth records more then 100 years old.
- Death records more then 50 years old.
- Marriage records more then 50 years old.
- Divorce records more then 50 years old

Tennessee Library And Archives
Archive Division
Nashville, TN 37243-0312
Phone: (615) 741-1763

Cost & Availability Of Certificates/Records

Money orders made payable to "Tennessee Vital Records".

- **Birth: $15.00 (long form), $8.00 (short form) Records since 1914/1881**
- **Death: $7.00 Records since 1917/1865**
- **Marriage: $15.00 Records since 1927. Keeps marriage records for 50 years. Some records available from County Clerk.**
- **Divorce: $15.00 Records since 1927. Keeps divorce records for 50 years. Some records available from the Clerk Of Court.**

Remarks: Additional copies of records ordered at the same time are $5.00 each. All requests must include a copy of government photo ID with signature. Earlier years are available. See instruction section for purchasing all certificates and records.

Texas

Address
Vital Statistics Unit
Texas Department Of Health
PO Box 12040
Austin, TX 78711-2040
Phone: (512) 458-7111 – (verify current fees)
Web Site: http://www.dshs.state.tx.us/vs

Cost & Availability Of Certificates/Records

Money orders made payable to "Vital Statistics Unit".

- **Birth: $22.00 Records since 1903.**
- **Death: $20.00 Records since 1903.**
- **Marriage: $20.00 (Fee for search and essential facts of marriage). Records since 1966. Some records available from County Clerk.**
- **Divorce: $20.00 (Fee for search and essential facts of divorce) Records since 1968. Some records available from Clerk Of The District Court.**

Remarks: Additional copies of death records ordered at the same time are $3.00, for birth records ordered at the same time are $22 each. Earlier years are available. See instruction section for purchasing all certificates and records.

Utah

Address
Office Of Vital Records And Statistics
Utah Department Of Health
288 North 1460 West
PO Box 141012
Salt Lake City, UT 84114-1012
Phone: (801) 538-6105
Web Site:
http://www.health.utah.gov/vitalrecords

Cost & Availability Of Certificates/Records

Money orders made payable to "Vital Records".

- **Birth: $18.00   Records since 1905.**
- **Death: $16.00   Records since 1905.**
- **Marriage: $16.00   Records since 1978. Some records available from County Clerk.**
- **Divorce: $16.00   Records since 1978. Some records available from County Clerk.**

Remarks: Mailed request must include an enlarged photo copy of the front and back sides of government photo identification. Additional copies of records ordered at the same time are $8.00 each. Earlier years are available. See instruction section for purchasing all certificates and records.

Vermont

Address
VT Department Of Health
Vital Records Section
PO Box 70
108 Cherry Street
Burlington, VT 05402-0070
Phone: (802) 863-7275 (Verify Fees)
Web Site:
http://www.healthvermont.gov/research/records/obtain_record.aspx

Older Records - As early as 1909 and 5 years old
VT State Archives And Records Administration
Office Of The Secretary
1078 US Route 2, Middlesex
Montpelier, VT 05633-7701
Money orders made payable to "Vermont Secretary Of State", for records more then five years and as early as 1909.
Phone: (802) 828-3286 (Verify Fees)
Web Site: http://vermont-archives.org/certifications

Cost & Availability Of Certificates/Records

Money orders made payable to "Vermont Department Of Health".

- **Birth: $10.00   Records for the most recent five years.   See state archives**

for older records.
- **Death: $10.00   Records for the most recent five years. See state archives for older records.**
- **Marriage: $10.00   Records for the most recent five years. See state archives for older records.**
- **Divorce: $10.00   Records for the most recent five years. See state archives for older records.**

Remarks: Additional copies of records ordered at the same time are $5.00 each. All requests must include a copy of photo ID. Earlier years are available. See instruction section for purchasing all certificates and records.

Virginia

Address
Division Of Vital Records
PO Box 1000
Richmond, VA 23218-1000
Phone: (804) 662-6200
Web Site: http://www.vdh.virginia.gov

Cost & Availability Of Certificates/Records

Money orders made payable to "State Health Department".

- **Birth: $9.00   Records since 1912/1853**
- **Death: $5.00   Records since 1912/1853**
- **Marriage: $5.00   Records since 1853. Some records are available from Clerk Of Court.**
- **Divorce: $5.00   Records since 1918. Some records are available from Clerk Of Court.**

Remarks: Certain records missing from 1897 to 1911. Earlier years are available. See instruction section for purchasing all certificates and records.

Virgin Islands

Birth Or Death St. Croix - $15 (Mail Request) $12 (In person). Records since 1840.

Department Of Health
Vital Statistics
Charles Harwood Memorial Hospital
St. Croix, VI 00820

Birth Or Death St. Thomas & St. John - $15 (Mail Request) $12 (In person). Records since 1906.

Department Of Health
Vital Statistics
Knud Hansen Complex
St. Thomas, VI 00802

Marriage & Divorce Records

Bureau Of Vital Records And Statistical Services
Virgin Islands Department Of Health
Charlotte Amalie
St. Thomas, VI 00801

Cost & Availability Of Certificates/Records

Money orders for birth and death made payable to "Department Of Health".
Money orders for marriage and divorce made payable to "Territorial Court Of The Virgin Islands".

- **Birth: $15 (Mail Request) $12 (In person) Records since 1906/1840.**
- **Death: $15 (Mail Request) $12 (In person) Records since 1906/1840.**
- **Marriage: $2.00**
- **Divorce: $2.00**

Remarks: Earlier years are available. See instruction section for purchasing all certificates and records.

Washington

Address
Department Of Health
Center For Health Statistics
PO Box 47814
Olympia, WA 98504-7814

Phone: (360) 236-4300
Web Site: http://www.doh.wa.gov

Cost & Availability Of Certificates/Records

Money orders made payable to "Department Of Health".

- **Birth: $20.00 Records since 1907.**
- **Death: $20.00 Records since 1907.**
- **Marriage: $20.00 Records since 1968. Some records available from County Auditor.**
- **Divorce: $20.00 Records since 1968. Some records available from County Clerk.**

Remarks: Earlier years are available. See instruction section for purchasing all certificates and records.

Washington District Of Columbia

Address
Vital Records Division
825 North Capitol Street, NE
5441 Commercial Boulevard, 1st Floor
Washington, DC 20002
Phone: (202) 671-5000
Web Site: http://www.dchealth.dc.gov

Cost & Availability Of Certificates/Records

Money orders made payable to "DC Treasurer for birth and death certificates.

- **Birth: $23.00 Records since 1874**
- **Death: $18.00 Records since 1874**
- **Marriage: $10.00 Records since 1956**
- **Divorce: $6.50 Records since 1956. Cost varies for records before 1956.**

Remarks: For Marriage and Divorce certificates write: DC Superior Court, 500 Indiana Avenue, NW, Room 4485, Washington, DC 20001. (202) 879-4840. Birth and death certificate requests must include a copy of a government issued picture ID. Earlier years are available.

See instruction section for purchasing all certificates and records.

West Virginia

Address
Vital Registration Office, Room 165
350 Capitol Street
Charleston, WV 25301-3701
Phone: (304) 558-2931
Web Site: http://www.wvdhhr.gor

Cost & Availability Of Certificates/Records

Money orders made payable to "Vital Registration".

- **Birth: $12.00 Records since 1917. Earlier records from Clerk Of County Court.**
- **Death: $12.00 Records since 1917. Earlier records from Clerk Of County Court.**
- **Marriage: $12.00 Records since 1921. Earlier as well as recent records available from County Clerk. Certified records from 1964.**
- **Divorce: $5.00 (fee for verifying some items) Records since 1968. Earlier records as well as recent records from Clerk Of The Circuit Court.**

Remarks: Earlier years are available. See instruction section for purchasing all certificates and records.

Wisconsin

Address
WI Vital Records Office
1 West Wilson Street
PO Box 309
Madison, WI 53701-0309
Phone: (608) 266-1371
Web Site:
http://www.dhfs.state.wi.us/vitalrecords

Cost & Availability Of Certificates/Records

Money orders made payable to "State Of Wisconsin Vital Records".

- **Birth: $20.00 Records since 1907/1857, Records before 1907 are incomplete.**
- **Death: $20.00 Records since 1907/1857. Records before 1907 are incomplete.**
- **Marriage: $20.00 Records since 1907/1857. Records before 1907 are incomplete.**
- **Divorce: $20.00 Records since 1907.**

Remarks: Additional copies of records ordered at the same time are $3.00 each. A stamped, self-addressed, business size (#10) should be included in each request. Earlier years are available. See instruction section for purchasing all certificates and records.

Wyoming

Address
Vital Statistics Services
Hathaway Building
Cheyenne, WY 82002
Phone: (307) 777-7591
Web Site: http://wdh.state.wy.us/vital_records

Older Records - More then 50 years old.
Wyoming State Archives
Phone: (307) 777-7826
Email: WyArchiv@state.wy.us

Cost & Availability Of Certificates/Records

Money orders made payable to "Vital Records Services".

- **Birth: $13.00 Records since 1909.**
- **Death: $10.00 Records since 1909. Records more then 50 years old from Wyoming State Archives.**
- **Marriage: $13.00 Records since 1941. Some records available from County Clerk.**
- **Divorce: $13.00 Records since 1941. Some records available from Clerk Of**

District Court.

Remarks:
Additional copies of records ordered at the same time are $5.00 each. All requests must include a copy of photo ID. Earlier years are available. See instruction section for purchasing all certificates and records.

Foreign, High-seas or Panama Canal Births and Deaths and certificates of citizenships.

Foreign Birth Records

Two different documents certify foreign birth records

- DS-1350 (Certification Of The Report Of Birth) **$30.00 for the first and $20.00 for each additional copy.**
- A replacement FS-240 (Report of birth abroad of a citizen of the United States and proof of citizenship) **$30.00**

Passport Services
Vital Records Section

U.S. Department Of State
111 19th Street, NW, Suite 510
Washington, DC 20522-1701

Certificate Of Citizenship & Alien Children Adopted By U.S. Citizens

Contact:
Immigration And Naturalization Service (INS)
20 Massachusetts Avenue, NW
Washington, DC 20529
Web Site: http://uscis.gov

Death Records Of U.S. Citizens Living In Foreign Countries.

Forms Used To Record Foreign Death

Form DS-2060 formerly OF-180

Address

A copy of the Report Of Death is filed with the Department Of State.

Passport Services, Vital Records Section,
U.S. Department Of State,
111 19th Street, NW
Washington, DC 20522-1705.

Records Of Birth & Death Occurring On Vessels Or Aircraft On The High Seas.

Address

Vital Records Section
U.S. Department Of State,
111 19th Street, NW
Washington, DC 20522-1705.

Records Maintained By Foreign Countries.

Contact the appropriate embassy in the country of the birth or death occurred. For a directory of addresses and contact information of U.S. embassies write the U.S. Government Printing Office.

Address
U.S. Government Printing Office
710 North Capitol Street, NW
Washington, DC 20401
Phone: (202) 512-0132
Fax: (202) 512-1355

National Birth, Death, Marriage and Divorce Website

The Centers For Disease Control And Prevention has detailed national and international information on birth, death, marriage and divorce records for American citizens naturalized American residents..

Contact

Centers for Disease Control and Prevention
1600 Clifton Rd. Atlanta, GA 30333, USA

Toll Free: 800-CDC-INFO (800-232-4636) TTY: (888)

Phone: 232-6348, 24 Hours/Every Day –

Email: cdcinfo@cdc.gov

Website: http://www.cdc.gov/nchs/w2w.htm

Chapter 10

Social Security & Medicare Programs

If you are unemployed and are looking for work, the following sources might be just what the doctor ordered. They can provide you with funds to pay your living expenses. One source I reveal to you in this section can also pay your moving expenses if you need to move. There are also many other entitlement programs included here that you may qualify for. You will be amazed at all the money the government can provide you with, if you know where to look.

Help For The Unemployed

You probably already know about Federal Unemployment Insurance. This program is financed by a tax on wages earned. Its purpose is to help people who are unemployed and searching for work. Such people may be unemployed for several different reasons including having been fired or laid off, or even having quit their previous job for a legitimate reason, such a substandard working conditions. Warning: If your local Employment Development Office does not consider your reason for being unemployed legitimate, it can make your attempt to receive benefits extremely difficult.

In order to become eligible for unemployment insurance benefits you must register with a state public employment office. You must be ready and able to accept a job, but you can not lose the benefits for refusing to accept a job which entails substandard working conditions or which requires that you join a company union.

Since each state administers its own program, the amount of benefits varies greatly. As in the other forms of insurance, the benefits are based on the worker's previous work history. The average benefit in 1986 was $135 per week, or over $540 per month. To find out if you are entitled to benefits you should contact your local Employment Development Office which should be listed under the "Government" section of the front of your phone book or contact the Department Of Labor.

DEPARTMENT OF LABOR
Department Of Labor
200 Constitution Ave., NW
Washington, DC 20210
Web Site: www.dol.gov
Toll Free: (866) 4-USA-DOL (866) 487-2365

Free Help If You Need To Move

If your unemployment benefits have run out, and you still have not found a job, there are many things that this program can do for you. You are eligible for the following benefits under the Job Training Placement Act. For more information, contact your local Employment Development Office.

- First, the local unemployment office should help you find a job.

- Second, they may help you retrain for a new job in your area. Not only does retraining help you get another job, but your training will be paid for by your state government.

- Third, if you have to go out of your area to look for a job, the state and federal government may pay 90 percent of your living expenses with a set limit.

- Fourth, after finding a job that is not near you, the government will pay your moving expenses. The government will pay 90 percent of you moving expenses for you and your family, including moving furniture.

- Fifth, after you move, the Government will also give you a lump sum of money that is worth many times your weekly wage at your old job. This lump sum payment is extended only to workers who have lost their jobs due to imports. These payments are funded under the Trade Adjustment Assistance program, which you also apply for at you Employment Development Office.

Low Income Programs

Supplemental Security Income

Supplemental Security Income is intended to assist those people who are over 65, disabled, or blind, and, also, have limited assets and income. This program does not require work credits and it is available to children as well as to adults. People who qualify for SSI are usually eligible for food stamps and Medicaid.

The basic federal monthly check is $674 for one person or $1011 for a couple. You may receive considerably more if you live in a state which augments the federal check. In some cases, you may receive less due to other income or benefits.

The amount of allowed earnings is extremely complicated. For one thing, the amount varies from state to state. Also, not all of your income is counted. All states do have a $2,000 limit on assets for one person and a $3,000 asset limit for a couple. There are many assets which are not included in this figure, however. For example, your home, and the property which it is on, do not count; your car should not count; and, among other things, savings set aside for burial expenses may not count.

Average SSI Payment Levels In Massachusetts, (2009)

Recipient	Total	Federal	State
Aged single	802.82	674.00	128.82
Member Of Aged couple	606.36	505.50	100.86
Blind single	823.74	674.00	149.74
Member Of Blind couple	823.74	505.50	90.03
Disabled single	788.39	674.00	114.39

Member Of Disabled couple	595.53	505.50	90.03

(Full cost of living)

Social Security Administration

For additional information on SSI, you should contact your local Social Security Administration Office which can be found in the beginning of the white pages phone book.
Visit their website at www.socialsecurity.gov or call toll free at 1-800-772-1213 or (for the deaf or hard of hearing, call the TTY number, 1-800-325-0778). You may also write the social security at: Social Security Administration, 6401 Security Blvd., Baltimore, MD 21235.

Aid to Families with Dependent Children

This is a combined federal-state program. The states, however, are allowed to set their own standards: they may choose the recipients, the type of aid, and the amount of aid. In general, the dependent child or children must be under the age of 18. Each state computes a standard of need, which is based on such things as the cost of housing, food, clothing, and other necessities. Ideally, the state will pay the difference between this standard and the family income, but it is not required to do so. AFDC recipients who are employable must register for work in the work incentive program and must work a specified number of hours in order to receive the aid.

Your local county welfare program will answer any questions you have regarding AFDC.

Food Stamps

The purpose of the food stamp program is to allow families to maintain a nutritional diet. In general, a household is eligible if its disposable assets are below $2,000, and if the household is not able to purchase an adequate diet with 30 percent of its countable cash income. The adequate diet is defined by the United States Department of Agriculture (USDA) in its Thrifty Food Plan. In 1988, nearly 20 million people received food stamp benefits which averaged $50 per month.

The federal government provides the funding for the program, but it delegates authority to the states, which, in turn, may delegate to the counties. Thus, eligibility may vary from state to state, or even from county to county, and it is best for each household to check its own eligibility with the local office.

The Food and Nutrition Service administers the food stamp program as a part of the Department of Agriculture. This department, also, administers a number of programs which are designed to provide inexpensive meals to children. The programs include the National School Lunch Program, the School Breakfast Program, the Summer Food Service Program, the Child Care Food Program, the Special Milk Program, and the Special Supplemental Food Program for Women, Infants, and Children. Also, there is a special program for the elderly.

Other Government Benefits

Disability Insurance

In 1956 the Social Security Administration was expanded to include help for those who lost their jobs due to disabilities. According to the Social Security definition, "A person is considered disabled when he or she has a severe physical or mental impairment or combination of impairments that prevents him or her from working for a year or more or that is expected to result in death. The work does not necessarily have to be the kind of work done before disability--it can be any gainful work found in the national economy." The definition of gainful work is flexible and depends on the needs and circumstances of the individual recipient.

There are numerous medical conditions which are usually considered severe enough to qualify for Social Security disability benefits. (It is important to realize that these requirements differ from those of other government and private programs.) Examples of these conditions are: diseases of the heart, lungs, or blood vessels which cause a limitation in the ability to work, despite medical attention; severe arthritis which limits mobility or the use of the hands; and (among many others) blindness. (Benefits due to blindness are considerably different than those due to other disabilities. Please contact your local Social Security office if you feel that you are entitled to disability benefits because of problems with your vision.)

Assuming that the worker qualifies as disabled, then the following people may be eligible to receive benefits on that individual's work history:

- A worker under 65 may receive benefits from disability insurance. (Disabled workers over the age of 65 may receive retirement benefits rather than disability benefits.)

- An unmarried child of the worker may receive benefits until the age of 18, or until 19 if attending a primary or secondary school full time.

- An unmarried child who is disabled before the age of 22 may be eligible for benefits on the work record of the parent. If you are a disabled child, under the age of 22, then you can receive benefits if one of your parents is receiving either old-age or retirement benefits, or as a survivor of a parent who earned OASDI coverage. Also, you should look to see if you quality for Supplemental Security Income (SSI).

- The spouse of a disabled worker can receive benefits if he or she is caring for the worker's child (age 16 or younger); or if he or she is disabled and also receiving benefits; or if he or she is age 62 or older.

- The worker's disabled widow or widower may receive benefits under survivors insurance, as listed above.

- The worker's disabled surviving divorced wife or husband may receive benefits as a disabled widow or widower if the marriage lasted at least 10 years.

As with old age and survivors insurance, disability insurance is connected to the amount of covered work which you have accumulated. The number of required credits, however, is different. If you are disabled prior to age 24, then you need six work credits in the three years immediately preceding the disability. Since, like the other OASDI programs, a maximum of four credits may be earned a year, this amounts to having worked for half of the previous three years. If you are between the ages of 24 and 31, then you must have credit for having worked half of the time between the age of 21 and the time when you became disabled. For example, if you become disabled at age 25, then you would need credit for two years, or eight credits; if you become disabled at age 27, they you would need credit for three years, or 12 credits. For workers who become disabled at an age over 31, the requirements vary greatly with age, but in general, you must have at least 20 work credits from the last 10 years. An exception is made for people who are disabled by blindness, they need only have earned sufficient credits since 1936 and do not need recent credits.

The amount of monthly benefits is, as for most of the other insurance programs, based on the worker's average covered earnings. In 1990 the average benefit for a disabled worker is $555 per month; for a disabled worker with a family the average monthly payment is $975. These benefits usually start with the sixth full month of disability. There is no waiting period for a person who is disabled before 22 and who qualifies on the Social Security record of a retired, disabled, or deceased parent.

The disability program also provides the opportunity for a trial work period. You may receive full benefits for up to a year while working. If, after nine months, it is apparent that you are not able to work at a substantial level, then your benefits will continue as normal.

Temporary Disability Insurance

This program is designed to assist workers who lose their wages due to a temporary disability which did not occur on the job. It is a state level supplement for those whose disability is not expected to last long enough to qualify for federal disability insurance. Temporary disability is expected to replace at least half of the worker's earnings for a maximum of 26-39 weeks a year. In 1984 it was estimated that approximately two-thirds of the country's workers had some form of protection for a temporary disability. Workers with occupational disabilities should be qualified for Workers' Compensation benefits.

Workers' Compensation

The workers' compensation program is designed to aid those workers who are injured while on the job. It also provides compensation to the families of those workers who are killed on the job. The compensation is payable regardless of who is at fault for causing the accident which resulted in the injury. This program is not financed by taxes, but rather, the burden falls on the employer to compensate you and your family in the event of an injury.

About 87 million workers were covered by compensation laws in 1986. The workers who are most commonly not covered by these laws are domestic, agricultural, and casual laborers.

The amount of compensation depends on the severity of the injury and often on the your earning power. An injury which causes total disability or death usually results in compensation of about two-thirds of the your earnings at the time of the injury, but the compensation can also be affected by the number of your dependents. An injury which causes what the government calls a "permanent partial disability" is classified as either a "schedule" injury or a "non-schedule" injury. Such an injury would be one that limits your ability to work at your previous level.

A schedule injury is one for which there is a payment schedule based on the injury itself, without regard to the lost earnings. A non-schedule injury is one which is harder to assess in a monetary manner. Compensation for this type of injury is the difference between earnings before and after the injury. Also, complete medical benefits are furnished by the workers' compensation program. In the event of a work-related injury you should call the claims department at the workers' compensation office in your state.

Black Lung Program

The Black Lung Program was created in 1969 in response to the extreme hazards faced by coal miners. It is designed to provide monthly benefits to miners who are totally disabled by black lung disease (pneumoconiosis), or to the survivors of those miners who die from the disease. Benefits are based on the wage scale for federal employees, rather than on the earnings of the miner. In 1987 the benefit for a disabled minor ranged from $338 per month to $676 per month for someone with three or more dependents. The program is financed from a trust fund which has been created with an excise tax on coal.

Your local Employment Development Office should be able to direct your questions regarding any of these employment programs. They are listed in the white pages under "Government."

Note: Your local Employment Development is also a great place to find work, especially government employment. Every available government job - federal, state, county and city, should be listed there.

Other Government Help

(OASDI) Social Security:
Old-Age, Survivors, and Disability Insurance

On August 14, 1935, Franklin Roosevelt signed the Social Security Act. The new law created the foundation for a system by which millions of United States citizens have enjoyed secure retirements. But retirement is not the only situation for which this insurance-like program is beneficial; spouses and dependents can benefit, also.

The basic tenet of the Social Security program is that, while working in a "covered job," you earn credits toward retirement benefits. About 95 percent of all jobs are currently covered. A covered job is one in which Social Security taxes are taken out of your check at the current level of 7.65 percent. Your employer then matches your tax out of his/her own pocket, and the money is sent to Uncle Sam. Any earnings above the current limit of $50,000 are not taxed by Social Security. This tax limit changes periodically and the maximum monthly benefits are payable to anyone who has consistently earned above the maximum amount. For example, even though you may have earned only $35,000 in 1965, you may have been above the limit which was established at that time.

Upon retirement you are, of course, entitled to receive the money back in monthly installments. It is as if the government is helping you create your own retirement account, or IRA. One of the best parts of the program, however, is that you do not necessarily have to be 65 and retired to receive the benefits which you deserve. The system has been expanded to cover elderly workers who retire before the age of 65; elderly workers who continue to work at a low income level; the surviving spouses and children of workers who have died; and, also, to cover workers who have a disability which prevents them from maintaining substantial employment.

Similar to an Individual Retirement Account (IRA), the more you pay in during the time you work, the more you are entitled to receive upon retirement. The amount of your benefits will be based on the average amount of your covered earnings. For example, if you averaged $35,000 a year in covered employment, then you will have paid more Social Security tax than someone who only averaged $25,000. You will, therefore, receive higher benefits. In order to qualify for retirement benefits, you must have worked a total of 10 years in covered jobs. For each year of work, you can gain four work credits. So, you need a total of 40 credits to qualify for old age benefits. As a disabled person, you may receive benefits with fewer than 10 years, and if you are a survivor of a family member, you may receive benefit even though that family member had acquired fewer than 10 years of covered work.

If, after reading the following listings, you still have questions or you feel that you are entitled to these benefits, then you should call your local Social Security Office or Visit their website at www.socialsecurity.gov or call toll free at 1-800-772-1213 or (for the deaf or hard of hearing, call the TTY number, 1-800-325-0778).

Old Age Benefits

The first thing to remember about the old age benefits is that you can receive them before ~OU are in full retirement. A person who retires at the age of 65, may receive full benefits while also having an annual outside income of $8,800. This income is that which YOU receive as wages or as earnings from self-employment, and it does not include income from savings and pensions, etc. If you earn above this limit, then your benefits will he adjusted downward, depending on the actual amount of your income. The total amount which you receive from working and benefits will not the lower than the benefits which you would receive without working. After the age of 70, there is no maximum limit to your earnings.

You may find it surprising that you can receive retirement benefits prior to reaching 65. It is possible to receive reduced payments at the age ol'62 (reduced means 80 percent of the amount to which you would be entitled if you retired at 65). The monthly payments are reduced to compensate for the additional payments made in the years between the ages of 62 and 65. You would continue to receive reduced benefits after you reach the age of 65. If you retire between 62 and 65, you may earn an annual outside income of $6480. The normal retirement age of 65 will he slowly moved up to 67, beginning in 2003.

The highest monthly rate for workers who retired in 1989 at the age of 65, and who consistently had earnings at or above the maximum amount is $899. All retirement payments are good for life.

Survivor's Benefits

Survivors benefits can be paid to the family or a deceased worker, in order to help ease the financial burden which may follow the death of a breadwinner. As with the retirement benefits, the amounts of these benefits are based on the work history of the deceased. Also like retirement benefits, the benefits can be reduced if there is a substantial source of outside income.

For recipients under 65, the maximum annual amount which can be earned without a reduction of benefits is $6,840. The amount is $9,360 for recipients between the ages of 65 and 69. After age 70 there is no reduction in benefits regardless of other income.

The major difference between retirement benefits and survivor's benefits is that, depending on the age of the deceased, the full survivor's benefits may be received without the 40 work credits. For example, the family of a woman who was born after 1929 and died at the age of 36, is entitled to benefits if she had accumulated as few as 14 work credits. Your family may qualify for benefits even if the deceased family member did not have sufficient credits. In this case they must have credit for working at least one and a half of the three years prior to death.

As with all Social Security programs, determining if you qualify, and for to how much you are entitled, is not an easy task (former Social Security Commissioner Dorcas R. Hardy described the program as the "most complex government program that God and Congress ever created"). The following are explanations of the various entitlements. Check with your local Social Security Office for more information.

Assuming that the deceased had a work record which qualified for benefits, then the following family members may be entitled to receive those benefits:

- A widow or widower is entitled to receive full monthly benefits at the age of 65. Reduced benefits may be received as early as age 60. Remarriage after the age of 60 will not stop the payment of benefits. The range of the benefit amounts varies greatly from case to case, depending on the age and work history of the deceased, including the deceased's salary. A widow or widower, who begins to take benefits at age 60, may realistically expect to receive between $600 and $800 a month. A divorced widow or widower will be treated as though they had not been divorced, if the marriage lasted for at least 10 years. The widow or widower is also entitled to a single 'lump sum death payment' of $255. This is in addition to the monthly survivor benefits. If there is not a surviving spouse, then the lump sum death payment is payable to whatever children are eligible for survivor benefits.

- A parent of the deceased's child may receive benefits if the parent is supporting the child, and if the child is either under the age of 16 or disabled. If the parent is the spouse of the deceased, then he or she is entitled to the benefits which would normally come due at age 65. The spouse's benefits will end when the child reaches age 16, but they will start again as the spouse reaches 65. The amount of a family's total benefits will depend on the number of children, as well as the work history. A widow or widower with two children could receive as much as $2000 per month.

- An unmarried child of the deceased is entitled to benefits up to the age of 18 (or 19 if he or she is a full time student in a primary or secondary school). The amount of benefits for a child is comparable to that of a widow or widower without children. A grandchild may be treated as a survivor in the event that the parents of the child are deceased, or the grandparent has assumed responsibility for the child.

- Disabled Survivors. Children and disabled widows or widowers of a deceased worker can receive extensions the period during which their benefits will be paid. A child who is disabled before age 22 may receive benefits as long as they remain disabled, instead of having them end at age 16. A widow or widower who is disabled within seven years of the death of a spouse may receive reduced benefits at the age of 50. If a widow or widower receives benefits as a spouse with dependent children (see above) and is then disabled within seven years of when the child reaches age 16, then he or she may receive benefits. A disabled widow or widower may be remarried after 50 without affecting these benefits.

Veteran Programs

The Veteran's Administration has two major programs to assist disabled or retired veterans:

- Service Connected Disabilities: Cash benefits are payable to veterans with disabilities which have been connected to their service in the armed forces. These benefits are also payable, upon the death of the veteran, to his or her spouse, parents, and children. The amount of compensation is based on the degree of disability, and the compensation is paid regardless of additional income. Payments for total disability are over $1400 monthly. In addition, certain severe disabilities may result in payments of $4000 a month. Veterans with service-connected disabilities of '30 percent' or more are entitled to an additional allowance for dependents.

- Veteran Pension: The pension benefits are designed for veterans with non-service-connected disabilities. Wartime veterans who are totally or permanently disabled and on a limited income may be eligible. Wartime veterans who are over 65 and not working may, also, be eligible. To quality you must have served at least 90 days in one of the five disputes which have occurred in this century (the Mexican border period through the Vietnam era) and you must have received other than a dishonorable discharge. Annual benefits begin at $6200 for a veteran without dependents.

- Veterans Loan Program: The Small Business Administration has loans which range up to $350,000 for Vietnam-era and disabled veterans. These loans are intended to help veterans with starting and maintaining their private businesses. For information, call or visit the website of the Office of Business Loans, SBA: (202) 205-6605 or http://www.sba.gov

- Veterans Administration Home Loans:This program is intended to help veterans secure loans in order to purchase or construct housing. You can either buy a home, build a home, refinance a home loan, or make home improvements. You must live in the house, or condo, for which you receive the loan. The interest rate will generally be fixed below the current market rate, and you may refinance the loan if lower interest rates become available. Also, veterans with permanent service disabilities may be eligible for grants, or additional loans, with which to adapt housing for their specific needs.

The eligibility requirements for this program are dependent on the time and the length of your enlistment. Any veteran who has been permanently disabled for service related reasons should be eligible. Veterans who served prior to September 7, 1980, must have served a minimum of either 90 or 181 days, depending on the dates of service. In general, a wartime veteran needs 90 days active service and a peacetime veteran needs 181 days active service. Veterans who served after September 7, 1980 need a minimum of two years of active duty. The unmarried widow or widower of a service person who has died in a service related incident, or the spouse of a service member who has been declared missing in action or a prisoner of war, may also qualify. Only those veterans who have received other than dishonorable discharge, or who are still active, are eligible for these loans.

To check your eligibility, contact your local Veterans Administration, at their website , www.va.gov or call toll free at (800) 827-1000.

Medical Programs

Medicare

Medicare is a program which helps to defray the costs of medical treatment for people who are receiving Social Security old age or disability benefits. A person must receive disability benefits for 24 months prior to becoming eligible for Medicare benefits in the 25th month. People who reach age 65 without qualifying for these benefits through the work credit system may enroll for Medicare insurance by paying a monthly premium. Also, people who are eligible for Medicare but have an income are required to pay a premium of $22.50 for each $150 of taxable income, not to exceed a total yearly premium of $800.

Medicare benefits are divided into two categories, Hospital Insurance and Supplemental Medical Insurance. Hospital Insurance is a mandatory program which is funded by a 1.45 percent payroll tax, just like the Social Security tax. It is designed to provide protection against the costs of hospitalization and some related costs, such as physical therapy and home health services. In 1989 the average Medicare hospital payment was $4700. Supplemental Medical Insurance is a voluntary program which requires a monthly premium of $27.90. The program covers such costs as the services of the physician and surgeon, outpatient programs, ambulance services, and others.

For general information on Medicare, you can call the Social Security Administration: Visit the website at www.socialsecurity.gov or call toll free at 1-800-772-1213 or (for the deaf or hard of hearing, call the TTY number, 1-800-325-0778).

Medicaid

Medicaid is a federal program which provides matching funds to states in order to help people with low incomes to pay for medical expenses. All people who receive help from Aid to Families with Dependent Children (AFDC) are covered by Medicaid, as are most people who are covered by Supplemental Security Income (SSI). Both AFDC and SSI are listed below.

Medicaid payments are made directly to the doctor or other care provider. In 1986, over 22 million people received assistance from the Medicaid program. Payments to providers reached nearly 41 billion dollars.

For additional information regarding the Medicaid program, you should contact your local county welfare office. For additional information regarding food stamps and the meal programs, you should contact your county welfare program.

Chapter 11

Free Rent Programs

As part of its domestic safety net, the Federal Government sponsors many programs which are intended to help in the creation and maintenance of affordable housing. These programs include ones which help investors and developers with their projects, and even one that helps tenants with their rent payments. The four programs under HUD's Section 8 programs, listed below, help thousands of low-income families and individuals pay their rents each month.

All of the following programs are under the auspices of either the Department of Housing and Urban Development (HUD), the Farmers' Home Administration (FmHA), or the Veterans' Administration (VA). To obtain further details on any of these programs you should call the local office of the appropriate agency. The local phone numbers of these agencies should be listed under government programs in your phone book.

Also, you can contact the home office of these agencies:

Department of Housing and Urban Development
451 7th St., SW
Washington, DC 20410
Web Site: www.hud.gov
Toll Free: (800) FED-INFO (800) 333-4636)

Department Of Veterans Affairs
810 Vermont Ave. NW
Washington, DC 20420
Web Site: www.va.gov
Toll Free: (800) 827-1000

Rural Development
Department of Agriculture
1400 Independence Ave SW
Washington, DC 20250
Web Site: www.usda.gov

Rental Program Descriptions

14.149 Rent Supplements -- Rental Housing for Lower-Income Families (HUD)

Objectives: This is a program which makes payments to landlords in order to help reduce rent payments for disadvantaged low-income tenants. If you qualify, this one will pay part part of your rent Payments every month.

Uses: HUD may make payments directly to the owner of the building, so that the occupant's rent may be lowered. The payment makes up the difference between 30 percent of the your adjusted income and what HUD determines is the fair market rent for the unit. This payment may not exceed 70 percent of the fair market value.

Eligibility: In general, to be eligible for public housing you must be a low-income family. A family may be a parent and a child, or a man and wife, or even an unmarried couple. If you are single, you can qualify for these programs if you are disabled or elderly. The definition of low-income depends on the size of the family and the cost of living in your area. The rent supplement program has the additional requirement that your household is disadvantaged. Disadvantaged refers to households who are either elderly, handicapped, displaced by government action, victims of national disaster, occupying substandard housing, or headed by a person who is serving on active military duty.

I4.195 Rental Property- Section 8 Lower-Income Rental Assistance (HUD)

Objectives: This program is intended to assist low- and very low-income families in finding decent, safe, and sanitary housing in private accommodations.

Uses: HUD will make up the difference between what it expects a low-income family to pay and the market rent. The amount which the family pays depends on its income and any welfare assistance which they receive specifically in order to pay housing costs.

Eligibility: Low-income families (Families may be anything from a married couple with children to an unmarried couple who are living together) are defined as those whose income does not exceed 80 percent of the median income for the area. The median income is that which half of the people in the area have an income above this amount and half of them have an income below this amount. HUD adjusts incomes, so you may be below 80 percent of the median income even though you have a fairly steady income.

14.871 Section 8 Existing Housing Voucher Program (HUD)

Objectives: to assist very low-income families find decent, safe, and sanitary housing in private accommodations.

Uses: The Existing Housing Voucher Program allows you to rent a unit which is above the fair market rent. Monthly payments make up the difference between a payment standard for the area (not the actual rent) and 30 percent of a family's monthly income.

Eligibility: This program is only for very low-income families (those with under 50 percent of the area's median income) and does not include low-income families (those with incomes between 50 percent and 80 percent of the median income).

14.856 Section 8 Moderate Rehabilitation Program (HUD)

Objectives: To assist very low-income families in finding decent, safe, and sanitary housing in private accommodations.

Uses: This program involves buildings which are approved for renovation projects. The rents are set on the basis of the overhead for operating the buildings.

Eligibility: Very low-income families (incomes of below 50 percent of the median for the area) are eligible. If you qualify for this program, you must pay the highest of either 30 percent of your adjusted income, 10 percent of your gross income, or the part of your welfare assistance which is designated for housing.

14.103 Interest Reduction Payments-- Rental and Cooperative Housing for Lower-Income Families. (HUD)

Objectives: To provide quality rental and cooperative housing for low- and moderate-income persons by reducing their interest payments.
Uses: limited to mortgages which are financed by state or local Housing Finance Associations
Eligibility: Families and individuals who are either elderly or handicapped may be eligible to benefit from the reductions, if they fall within certain locally-determined income levels. Investors may receive the interest reductions if they are sponsoring the project.

14.169 Counseling for Homebuyers, Homeowners, and Tenants (HUD)

Any family or individual who is part of a HUD program is eligible for free counseling.
Counseling services are intended to help homeowners and tenants to improve their housing conditions and to meet their responsibilities. These services include help with buying and maintaining a home, and referrals for: financial assistance, food, medical care, family guidance, job training, and for job placement. For additional information, you can reach HUD

> Department of Housing and Urban Development
> 451 7th St., SW
> Washington, DC 20410
> **Web Site:** www.hud.gov
> **Toll Free**: (800) FED-INFO (800) 333-4636)

10.415 Rural Rental Housing Loans (USDA)

Objectives: To provide economically designed and constructed rental and cooperative housing and related facilities suited for independent living for rural residents.
Uses: Loans may be used to construct, purchase, improve, or repair rental or cooperative housing or to develop manufactured housing projects.
Eligibility: Applicants must be able to assume the obligations of the loan, furnish adequate security and have sufficient income for repayment. Available in rural areas only.

10.427 Rural Rental-Assistance Payments (USDA)

Objectives: to reduce the rents paid by low-income families in eligible rural housing projects.
Uses: Rental assistance may be used to reduce the rent payments of low-income senior citizens or families and domestic farm laborers whose rent exceeds 30 percent of their adjusted income.
Eligibility: Any low-income family, handicapped individuals, or senior citizen that is unable to pay the approved rental rate for an eligible USDA rental assistance unit with 30 percent, or less, of their adjusted monthly income.

14.134 Mortgage Insurance-- Rental Housing (HUD)

Objectives: To provide good quality rental housing for middle-income families
Uses: These loans may be used to finance the construction or rehabilitation of rental structures which consist of five or more units.
Eligibility: All investors, builders, and developers are eligible to apply for these loans.

14.135 Mortgage Insurance-- Rental and Cooperative Housing for Moderate-Income Families and the Elderly, Market Rate (HUD)

Objectives: to provide good quality rental or cooperative housing for moderate-income families and the elderly.
Uses: These loans may be used to finance construction or rehabilitation of rental or cooperative housing which contains five or more units.
Eligibility: All investors are eligible to apply for these loans.

14.138 Mortgage Insurance-- Rental Housing for the Elderly (HUD)

Objectives: To provide good quality rental housing for the elderly
Uses: These loans may be used to finance the construction or rehabilitation of rental housing designed for occupancy by elderly or handicapped individuals and consisting of eight or more units.
Eligibility: All investors are eligible to apply for these loans.

14.139 Mortgage Insurance -- Rental Housing in Urban Renewal Areas (HUD)

Objectives: To provide good quality rental housing in urban renewal areas
Uses: These loans may be used to finance the construction or rehabilitation of rental housing in Urban Renewal areas, or to finance the purchase of properties which have been rehabilitated by a public agency.
Eligibility: All investors are eligible to apply for these loans.

14.151 Supplemental Loan Insurance-- Multifamily Rental Housing (HUD)

Objectives: to finance repairs, additions, and improvements to multifamily projects already insured by HUD
Uses: Loans may be used to finance additions to and improvements of multifamily housing projects, or to finance energy conservation improvements.
Eligibility: Owners of multifamily projects which are already subject to HUD mortgages are eligible.

14.155 Mortgage Insurance for the Purchase or Refinancing of Existing Multifamily Housing Projects (HUD)

Objectives: To provide mortgage insurance to facilitate the purchase or refinancing of existing multifamily housing projects

Uses: Only housing projects not requiring substantial rehabilitation are eligible for this program.
Eligibility: All investors are eligible to apply for this program.

14.157 Housing for the Handicapped and the Elderly (HUD)

Objectives: to provide rental and cooperative housing and related facilities for the elderly and the handicapped.
Uses: The loans may be used to finance the purchase, construction, or rehabilitation of rental and cooperative housing for the elderly and the handicapped.
Eligibility: Private nonprofit organizations and consumer cooperatives are eligible.

Chapter 12

Home & Real Estate Buying Programs

Government Housing Programs

Urban Homesteading Program (HUD)-- $1 Homes

Program: Urban homesteading was a federal program and now is a city program to improve deteriorating urban areas by offering abandoned or foreclosed houses to persons who agree to repair them and live in them for a specified number of years. This federal run program is now run by local government who want to improve the property values of run down or rehabilitated neighborhoods. Cities like Detroit and Baltimore have these types of programs. Contact the department of urban renewal in from a branch of the city hall of various cities.

Objectives: To revitalize declining neighborhoods by transferring vacant and unrepaired single family properties to new homeowners for rehabilitation

Uses: Federally owned properties are transferred to local governments which have developed homesteading programs with HUD's approval. These governments then transfer the properties to eligible individuals or families for a nominal sum. These transfers have occurred for as low as a single dollar with the stipulation that you invest in the property with renovations.

Eligibility: Homesteaders must occupy the residence for at least five years after the transfer and must bring the property up to area code standards within three years. The local governments are allowed to set their own requirements, but in general, precedence will be given to people who live in the area already and are first-time homebuyers who are unable to afford a home through conventional means. Also, the applicants must be able to qualify for a rehabilitation loan to ensure that they will be able to renovate the house.

14.117 Mortgage Insurance-- Homes (HUD)

Objectives: to help families become homeowners
Uses: The loans may be used to finance the purchase of one- to four-family housing, to build similar housing, or to refinance loans on existing property. (This can save you hundreds every month.)
Eligibility: All families are eligible, provided they intend to live in the property.

14.119 Mortgage Insurance-- Homes for Disaster Victims (HUD)

Objectives: to help the victims of major disasters become home owners on a sound financial basis.
Uses: These loans may be used by disaster victims to purchase or refinance existing housing, or to build single-family housing.

Eligibility: Families which have been victims of disasters which the President has designated as major are eligible for this program.

14.172 Mortgage Insurance-- Growing Equity Mortgages (HUD)

Objectives: To help homebuyers receive a shorter mortgage term by increasing payments over a ten-year period.
Uses: These loans may be used to finance the purchase of proposed or existing single-family housing, as well as to refinance existing loans on existing housing.
Eligibility: All persons are eligible to apply, providing they intend to live in the property.

14.108 Rehabilitation Mortgage Insurance (HUD)

Objectives: To help families repair, improve, purchase, or refinance existing residential structures which are more than one year old.
Uses: Loans may be used only in connection with improving an existing one- to four-unit residential property. This may include moving such a structure to a new location and making improvements, or refinancing it in order to make the improvements.
Eligibility: Individual purchasers or investors are eligible.

14.110 Manufactured Home Loan Insurance (HUD)

Objectives: to create a reasonable means of financing mobile homes.
Uses: The loans may be used to purchase a manufactured home only on the condition that the buyer uses the home as a primary residence. The maximum loan amount is $40,500.
Eligibility: All persons are eligible to apply.

14.112 Mortgage Insurance for Construction Or Rehabilitation of Condominium Projects. (HUD)

Objectives: to enable investors to develop condominium projects for sale to individuals
Uses: The loans may be used to finance the construction or rehabilitation of multifamily housing structures by an investor who intends to sell the units as condominiums.
Eligibility: Private investors are eligible for this program.

14.133 Mortgage Insurance-- Purchase of Units in Condominiums (HUD)

Objectives: to enable families to purchase units in condominiums
Uses: These loans may be used to purchase individual units in proposed or existing condominium projects which consist of four or more units.
Eligibility: All families are eligible.

14.122 Mortgage Insurance-- Homes in Urban Renewal Areas (HUD)

Objectives: to help families purchase or rehabilitate homes which are in urban renewal areas.
Uses: These loans may be used to purchase one- to 11-family housing in approved urban development areas.
Eligibility: All families are eligible to apply.

14.123 Mortgage Insurance-- Housing in Older, Declining Areas (HUD)

Objectives: To assist in the purchase and rehabilitation of housing in older, declining urban areas.
Uses: These loans may be used to finance the purchase, repair, rehabilitation, and construction of housing in certain older, declining urban areas.
Eligibility: All families are eligible to apply.

14.127 Mortgage Insurance-- Manufactured Home Parks (HUD)

Objectives: To make possible the financing of construction or rehabilitation of manufactured home parks.
Uses: These loans may be used to finance the construction or rehabilitation of manufactured home parks which include five or more spaces.
Eligibility: Loans may be assumed by investors, builders, and developers who meet HUD loan requirements.

14.142 Property Improvement Loan Insurance for Existing Structures (HUD)

Objectives: To facilitate the financing of improvements to homes and other existing structures
Uses: These loans may be used to finance alterations, repairs, and improvements to existing structures.
Eligibility: Eligible borrowers include the owner of the property, a resident who has a long-term lease, or a potential buyer of the property.

14.159 Graduated Payment Mortgage Program (HUD)

Objectives: to help households who expect their incomes to rise purchase homes now. **Uses**: The program allows homeowners to make smaller monthly payments in the beginning and to slowly increase the amounts of these payments. Loans may be used to finance the purchase of proposed or existing single-family housing or condominiums.
Eligibility: All persons are eligible to apply for these loans. Applicants must plan to live on the property.

14.162 Mortgage Insurance— Manufactured Home Lot Loans (HUD)

Objectives: to make possible reasonable financing for the purchase of a manufactured home and a lot on which to place the home.
Uses: These loans may be used to purchase manufactured homes and lots for buyers in-tending to use them as principle places of residence.
Eligibility: All persons are eligible to apply.

14.175 Adjustable Rate Mortgages (HUD)

Objectives: To provide mortgage insurance for an adjustable rate mortgage which offers consumer protection features.
Uses: These loans may be used to finance the purchase of existing one- to four-family housing, the construction of such housing, or the refinancing of a loan on existing housing. **Eligibility**: All persons who intend to occupy the property are eligible to apply for these loans.

14.169 Counseling for Homebuyers, Homeowners, and Tenants (HUD)

Any family or individual who is part of a HUD program is eligible for free counseling. Counseling services are intended to help homeowners and tenants improve their housing conditions and meet their responsibilities. These services include help with buying and maintaining a home, and referrals for: financial assistance, food, medical care, family guidance, job training, and for job placement.

For additional information, you can reach HUD by calling (202) 708-4534, or by writing U.S. Department of Housing and Urban Development, Washington, D.C. 20410-4000. Also, your phone book will list the HUD office nearest you under Government.

10.417 Very Low-Income Housing Repair Loans and Grants (USDA)

Objectives: To give very low-income rural homeowners an opportunity to make essential repairs to their homes in order to make them safe and to remove health hazards.

Uses: Grant funds may only be used to make the homes of low-income owner-occupants safe and sanitary. Loans bear an interest rate of one percent (which amounts to USDA paying a portion of your mortgage payment) and are for a term of 20 years.

Eligibility: Loan applicants must own and occupy a home in a rural area; have sufficient income to repay the loan; and be a citizen or permanent resident of the U.S. Grant recipients must be 62 years old and be unable to repay the portion received as a grant.

10.433 Rural Housing Preservation Grants (USDA)

Objectives: To assist low-income rural homeowners in obtaining adequate housing by providing the necessary assistance to repair or rehabilitate their housing.

Uses: to repair and rehabilitate the housing of low-income rural homeowners.

Eligibility: Low-income rural individuals and families who are homeowners and need resources to bring their housing up to code are eligible.

10.437 Interest Rate Reduction Program (USDA)

Objectives: To aid family-sized farms in obtaining credit when they are temporarily unable to make ends meet without getting a reduction in interest rate.

Uses: May be used to refinance the purchase, improvement or enlargement of farms; or the construction, improvement, or repair of farm homes and service buildings.

Eligibility: individuals, partnerships, or joint ventures that are, or will be, conducting family-size farming or ranching operations.

64.106 Specially Adapted Housing For Disabled Veterans (VA)

Objectives: to assist certain severely disabled veterans acquire suitable housing with special fixtures and facilities which are made necessary by the nature of the veterans' disabilities.

Uses: The program provides a 50-percent grant to cover the cost of construction of a specially-equipped home or the substantial rehabilitation of an existing home, not to exceed $50,000. Also, the program will pay full costs, not to exceed $10,000, of adaptations to a veteran's home.

Eligibility: The eligibility requirements are complicated, but include injuries which necessitate the use of a cane, crutches, or wheelchair, or which result in legal blindness.

64.114 Veterans Administration Home Loans (VA)

Objectives: to help veterans secure loans in order to purchase or construct housing.

Uses: Loans may be used to buy, build, or improve a home, or to refinance an existing home loan.

Eligibility: Veterans must reside in the home for which they are receiving the loan. The eligibility requirements for this program are dependent on the time and the length of your enlistment. Any veteran who has been permanently disabled for service related reasons should be eligible. The unmarried widow or widower of a service person who has died in a service related incident, or the spouse of a service member who has been declared missing in action or a prisoner of war, may also qualify. Only those veterans who have received other than dishonorable discharge, or who are still active, are eligible for these loans.

Also, veterans with permanent service disabilities may be eligible for grants, or additional loans, with which to adapt housing for their specific needs.

64.118 Veterans Housing-- Direct Loans for Disabled Veterans (VA)

Objectives: to provide certain severely disabled veterans with direct housing credit in connection with grants for specially adapted housing which is made necessary by the nature of their disabilities (see program 64.106 above).

Uses: These loans, of up to $33,000, may be used by the veteran to purchase, construct, or rehabilitate a home which he or she intends to occupy.

Eligibility: The eligibility requirements are complicated, but include injuries which necessitate the use of a cane, crutches, or wheelchair, or which result in legal blindness.

64.119 Veterans Housing-- Manufactured Home Lots (VA)

Objectives: to assist veterans, service persons, and certain unmarried surviving spouses of veterans obtain credit for the purchase of a manufactured home on better terms than the general public

Uses: These loans may be used to purchase a new or used manufactured home and/or to buy or improve a lot on which to place the manufactured home. Also, the loans may be used to refinance a previous loan on the manufactured home and/or lot.

Eligibility: The eligibility requirements for this program are dependent on the time and the length of your enlistment. Any veteran who has been permanently disabled for service related reasons should be eligible. The unmarried widow or widower of a service person who has died in a service related incident, or the spouse of a service member who has been declared missing in action or a prisoner of war, may also qualify. Only those veterans who have received other than dishonorable discharge, or who are still active, are eligible for these loans.

Chapter 13

Free Grants & Loans For Education

Education grants and loans

Many people who are entering school or who want to go to school. Many people do not go to the school they want, or skip school all together because of money. Some people don't apply for grants and loans for education because they don't know what's available. Others think they or their parents are too well off to be eligible. But after a careful look, students find that there's more government money out there than most people think there is available.

With the federal programs out there, you shouldn't have to worry about money if you want to go to trade school, community college, vocational school or college.

The federal government has eleven main programs for people needing money to go to college. They are: The Federal Pell Grant, Federal Supplemental Education Opportunity Grant (FSEOG), Academic Competitiveness Grant (ACG), National Science and Mathematics Access to Retain Talent Grant (National SMART Grant), Teacher Education Assistance for College and Higher Education (TEACH) grant, Iraq and Afghanistan Service Grant, Federal Work-Study, Federal Perkins Loan, Subsidized Direct or FEEL Stafford Loan, Unsubsidized Direct or FEEL Stafford Loan and the last Direct or FEEL PLUS Loan.

The government defines grants as "awards you do not have to pay back." Work study "gives you the chance to work and earn money to help pay for school. Loans from the government "are borrowed money that you must repay with interest."

For more information on federal loans and grants contact the department of education or state educational agencies.

Department of Education
400 Maryland Ave, SW
Washington, DC 20202
Website: www.ed.gov
Toll Free: (800) 872-5327
Toll Free: TTY (800) 437-0833

Student Grant Programs

	Program	Type Of Assistance	Amount Of Benefits
1	1. Federal Pell Grant	Grant – No repayment of money.	2010 -11 $609-$5,550
2	2. Federal Supplemental Educational Opportunity Grant (FSEOG)	Grant – No repayment of money.	$100-$4,000
3	3. Academic Competitiveness Grant (ACG)	Grant – No repayment of money.	1st year up to $750. 2nd year up to $1,300
4	4. National Science and Mathematics Access to Retain Talent Grant (National SMART Grant)	Grant – No repayment of money.	Up to $4,000 a year.
5	5. Teacher Education Assistance for College and Higher Education (TEACH) Grant.	Grant – No repayment of money.	Up to $4,000 a year. Undergraduate total may not exceed $16,000. Graduate total may not exceed $8,000.
6	6. Iraq and Afghanistan Service Grant	Grant – No repayment of money.	$609-$5,550

Student Loan Programs

	Program	Type Of Assistance	Amount Of Benefits
1	1. Federal Work-Study	Loan – Money must be repaid.	No annual minimum or maximum amounts.
2	2. Federal Perkins Loan	Loan – Money must be repaid.	Undergraduate students up to $5,500 and professional students up to $8,000.
3	3. Subsidized Direct* or FFEL** Stafford Loan.	Loan – Money must be repaid.	$3,500 to $8.500 based on grade level.
4	4. Unsubsidized Direct* or FFEL** Stafford Loan	Loan – Money must be repaid.	$5,500 - $20,500 (less subsidies received for the same period.)
5	5. Direct* or FFEL**PLUS Loans For Parents	Loan – Money must be repaid.	Maximum amount is cost of attendance to school less any other financial aid received by student.

State Higher Education Agencies

Listed below for each state are the agencies responsible for administering state financial aid programs. You should encourage students to apply for any available state aid as well as federal aid and private scholarships. There also is a list of state education agency contact information at www.ed.gov/Programs/bastmp/SHEA.htm (this URL is case-sensitive).

State Higher Education Agencies List:

Alabama
Alabama Commission on Higher Education
Toll-free: 1-800-960-7773
Web site: www.ache.state.al.us

Alaska
Alaska Commission on Postsecondary Education
Toll-free: 1-800-441-2962
Web site: www.alaskaadvantage.state.ak.us

Arizona
Arizona Commission for Postsecondary Education
Phone: 602-258-2435
Web site: www.azhighered.org

Arkansas
Arkansas Department of Higher Education
Toll-free: 1-800-54-STUDY
Web site: www.arkansashighered.com
http://www.adhe.ed/student/pages/students.aspx#1

California
California Student Aid Commission
Toll-free: 1-888-224-7268
Web site: www.csac.ca.gov

Colorado
Colorado Commission on Higher Education
Phone: 303-866-2723
Web site: www.state.co.us/cche
http://highered.colorado.gov/finance/financialaid/

Connecticut
Connecticut Department of Higher Education
Phone: 860-947-1855
Web site: www.ctdhe.org

Delaware
Delaware Higher Education Commission
Toll-free: 1-800-292-7935

Web site: www.doe.state.de.us/high-ed

District of Columbia Office of the State
Superintendent of Education
Phone: 202-727-2824
Web site: www.seo.dc.gov

Florida
Office of Student Financial Assistance, Florida Department of Education
Toll-free: 1-888-827-2004
Web site: www.floridastudentfinancialaid.org

Georgia
Georgia Student Finance Commission
Toll-free: 1-800-505-4732
Web site: www.gsfc.org

Hawaii
University of Hawaii System
Phone: 808-956-7251
Web site: www.hawaii.edu/admissions/aid.html

Idaho
Idaho State Board of Education
Phone: 208-332-1574
Web site: www.boardofed.idaho.gov/scholarships

Illinois
Illinois Student Assistance Commission
Toll-free: 1-800-899-4722
Web site: www.collegezone.com

Indiana
State Student Assistance Commission of Indiana
Toll-free: 1-888-528-4719
Web site: www.in.gov/ssaci

Iowa
Iowa College Student Aid Commission
Toll-free: 1-877-272-4456
1-515-725-3400

Web site: www.iowacollegeaid.org

Kansas
Kansas Board of Regents
Phone: 785-296-3421
Web site: www.kansasregents.org

Kentucky
Kentucky Higher Education Assistance Authority
Toll-free: 1-800-928-8926
Web site: www.kheaa.com

Louisiana
Louisiana Office of Student Financial Assistance
Toll-free: 1-800-259-5626
Web site: www.osfa.state.la.us

Maine
Finance Authority of Maine
Toll-free: 1-800-228-3734
Web site: www.famemaine.com

Maryland
Maryland Higher Education Commission
Toll-free: 1-800-974-1024
Web site: www.mhec.state.md.us

Massachusetts
Massachusetts Board of Higher Education, Office of Student Financial Assistance
Phone: 617-727-9420
Web site: www.osfa.mass.edu

Michigan
Student Financial Services Bureau
Toll-free: 1-800-642-5626, ext. 37054
Web site: www.michigan.gov/mistudentaid

Minnesota
Minnesota Office of Higher Education
Toll-free: 1-800-657-3866
Web site: www.ohe.state.mn.us

Mississippi
Mississippi Office of Student Financial Aid, Mississippi Institutions of Higher Learning
Toll-free: 1-800-327-2980
Web site: www.mississippi.edu/riseupms/

financialaid-state.php

Missouri
Missouri Department of Higher Education
Toll-free: 1-800-473-6757
Web site: www.dhe.mo.gov

Montana
Montana Guaranteed Student Loan Program
Toll-free: 1-800-537-7508
Web site: www.mgslp.state.mt.us

Nebraska
Nebraska Coordinating Commission for Postsecondary Education
Phone: 402-471-0032
Web site: www.ccpe.state.ne.us

Nevada
Office of the State Treasurer
Toll-free: 1-888-477-2667
Web site: www.nevadatreasurer.gov

New Hampshire
New Hampshire Postsecondary Education Commission
Phone: 603-271-2555
Web site: www.nh.gov/postsecondary/financial/index.html

New Jersey
New Jersey Higher Education Student Assistance Authority
Toll-free: 1-800-792-8670
Web site: www.hesaa.org

New Mexico
New Mexico Higher Education Department
Toll-free: 1-800-279-9777
Web site: www.hed.state.nm.us

New York
New York State Higher Education Services Corporation
Toll-free: 1-888-697-4372
Web site: www.hesc.org

North Carolina
College Foundation of North Carolina

Toll-free: 1-866-866-2362
Web site: www.cfnc.org

North Dakota
North Dakota University System
Phone: 701-328-2960
Web site: www.ndus.edu

Ohio
Ohio Board of Regents
Toll-free: 1-888-833-1133
(for information specifically about Ohio
programs)
Toll-free: 1-877-428-8246
(for information about other sources of financial
aid)
Web site: regents.ohio.gov/sgs/index.php

Oklahoma
Oklahoma State Regents for Higher Education
Toll-free: 1-800-858-1840
Web site: www.okhighered.org

Oregon
Oregon Student Assistance Commission
Phone: 541-687-7400
Toll-free: 1-800-452-8807
Web site: www.osac.state.or.us

Pennsylvania
Pennsylvania Higher Education
Assistance Agency
Toll-free: 1-800-692-7392
Web site: www.pheaa.org

Rhode Island
Rhode Island Higher Education
Assistance Authority
Toll-free: 1-800-922-9855
Web site: www.riheaa.org/borrowers

South Carolina
South Carolina Commission
on Higher Education
Toll-free: 803-737-2260
Web site: www.che.sc.gov

South Dakota
South Dakota Board of Regents
Phone: 605-773-3455
Web site: www.sdbor.ed/student/

prospective

Tennessee
Tennessee Student Assistance Corporation
Toll-free: 1-800-342-1663
Web site: www.collegepaystn.com

Texas
Texas Higher Education Coordinating Board;
Texas Financial Aid Information Center
Toll-free: 1-888-311-8881
Web site: www.collegefortexans.com

Utah
Utah Higher Education Assistance Authority
Toll-free: 1-877-336-7378
Web site: www.uheaa.org

Vermont
Vermont Student Assistance Corporation
Toll-free: 1-800-642-3177
Web site: www.vsac.org

Virginia
State Council of Higher Education for Virginia
Toll-free: 1-877-516-0138
Web site: www.schev.edu

Washington
Washington State Higher Education
Coordinating Board
Toll-free: 1-888-535-0747
Web site: www.hecb.wa.gov

West Virginia
West Virginia Higher Education Policy
Commission
Toll-free: 1-888-825-5707
Web site: www.hepc.wvnet.edu

Wisconsin
Wisconsin Higher Educational Aids Board
Phone: 608-267-2206
Web site: www.heab.wisconsin.gov

Wyoming
Wyoming Department of Education
Phone: 307-777-7690
Web site: http://www.k12.wy.us/
grants.asp

U.S. Territories American Samoa
American Samoa Community College
Phone: 011-684-699-9155
Web site: www.ascc.as

Commonwealth of the Northern Mariana Islands
Northern Marianas College Financial Aid Office
Phone: 011-670-234-5498
Web site: www.nmcnet.edu
Federated States of Micronesia

Federated States of Micronesia
Department of Education
Phone: 011-691-320-2609
Web site: www.literacynet.org/
micronesia/doe.html

Guam
University of Guam
Phone: 011-671-735-2288
Web site: www.uog.edu

Puerto Rico
Puerto Rico Council on Higher Education
Phone: 1-787-641-7100
Web site: www.ces.gobierno.pr

Republic of Palau
Republic of Palau Ministry of Education
Phone: 011-680-488-2471
Web site: www.palaumoe.net

Republic of the Marshall Islands
Marshall Islands Scholarship Grant and Loan Board
Phone: 011-692-625-5770
Web site: www.rmischolarship.net

Virgin Islands
Virgin Islands Department of Education
Phone: 340-774-0100
Web site: www.doe.vi

Chapter 14

SBA Small Business Financing

SBA Guaranteed Loans

While SBA itself does not make loans, it does guarantee loans made to small businesses by private and other institutions. Banks and other lending institutions offer a number of SBA guaranteed loan programs to assist small businesses.

7(a) Loan Guaranty Program –

The 7(a) Loan Guaranty Program is one of SBA's primary lending programs. This is SBA's primary and most flexible loan program, with financing guaranteed for a variety of general business purposes. It is designed for start-up and existing small businesses, and is delivered through commercial lending institutions.
It provides loans to small businesses unable to secure financing on reasonable terms through normal lending channels. The program operates through private-sector lenders that provide loans which are, in turn, guaranteed by the SBA - the Agency has no funds for direct lending or grants.

The major types of 7(a) loans are:

- Express Programs
- Export Loan Programs
- Rural Lender Advantage Program
- Special Purpose Loans Program

Most lenders are familiar with SBA loan programs, so interested applicants should contact their local lender for further information and assistance in the SBA loan application process. Information on the SBA loan programs, as well as the management counseling and training services offered by the agency, is also available from the local office.

Certified Development Company (504) Loan Program –

This program provides long-term, fixed-rate financing to acquire fixed assets (such as real estate or equipment) for expansion or modernization. It is designed for small businesses requiring "brick and mortar" financing, and is delivered by CDCs (Certified Development Companies)—private, non-profit corporations set up to contribute to the economic development of their communities. CDCs work with the

SBA and private-sector lenders to provide financing to small businesses. There are about 270 CDCs nationwide. Each CDC covers a specific geographic area.

Typically, a 504 project includes a loan secured with a senior lien from a private-sector lender covering up to 50 percent of the project cost, a loan secured with a junior lien from the CDC (backed by a 100 percent SBA-guaranteed debenture) covering up to 40 percent of the cost, and a contribution of at least 10 percent equity from the small business being helped. The maximum SBA debenture is $1,000,000 for meeting the job creation criteria or a community development goal. Generally, a business must create or retain one job for every $35,000 provided by the SBA.

Prequalification Loan Program –

The Prequalification Pilot Loan Program uses intermediaries to assist prospective borrowers in developing viable loan application packages and securing loans. Once the loan package is assembled, it is submitted to the SBA for expedited consideration; a decision usually is made within three days. If the application is approved, the SBA issues a letter of prequalification stating the SBA's intent to guarantee the loan. The maximum amount for loans under the program is $250,000; the SBA will guarantee up to 80 percent for loans up to & including $100,000 and 75 percent for loans over $100,000. The intermediary (usually a Small Business Development Center) then helps the borrower locate a lender offering the most competitive rates. Small Business Development Centers serving as intermediaries do not charge a fee for loan packaging. For-profit organizations will charge a fee.

SBA Export Express –

SBA Export Express combines the SBA's small business lending assistance with its technical assistance programs to help small businesses that have traditionally had difficulty in obtaining adequate export financing. The pilot program is available throughout the country and is expected to run through September 30, 2005.

Microloan Program –

This program provides small (up to $35,000) short-term loans for working capital or the purchase of inventory, supplies, furniture, fixtures, machinery and/or equipment. It is designed for small businesses and not-for-profit child-care centers needing small-scale financing and technical assistance for start-up or expansion, and is delivered through specially designated intermediary lenders (nonprofit organizations with experience in lending and technical assistance). The average loan size is about $10,500. Applications are submitted to the local intermediary and all credit decisions are made on the local level.

Disaster Assistance Loan Program:

This program provides low-interest loans to homeowners, renters, businesses of all sizes and most private non-profit organizations to repair or replace real estate, personal property, machinery and equipment, inventory and business assets that have been damaged or destroyed in a declared disaster.

SBA Bonding Program

A surety bond is a three-party instrument between a surety (someone who agrees to be responsible for the debt or obligation of another), a contractor and a project owner. The agreement binds the contractor to comply with the terms and conditions of a contract. If the contractor is unable to successfully perform the contract, the surety assumes the contractor's responsibilities and ensures that the project is completed.

SBA does not issue surety bonds; rather, it provides and manages surety bond guarantees for qualified small and emerging businesses through the Surety Bond Guarantee (SBG) Program. SBA reimburses a participating surety (within specified limits) for the losses incurred as a result of a contractor's default on a bond. The SBG Program is administered through the <u>Office of Surety Guarantees (OSG)</u> in a public-private partnership with surety companies and their agents, utilizing the most efficient and effective operational policies and procedures.

The SBG Program was developed to help small and minority contractors who cannot obtain surety bonds through regular commercial channels. Through the program, SBA makes an agreement with a surety guaranteeing that SBA will assume a predetermined percentage of loss in the event the contractor should breach the terms of the contract. SBA's guarantee gives sureties an incentive to provide bonding for eligible contractors, thereby strengthening a contractor's ability to obtain bonding and greater access to contracting opportunities.

SBA Venture Capital

Venture capital is a type of equity financing that addresses the funding needs of entrepreneurial companies that for reasons of size, assets, and stage of development cannot seek capital from more traditional sources, such as public markets and banks. Venture capital investments are generally made as cash in exchange for shares and an active role in the invested company.

Venture capital differs from traditional financing sources in that venture capital typically:

- Focuses on young, high-growth companies;
- Invests equity capital, rather than debt;
- Takes higher risks in exchange for potential higher returns;
- Has a longer investment horizon than traditional financing;
- Actively monitors portfolio companies via board participation, strategic marketing, governance, and capital structure.

SBA provides venture capital through the Small Business Investment Company (SBIC) Program, a unique public-private investment partnership. SBA itself does not make direct investments. It works with SBICs, which are privately owned and managed investment firms licensed by SBA to provide financing to small businesses with private capital they raise and with funds borrowed at favorable rates through SBA.

SBA Federal Contracting

8(a) Business Development - offers a broad scope of assistance to socially and economically disadvantaged firms.

HubZone Empowerment Contracting Program - The HUBzone Empowerment Contracting program provides federal contracting opportunities for qualified small businesses located in distressed areas.

Subcontracting Opportunities Directory - A listing of prime contractors doing business with the federal government.

Procurement Technical Assistance Centers (PTACs) - A listing of Department of Defense Procurement Technical Assistance Centers.

SBA's Procurement Center Representatives (PCR's) - located in SBA area offices, review and evaluate the small business programs of federal agencies and assist small businesses in obtaining federal contracts and subcontracts.

SBA's Commercial Market Representatives (CMR's) - located in SBA area offices, assist small businesses in obtaining subcontracts by marketing small businesses and matching them with large prime contractors.

Offices of Small & Disadvantaged Business Utilization - the OSDBUs offer small business information on procurement opportunities, guidance on procurement procedures, and identification of both prime and subcontracting opportunities.

CCR – You must be registered in CCR to compete in the Federal marketplace. CCR is the search engine for government contracting officers, a marketing tool for small firms and a "link" to procurement opportunities and important information.

Sub-Net - Prime contractors use SUB-Net to post subcontracting opportunities. These may or may not be reserved for small business, and they may include either solicitations or other notices -- for example, notices of sources sought for teaming partners and subcontractors on future contracts. Small businesses can review this web site to identify opportunities in their areas of expertise. While the web site is designed primarily as a place for large businesses to post solicitations and notices, it is also used by Federal agencies, state and local Governments, non-profit organizations, colleges and universities, and even foreign Governments for the same purpose.

The new web site has shifted the traditional marketing strategy from the shotgun approach to one that is more focused and sophisticated. Instead of marketing blindly to hundreds of prime contractors, with no certainty that any given company has a need for their product or service, small businesses can now use their limited resources to identify concrete, tangible opportunities and then bid on them.

Tech-Net - Tech-Net is an electronic gateway of technology information and resources for and about small high tech businesses. It is a search engine for researchers, scientists, state, federal and local government officials, a marketing tool for small firms and a potential "link" to investment opportunities for investors and other sources of capital.

SBA Counseling & Assistance

The SBA provides small business counseling and training through a variety of programs and resource partners, located strategically around the country.

For Free Business Counseling and business assistance contact the SBA at SBA.gov. Counseling and Assistance Programs available from the Small Business Administration.

SCORE fa

The SCORE Association "Counselors to America's Small Business" is a resource partner of the SBA dedicated to entrepreneur education and the formation, growth and success of small businesses nationwide. There are more than 12,400 SCORE volunteers in 364 chapters operating in over 800 locations who assist small businesses with business counseling and training. SCORE also operates an active online counseling initiative at www.score.org.

Small Business Development Centers (SBDCs)

The Office of Small Business Development Centers (SBDC) provides management assistance to current and prospective small business owners. SBDCs offer one-stop assistance to individuals and small businesses by providing a wide variety of information and guidance in central and easily accessible branch locations. The program is a cooperative effort of the private sector, the educational community and federal, state and local governments and is an integral component of Entrepreneurial Development's network of training and counseling services.

U.S. Export Assistance Centers

U.S. Export Assistance Centers, located in major metropolitan areas throughout the United States, are one-stop shops ready to provide your small- or medium-sized business with local export assistance. Receive personalized assistance by professionals from the U.S. Small Business Administration, the U.S. Department of Commerce, the U.S. Export-Import Bank and other public and private organizations. It's a partnership that makes it easier to get the help you need to compete and succeed in the global marketplace.

Women's Business Centers (WBCs)

Women's Business Centers represent a national network of nearly 100 educational centers designed to assist women start and grow small businesses. WBCs operate with the mission to level the playing field for women entrepreneurs, who still face unique obstacles in the world of business.

SBA Publications

For free small business publications contact the SBA.gov. Free publications include:

General SBA Publications:
- The Small Business Advantage
- The Small Business Advantage (Spanish Language)

- **Small Business Management Series**:

- Management And Planning Series
- Financial Management Series
- Marketing Series
- Products/Ideas/Inventions Series
- Personnel Management Series
- Crime Prevention Series

- Emerging Business Series
-

Government Contracting:
- Opening Doors to Federal Government Contracting Opportunities
- Women-Owned Business (WOB)

- Opportunities in Contracting
- HUBZones and Federal Contracting
- Service-Disabled Veteran-Owned Small Business
- (SDVOSB) Opportunities in Contracting

Contact The Small Business Administration

To reach SBA by Mail:	To reach SBA by phone or e-mail:
US Small Business Administration **409 3rd Street, SW** **Washington, DC 20416** **http://www.sba.gov**	SBA Answer Desk 1-800-U-ASK-SBA (1-800-827-5722) Send e-mails to: answerdesk@sba.gov Answer Desk TTY: (704) 344-6640

SBA District Offices

In addition to its resource partners, the SBA operates full service district offices in every state of the country. Locate the district office closest to you.

Chapter 15

Business, Energy & Emergency Tax Credits

Business Tax Credits

Getting business credit is like getting a business refund. A refund check is revenue in the bank. Take all of the business credits that you can for your business. Your general business credit for the year consists of your carry forward of business credits from prior years plus the total of your current year business credits. The total business credit could sum up to a very large amount. In addition, your general business credit for the current year could be increased at a later time by the carry back of business credits from later years. You subtract this credit directly from your tax. Make it a point to pay close attention to business credits.

All of the following credits, with the exception of the electric vehicle credit, are part of the general business credit. The form you use to figure each credit is shown below. Look at the energy tax credit list for more business tax credits.

Business Tax Credit Programs

Farmer's Tax Guide
Publication 225,
For an agricultural producer/farmer, dairy farmer or the owner or tenant operator of a family farm.
Web Site: http://www.irs.gov/publications/p225/index.html
Go to http://irs.gov or call 1-800-829-3676 or write the IRS to place your order.

Tax Guide for Small Business
Publication 334
Web Site: http://www.irs.gov/publications/p334/index.html
Go to http://irs.gov or call 1-800-829-3676 or write the IRS to place your order.

Electric Vehicle Credit in Publication
Publication 535
Web Site: http://www.irs.gov/publications/p535/index.html

Go to http://irs.gov or call 1-800-829-3676 or write the IRS to place your order.

General Business Credit (PDF)
Form 3800
Web Site: http://www.irs.gov/pub/irs-pdf/f3800.pdf
Go to http://irs.gov or call 1-800-829-3676 or write the IRS to place your order.

Investment Credit (PDF)
Form 3468
This consists of the sum of the rehabilitation, energy, and reforestation credits.
Web Site: http://www.irs.gov/pub/irs-pdf/f3468.pdf
Go to http://irs.gov or call 1-800-829-3676 or write the IRS to place your order.

American Samoa Economic Development Credit (PDF)
Form 5735
Web Site: http://www.irs.gov/pub/irs-pdf/f5735.pdf
Go to http://irs.gov or call 1-800-829-3676 or write the IRS to place your order.

Work Opportunity Credit (PDF)
Form 5884
Web Site: http://www.irs.gov/pub/irs-pdf/f5884.pdf
Go to http://irs.gov or call 1-800-829-3676 or write the IRS to place your order.

Credit for Increasing Research Activities (PDF)
Form 6765
Web Site: http:// www.irs.gov/pub/irs-pdf/f6765.pdf
Go to http://irs.gov or call 1-800-829-3676 or write the IRS to place your order.

Low-Income Housing Credit (PDF)
Form 8586
Web Site: http://www.irs.gov/pub/irs-pdf/f8586.pdf
Go to http://irs.gov or call 1-800-829-3676 or write the IRS to place your order.

Recapture of Low-Income Housing Credit (PDF)
Form 8611,
Web Site: http://www.irs.gov/pub/irs-pdf/f8611.pdf
Go to http://irs.gov or call 1-800-829-3676 or write the IRS to place your order.

Orphan Drug Credit (PDF)
Form 8820
Web Site: http://www.irs.gov/pub/irs-pdf/f8820.pdf
Go to http://irs.gov or call 1-800-829-3676 or write the IRS to place your order.

Disabled Access Credit (PDF)
Form 8826
Web Site: http://www.irs.gov/pub/irs-pdf/f8826.pdf
Go to http://irs.gov or call 1-800-829-3676 or write the IRS to place your order.

Empowerment Zone Employment Credit (PDF)
Form 8844
Web Site: http://www.irs.gov/pub/irs-pdf/f8844.pdf

Go to http://irs.gov or call 1-800-829-3676 or write the IRS to place your order.

Indian Employment Credit (PDF)
Form 8845
Web Site: http://www.irs.gov/pub/irs-pdf/f8845.pdf
Go to http://irs.gov or call 1-800-829-3676 or write the IRS to place your order.

Credit for Employer Social Security and Medicare Taxes Paid on Certain Employee Tips (PDF)
Form 8846
Web Site: http://www.irs.gov/pub/irs-pdf/f8846.pdf
Go to http://irs.gov or call 1-800-829-3676 or write the IRS to place your order.

Credit for Contributions to Selected Community Development Corporations (PDF)
Form 8847
Web Site: http://www.irs.gov/pub/irs-pdf/f8847.pdf
Go to http://irs.gov or call 1-800-829-3676 or write the IRS to place your order.

New Markets Credit (PDF)
Form 8874
Web Site: http://www.irs.gov/pub/irs-pdf/f8874.pdf
Go to http://irs.gov or call 1-800-829-3676 or write the IRS to place your order.

Credit for Small Employer Pension Plan Startup Costs (PDF)
Form 8881
Web Site: http://www.irs.gov/pub/irs-pdf/f8881.pdf
Go to http://irs.gov or call 1-800-829-3676 or write the IRS to place your order.

Credit for Employer-Provided Childcare Facilities and Services (PDF)
Form 8882
Web Site: http://www.irs.gov/pub/irs-pdf/f8882.pdf
Go to http://irs.gov or call 1-800-829-3676 or write the IRS to place your order.

Qualified Railroad Track Maintenance Credit (PDF)
Form 8900
Web Site: http://www.irs.gov/pub/irs-pdf/f8900.pdf
Go to http://irs.gov or call 1-800-829-3676 or write the IRS to place your order.

Mine Rescue Team Training Credit (PDF)
Form 8923
Web Site: http://www.irs.gov/pub/irs-pdf/f8923.pdf
Go to http://irs.gov or call 1-800-829-3676 or write the IRS to place your order.

Fisherman Tax Program
The Capital Construction Fund (CCF) Program enables fishermen to construct, reconstruct, or under limited circumstances, acquire fishing vessels with before-tax, rather than after-tax dollars. The program allows fishermen to defer tax on income from the operation of their fishing vessels.

CCF Program, Financial Services Division (F/MB5)
National Marine Fisheries Service
1315 East West Highway
Silver Spring, MD 20910

Web Site: http://www.nmfs.noaa.gov/mb/financial_services/ccf.htm
Phone: 301-713-2393

Tax Relief Emergency Situations

For taxpayers impacted by a disaster, the tax code may provide necessary relief. The law permits the IRS to grant taxpayers affected by a federally declared disaster additional time to perform certain time sensitive acts, including filing returns and paying taxes when the original or extended due date of the return falls within the disaster period. In addition, affected individual and business taxpayers in a federally declared disaster area can more quickly obtain a refund by claiming losses related to the disaster on the tax return for the previous year, usually by filing an amended return. For more information on how to calculate and claim a disaster loss please refer to Publication 547, Casualties, Disasters and Thefts, and Publication 4492, Information for Taxpayers Affected by Hurricanes Katrina, Rita and Wilma, Publication 4492–A, Information for Taxpayers Affected by the May 4, 2007, Kansas Storms and Tornados, and Publication 4492–B, Information for Affected Taxpayers in the Midwestern Disaster Areas. You may also refer to Disaster Assistance and Emergency Relief for Individuals and Businesses on the irs.gov web site.

Casualties, Disasters and Thefts
Publication 547: http://www.irs.gov/publications/p547/index.html
Go to http://irs.gov or call 1-800-829-3676 or write the IRS to place your order.

Information for Taxpayers Affected by Hurricanes Katrina, Rita and Wilma
Publication 4492: http://www.irs.gov/publications/p4492.pdf
Go to http://irs.gov or call 1-800-829-3676 or write the IRS to place your order.

Information for Taxpayers Affected by the May 4, 2007, Kansas Storms and Tornado
Publication 4492-A: http://www.irs.gov/publications/p4492a.pdf
Go to http://irs.gov or call 1-800-829-3676 or write the IRS to place your order.

Information for Affected Taxpayers in the Midwestern Disaster Areas
Publication 4492-B: http://www.irs.gov/publications/p4492b.pdf
Go to http://irs.gov or call 1-800-829-3676 or write the IRS to place your order.

Disaster Assistance and Emergency Relief for Individuals and Businesses:
http://www.irs.gov/business/small/article/0,,id=156138,00.html
Go to http://irs.gov or call 1-800-829-3676 or write the IRS to place your order.

General Tax Credits

Recovery Rebate Credit (2008)
Recovery Rebate Credit, claimed on Form 1040 Line 70, Form 1040A Line 42 and Form 1040EZ Line 9. FS-2009-3 has further details.
Web Site: http://www.irs.gov/newsroom/article/0,,id=186065,00.html
Go to http://irs.gov or call 1-800-829-3676 or write the IRS to place your order.

Credit for prior year minimum tax (2008)
Credit for prior year minimum tax, claimed on Form 8801.
Web Site: http://www.irs.gov/pub/irs-pdf/f8801.pdf

Go to http://irs.gov or call 1-800-829-3676 or write the IRS to place your order.

Foreign Tax Credit (2008)
Foreign tax credit, claimed on Form 1040 Line 47
Go to http://irs.gov or call 1-800-829-3676 or write the IRS to place your order.

Economic Stimulus Payments Not Yet Claimed
You must file by October 15, 2008 to get your stimulus payment this year for veterans and retirees.
Web Site: http//www.irs.gov/newsroom/article,,id=184928,00.html
Go to http://irs.gov or call 1-800-829-3676 or write the IRS to place your order.

How to Claim the Tax Credits

To claim a general business credit, you will first have to get the forms you need to claim your current year business credits.
In addition to the credit form, in most cases you may also need to file Form 3800.
Go to http://irs.gov or call 1-800-829-3676 or write the IRS to place your order.

Tax Deductions

Charitable Contributions

Charitable contributions are good for people that can afford them. If you can't afford a charitable contribution definitely don't undertake the expense.   Charitable contributions are for the rich. The rich that have considerable junk with value and want to get rid of their valuables with some type of profit, then charitable contributions is a good method of disposing of junk with value.

Charitable contributions are deductible only if you itemize deductions on Form 1040, Schedule A.

U.S. Individual Income Tax Return
Form 1040 Schedule A: http://www.irs.gov/pub/irs-pdf/f1040sa.pdf
Go to http://irs.gov or call 1-800-829-3676 or write the IRS to place your order.

To be deductible, charitable contributions must be made to qualified organizations. See Publication 526, Charitable Contributions.

Charitable Contributions
Publication 526: http://www.irs.gov/publications/p526/index.html
Go to http://irs.gov or call 1-800-829-3676 or write the IRS to place your order.

If your contribution entitles you to merchandise, goods, or services, including admission to a charity ball, banquet, theatrical performance, or sporting event, you can deduct only the amount that exceeds the fair market value of the benefit received. For a contribution of cash, check, or other monetary gift (regardless of amount), you must maintain as a record of the contribution either a bank record or a written communication from the qualified organization containing the date and amount of the contribution and the name of the organization. You generally can deduct the fair market value of any property you donate, as well as your cash contributions, to qualified organizations. See Publication 561, Determining the Value of Donated Property. For any contribution of $250 or more (including contributions of cash or property), you must obtain and keep in your records a contemporaneous written acknowledgment from the qualified organization indicating the amount of the cash and a description of any property contributed, and whether the organization provided any goods or services in exchange for the gift. One document from the qualified organization may satisfy both the written communication requirement for monetary gifts and the contemporaneous written acknowledgment requirement for all contributions of $250 or more.

Determining the Value of Donated Property
Publication 561: http://www.irs.gov/publications/p561/index.html
Go to http://irs.gov or call 1-800-829-3676 or write the IRS to place your order.

You must fill out Form 8283 (PDF), and attach it to your return, if your total deduction for all noncash contributions is more than $500. If you claim a deduction for a contribution of noncash property worth $5,000 or less, you must fill out Form 8283, Section A. If you claim a deduction for a contribution of noncash property worth more than $5,000, you will need a qualified appraisal of the noncash property and must fill out Form 8283, Section B. If you claim a deduction for a contribution of noncash property worth more than $5,000,000, you will also need to attach the qualified appraisal to your return.

Non Cash Charitable Contributions
Form 8283: http://www.irs.gov/pub/irs-pdf/f8283.pdf
Go to http://irs.gov or call 1-800-829-3676 or write the IRS to place your order.

For more information refer to Form 8283 and its instructions, as well as Publication 526, Charitable Contributions. For information on determining value, refer to Publication 561, Determining the Value of Donated Property.

Charitable Contributions
Publication 526: http://www.irs.gov/publications/p526/index.html
Go to http://irs.gov or call 1-800-829-3676 or write the IRS to place your order.

Determining the Value of Donated Property
Publication 561: http://www.irs.gov/publications/p561/index.html
Go to http://irs.gov or call 1-800-829-3676 or write the IRS to place your order.

IRS Energy Tax Credits

Non-business Energy Property Credit

Winterize and make your home more energy efficient with this tax credit. The new energy-efficient improvements that could qualify for this tax credit includes insulation, exterior windows, exterior doors, water heaters, heat pumps, central air conditioners, furnaces and hot water boilers. This credit equals 30 percent of what a homeowner spends on eligible energy-saving improvements, up to a maximum tax credit of $1,500 over a maximum of two tax years. The cost of certain high-efficiency heating and air conditioning systems, water heaters and stoves that burn biomass all qualify, along with labor costs for installing these items. In addition, the cost of energy-efficient windows and skylights, energy-efficient doors, qualifying insulation and certain roofs also qualify for the credit, though the cost of installing these items does not count. The limit for these energy credits is $1,500, so after even spending over $4,500, you only get $1,500 in credits.   Due to limits based on tax liability, other credits claimed by a particular taxpayer and other factors, actual tax savings will vary. These tax savings are on top of any energy savings that may result.

Residential energy efficient property credit

You can get a 30% tax credit for going green and buying alternative energy equipment such as qualifying property such as solar electric systems, solar hot water heaters, geothermal heat pumps, wind turbines, and fuel cell property. Generally, labor costs are included when calculating this credit. Also, no cap exists on the amount of credit available except in the case of fuel cell property. These are energy improvements that you make to increases energy efficiency. Not all energy-efficient improvements qualify for these tax credits. For that reason, homeowners should check the manufacturer's tax credit certification statement before purchasing or installing any of these improvements. The certification statement can usually be found on the manufacturer's website or with the product packaging. Normally, a homeowner can rely on this certification. The IRS cautions that the manufacturer's certification is different from the Department of Energy's Energy Star label, and not all Energy Star labeled products qualify for the tax credits. Most contractors or manufactures of solar or wind energy equipment will post the tax credits on their web sites. If you made these innovative energy solar or wind energy improvements in 2009 then you can claim this tax credit on your 2009 tax return.

> **Residential energy efficient property credit**
> **Form 5695:** http://www.irs.gov/pub/irs-pdf/f5695.pdf
> Go to http://irs.gov or call 1-800-829-3676 or write the IRS to place your order.
>
> **Alternative motor vehicle (including hybrids) credit. (2008)**
> **Form 8910:** http://www.irs.gov/pub/irs-pdf/f8910.pdf
> Go to http://irs.gov or call 1-800-829-3676 or write the IRS to place your order.

More IRS Energy Tax Credits

One Billion In Tax Credits For Clean Coal Products
Web Site: http://www.irs.gov/newsroom/article/0,,id=164595,00.html
Go to http://irs.gov or call 1-800-829-3676 or write the IRS to place your order.

Electric Vehicle Credit in Publication
Publication 535:
Web Site: http://www.irs.gov/publications/p535/index.html
Go to http://irs.gov or call 1-800-829-3676 or write the IRS to place your order.

Credit for Alcohol Used as Fuel (PDF)
Form 6478
Web Site: http:// www.irs.gov/pub/irs-pdf/f6478.pdf
Go to http://irs.gov or call 1-800-829-3676 or write the IRS to place your order.

Qualified Electric Vehicle Credit (PDF)
Form 8834
Web Site: http://www.irs.gov/pub/irs-pdf/f8834.pdf
Go to http://irs.gov or call 1-800-829-3676 or write the IRS to place your order.

Renewable Electricity Production Credit (PDF)
Form 8835
Web Site: http://www.irs.gov/pub/irs-pdf/f8835.pdf
Go to http://irs.gov or call 1-800-829-3676 or write the IRS to place your order.

Biodiesel and Renewable Diesel Fuels Credit (PDF)
Form 8864
Web Site: http://www.irs.gov/pub/irs-pdf/f8864.pdf
Go to http://irs.gov or call 1-800-829-3676 or write the IRS to place your order.

Low Sulfur Diesel Fuel Production Credit (PDF)
Form 8896
Web Site: http://www.irs.gov/pub/irs-pdf/f8896.pdf
Go to http://irs.gov or call 1-800-829-3676 or write the IRS to place your order.

Distilled Spirits Credit (PDF)
Form 8906
Web Site: http://www.irs.gov/pub/irs-pdf/f8906.pdf
Go to http://irs.gov or call 1-800-829-3676 or write the IRS to place your order.

Nonconventional Source Fuel Credit (PDF)
Form 8907
Web Site: http://www.irs.gov/pub/irs-pdf/f8907.pdf
Go to http://irs.gov or call 1-800-829-3676 or write the IRS to place your order.

Energy Efficient Home Credit (PDF)
Form 8908
Web Site: http://www.irs.gov/pub/irs-pdf/f8908.pdf
Go to http://irs.gov or call 1-800-829-3676 or write the IRS to place your order.

Alternative Motor Vehicle Credit (PDF)
Form 8910
Web Site: http://www.irs.gov/pub/irs-pdf/f8910.pdf
Go to http://irs.gov or call 1-800-829-3676 or write the IRS to place your order.

Alternative Fuel Vehicle Refueling Property Credit (PDF)
Form 8911
Web Site: http://www.irs.gov/pub/irs-pdf/f8911.pdf
Go to http://irs.gov or call 1-800-829-3676 or write the IRS to place your order.

Energy Tax Credits at:
IRS Web Site: **http://www.irs.gov/recovery**

Order IRS Forms And Publications By Mail Or Phone.

If you need a prior year form or cannot locate an IRS product, visit the IRS Forms and Publications page to download products or call 1-800-829-3676 to place your order or write the Internal Revenue Service, 1111 Constitution Avenue, NW, Washington, DC 20224 and specify the number of the publications and forms you would like to order.

How to Order IRS Products

You may order up to 10 different products from the IRS and you will receive two copies of each ordered form and one copy of each ordered publication. The IRS will automatically include applicable instructions in your order. (If you need more than the quantity allowed, please call 1-800-829-3676 to place your order.) **Be aware that not all tax products are available through the IRS Web page and that quantities are limited.**

To place an order, enter the product number or a keyword in the search box. For example, if you need Form 2441, Child and Dependent Care Expenses, you could search for 2441, child, dependent, etc. Your search will produce a list of products matching the search criteria. Check the box next to the product and follow the instructions to finish your order or select more products.

Please allow 7 to 15 days for the IRS to process and ship your order. If a product is not available when you place your order, the IRS will send it as soon as it becomes available. Please do not place another order.

Internal Revenue Service
1111 Constitution Avenue, NW
Washington, DC 20224
Web Site: http://www.irs.gov
Toll Free: (800) 829-1040 (Tax Information)
Toll Free: (800) 829-3676 (Forms & Booklets)
Toll Free: (800) 829-0433 (Criminal Investigation)

Web Pages For Internet Form and Publication Articles and Indexes

IRS Forms And Publications: http://www.irs.gov/formspubs/index.html
IRS Forms And Publications Article: http://www.irs.gov/formspubs/article/0,,id=128717,00.html
Download or order by telephone or write the IRS.

Chapter 16

Personal
Tax Credits & Refunds

Credits can save every taxpayer a lot of money. Tax credits can be used to pay part of the cost of buying a new home, raising a family, going to college, saving for retirement, making energy-saving improvements to your home and getting daycare so you can work or go to school.

These credits can increase a refund or reduce a tax bill. Usually, credits can only lower a tax liability to zero. But some credits, such as the EITC, the child tax credit, the Recovery Rebate Credit and the first-time homebuyer credit, are refundable — in other words, they can make the difference between a balance due and a refund.

Each year, many taxpayers overlook them, even though they often qualify for one or more of these credits. Though both tax deductions and credits can save you money, they do it in different ways. A deduction lowers the income on which tax is figured, while a credit lowers the tax itself. Take time now to review your records and see if you qualify for one of these popular but often overlooked tax credits.

Although some credits are available to people at all income levels, others have income restrictions. These include the EITC, the Recovery Rebate Credit, the saver's credit, the first-time homebuyer credit, the education credits and the child tax credit.

A taxpayer who qualifies can claim any credit, regardless of whether he or she itemizes deductions. Any credit can be claimed on Form 1040, sometimes referred to as "the long form." Alternatively, many credits can also be claimed on the 1040A "short form." The EITC and Recovery Rebate Credit can even be claimed on Form 1040EZ. The instruction booklet for each of these forms contains information about these and other tax credits.

Go to http://irs.gov or call 1-800-829-3676 or write the IRS to place your order.

Home Buyer Credits

First-Time Homebuyer Credit   (2010)

You should consider buying a new home. For first time homebuyers, there is a refundable credit equal to 10 percent of the purchase price up to a maximum of $8,000 ($4,000 if married filing separately). Buying a home may qualify for the first-time homebuyer credit. Normally, a taxpayer qualifies if she didn't own a main home during the prior three years. This unique credit of up to $8,000 works much like a 15-year interest-free loan. It is available for a limited time only — on homes bought from April 9, 2008, to June 30, 2009, but it is being extended for future years.. This new tax program for 2010 offers to give you up to an $8,000 tax credit. It can be claimed on new Form 5405 and is repaid each year as an additional tax. Income limits and other special rules apply. The First-Time Homebuyer Credit Information Center has more details. The same tax credit has gone up to a limit of $8,000 for 2010.

> **Form 5405 Instructions:** http://www.irs.gov/pub/irs-pdf/i5405.pdf
> Go to http://irs.gov or call 1-800-829-3676 or write the IRS to place your order.
>
> **Form 5405:** http://irs.gov/pub/irs-pdf/f5405.pdf
> Go to http://irs.gov or call 1-800-829-3676 or write the IRS to place your order.

Rules For First Time Home Buyer Credit

A first-time homebuyer is an individual who, with his or her spouse if married, has not owned any other principal residence for three years prior to the date of purchase of the new principal residence for which the credit is being claimed.

There are several situations in which a taxpayer cannot claim the credit:

- The taxpayer is a nonresident alien;
- The taxpayer purchases a home located outside the United States;
- The taxpayer sells the home or if it stops being the taxpayer's principal residence in the year the taxpayer purchased the home;
- The taxpayer receives the home, or any portion of the home, as a gift or as an inheritance; and
- The taxpayer exceeds the income limits.

Selling the Home and Other Events that Require Repaying the Credit

Taxpayers who bought homes in 2009 or 2010 and sold them within a 36 month period that begins on the purchase date, must repay the credit. They also must repay the credit if they convert the home to a business or rental property or the lender forecloses on the home. The taxpayer repays the credit by including the amount of the credit as additional tax on the tax return for the year in which the repayment event occurs.
However, taxpayers do not have to repay all or a portion of the credit under the following circumstances:

- Taxpayers sell the home to someone who is not related to them, the repayment in the year of sale is limited to the amount of gain on the sale;
- If the home is destroyed, condemned, or disposed of under threat of condemnation and the taxpayer acquires a new principal residence within 2 years of the event, the taxpayer does not have to repay the credit; and
- If, as part of a divorce settlement, the home is transferred to a spouse or former spouse, the spouse who receives the home is responsible for repaying the credit if required.

Rule Changes For Qualified Purchases Made After November 6, 2009:

- Credit Limitation: The credit limit remains $8,000 for qualified first-time homebuyers, however, long-time residents who owned and used the same principal residence for any 5 consecutive years of the last 8 years prior to purchasing a subsequent new principal residence, may now qualify for a tax credit of up to $6,500.

- Income Limitation Is Increased: The Modified Adjusted Gross Income Limitation at which the credit will begin to be phased-out is increased to $125,000 for single taxpayers and $225,000 for joint taxpayers.
- Purchase Price Limitation: No credit shall be allowed for the purchase of any residence if the purchase price of such residence exceeds $800,000.
- Restriction for Age and Dependents: No credit shall be allow for the purchase of any residence unless the homebuyer (or spouse if married) has attained age 18 as of the date of such purchase. In addition, no buyer may take a credit if he or she can be claimed as a dependent on someone else's return.
- Documentation Requirement: Buyers will be required to submit a copy of their settlement statement to claim the tax credit.
- Claiming the Credit: Under the new law, as under the old, 2009 homebuyers may claim the credit on either their 2008 or 2009 returns, and 2010 buyers may claim their credit on either their 2009 or 2010 returns.

For more information on the new rules for 2009 and 2010 you may refer to the following references on the IRS Website at www.irs.gov.: The Form 5405 Instructions, the 2009 IRS News Release (IR-2009-14, Feb. 25, 2009), the First-Time Homebuyer Credit Information Center article, and additional topics on this subject.

Claiming the Credit

The credit is claimed on Form 5405, First-Time Homebuyer Credit, and attached to your 2008 Form 1040.

Form 5405 Instructions: http://www.irs.gov/pub/irs-pdf/i5405.pdf
Go to http://irs.gov or call 1-800-829-3676 or write the IRS to place your order.

Form 5405: http://irs.gov/pub/irs-pdf/f5405.pdf
Go to http://irs.gov or call 1-800-829-3676 or write the IRS to place your order.

IR-2009-14, Feb, 25 2009:
Article: http://www.irs.gov/newsroom/article/0,,id=204672,00.html
Go to http://irs.gov or call 1-800-829-3676 or write the IRS to place your order.

First Time homebuyer Credit Information:
Article: http://www.irs.gov/newsroom/article/0,,id=187935,00.html
Go to http://irs.gov or call 1-800-829-3676 or write the IRS to place your order.

U.S. Individual Tax Return
Form 1040: http://www.irs.gov/pub/irs-pdf/f1040.pdf
Go to http://irs.gov or call 1-800-829-3676 or write the IRS to place your order.

Washington, DC Homebuyer Tax Credit (2008)

District of Columbia first-time homebuyer credit, claimed on Form 8859.
Web Site: http://www.irs.gov/pub/irs-pdf/f8859.pdf
Go to http://irs.gov or call 1-800-829-3676 or write the IRS to place your order.

Form 8859: http://www.irs.gov/pub/irs-pdf/f8859.pdf
Go to http://irs.gov or call 1-800-829-3676 or write the IRS to place your order.

Earned Income Tax Credit (EITC)

Earned Income Tax Credit (EITC)   (2008)

If you file a Form 1040 Schedule C, you may be eligible to claim the Earned Income Tax Credit (EITC). To learn more about EITC, refer to the IRS website.

The Earned Income Tax Credit (EITC) helps people who work but do not earn a lot of money. Working families with incomes below $41,646 and childless workers with incomes under $15,880 often qualify for the EITC tax credit. Generally, you must have earned income as an employee, independent contractor, farmer or business owner to qualify. Taxpayers under the minimum retirement age who receive disability payments from an employer plan may also be eligible. Use the EITC Assistant, available in mid-January, can help you see if you qualify.

Qualifying For The Earned Income Tax Credit:
http://irs.gov/individuals/article/0,,id=96406,00.html
Go to http://irs.gov or call 1-800-829-3676 or write the IRS to place your order.

EITC Assistant: http://www.irs.gov/individuals/article/0,,id=130102,00.html
Go to http://irs.gov or call 1-800-829-3676 or write the IRS to place your order.

Elderly & Disabled Tax Credits

Credit for the elderly or the disabled. (2008)

Credit for the elderly or the disabled, claimed on Form 1040 Schedule R
Go to http://irs.gov or call 1-800-829-3676 or write the IRS to place your order.

Child Care Tax Credits

Child Tax Credit   (2008)

This child tax credit, which can be as much as $1,000 per eligible child, is in addition to the regular $3,500 exemption claimed for each dependent. To qualify for this tax credit a tax payer must have a dependent child under age 17. A change in the way the credit is figured means that more low- and moderate-income families will qualify for the full credit on their 2008 and other returns. Don't confuse the child tax credit with the child care credit. For details on figuring and claiming the child tax credit. The child tax credit is not the same as the child care credit. Details on figuring and claiming the child tax credit can be found in IRS Publication 972 (PDF format).

Child Tax Credit
Publication 972: http://irs.gov/pub/irs-pdf/p972.pdf
Go to http://irs.gov or call 1-800-829-3676 or write the IRS to place your order.

Credit for Child and Dependent Care Expenses (2008)

The tax credit is available for an individual who pays for someone to care for a child so he or she can work or look for work probably qualifies for the child and dependent care credit. Normally, the child must be the taxpayer's dependent and under age 13. Though often referred to as the child care credit, this credit is also available to those who pay someone to care for a spouse or dependent, regardless of age, who is unable to care for him- or herself. In most cases, the care provider's Social Security Number or taxpayer identification number must be obtained and entered on the return.

Form 1040 filers claim the credit for child and dependent care expenses on Form 2441. Form 1040A filers claim it on Schedule 2. IRS Publication 503 (PDF version) has more information.

> **Credit For Child And Dependent Care Expense**
> **Publication 503:** http://irs.gov/pub/irs-pdf/p503.pdf
> Go to http://irs.gov or call 1-800-829-3676 or write the IRS to place your order.

> **Credit For Child And Dependent Care Expense**
> **Form 2441:** http://www.irs.gov/pub/irs-pdf/f2441
> Go to http://irs.gov or call 1-800-829-3676 or write the IRS to place your order.

Health Care Tax Credits (2010)

The "Affordable Care Act" of 2010 Offers Employers New Tax Deductions and Credits

A variety of new business tax deductions and credits for employers were created by the Affordable Care Act which was passed into law on March 23, 2010. It contains some tax provisions that take effect in 2010, and more that will be implemented during the next several years. The information under the following headings briefly explains some of the key provisions of the new legislation that are now in effect.

The Small Business Health Care Tax Credit (2010)

This new credit helps small businesses and small tax-exempt organizations afford the cost of covering their employees, and specifically targets those businesses with low and moderate income workers. The credit is designed to encourage small employers to offer health insurance coverage for the first time or maintain coverage they already have. For the 2010 tax year the credit generally is available to small employers who pay at least half the cost of single coverage for their employees.
Web Site: http://www.irs.gov

Health Coverage for Older Children (2010)

Health coverage for an employee's children who do not turn 27 years of age at any time during the taxable year is now generally tax free to the employee. This expanded health care benefit applies to various work place and retiree health plans. These changes immediately allow employers with cafeteria plans (plans that allow employees to choose from a menu of tax-free benefit options and cash or taxable benefits) to permit employees to begin making pre-tax contributions to pay for this expanded benefit. This also applies to self-employed individuals who qualify for the self-employed health insurance deduction on their federal income tax return.
Web Site: http://www.irs.gov

Medicare Part D Coverage Gap "donut hole" Rebate   (2010)

The Affordable Care Act provides a one-time $250 rebate in 2010 to assist Medicare Part D recipients who have reached their Medicare drug plan's coverage gap. This payment is not made by the IRS, and it is not taxable. More information on the rebate can be found at www.medicare.gov.
Medicare Rebate: http://www.medicare.gov

Therapeutic Discovery Project Program   (2010)

This program is provides tax credits and grants to taxpayers with no more than 250 employees engaged in therapeutic discovery projects that show a reasonable potential to:

- Result in new therapies to treat areas of unmet medical need or prevent, detect or treat chronic or acute diseases and conditions
- Reduce the long-term growth of health care costs in the United States, or
- Significantly advance the goal of curing cancer within 30 years

Allocation of the credit will also take into consideration which projects show the greatest potential to create and sustain (directly or indirectly) high-quality, high paying U.S. jobs and to advance U.S. competitiveness in life, biological and medical sciences.

IRS guidance describes the process by which firms can apply to have their research projects certified as eligible for the credit or grant. Companies may submit applications for certification beginning June 21, 2010. Applications must be postmarked no later than July 21, 2010.

For more information on these business credits and benefits click the following link: Affordable Care Act of 2010

IRS Guidance: Internet Link: http://irs.gov/newsroom/article/0,,id=224513,00.html
Affordable Care Act Of 2010: Internet Link: http://irs.gov/newsroom/article/0,,id=222814,00.html

Telephone Tax Credit

Telephone Excise Tax Refund: (2006)

 This is a one-time refund of long distance excise taxes available on 2006 income tax returns. The refund applies to charges billed from March 2003 through July 2006. The IRS offers a standard refund amount of $30 to $60, or taxpayers can calculate the actual tax paid. Even if the taxpayer does not normally have to file a return, Form 1040EZ-T can be used to request this refund. Businesses and exempt organizations can also request it. Taxpayers can visit IRS.gov for more information on this special payment.
Go to http://irs.gov or call 1-800-829-3676 or write the IRS to place your order.

Education Tax Credits

Education Credits   (American Opportunity, Hope and Lifetime Learning Credits) **(2008)**

The Hope credit and the lifetime learning credit help parents and students pay for post-secondary education. Normally, a taxpayer can claim both his or her own tuition and required enrollment fees, as well as those for a dependent's college education. The Hope credit targets the first two years of post-secondary education, and an eligible student must be enrolled at least half time. A taxpayer can also choose the lifetime learning credit, even if they are only taking one course.

In some cases, however, she may do better by claiming the tuition and fees deduction, instead. The education credit and the tuition and fees deduction cannot both be claimed for the same student in the same year. Special rules, including income limits, apply to each of these tax breaks.

Education credits are claimed on Form 8863. Details on these and other education-related tax breaks are contained in Publication 970 (PDF version).

> **Education credits (American Opportunity, Hope, and Lifetime Learning Credits)**
> **Form 8863:** http://irs.gov/pub/irs-pdf/f8863
> Go to http://irs.gov or call 1-800-829-3676 or write the IRS to place your order.
>
> **Tax Benefits For Education**
> **Publication 970:** http://irs.gov/pub/irs-pdf/p970.pdf
> Go to http://irs.gov or call 1-800-829-3676 or write the IRS to place your order.

Education Tax Credits.

The IRS will give you a tax credit for your educational expenses.
Web Site: http://www.irs.gov/individuals/article/0,,id=121452,00.html

Continuing Education Tax Credits

The IRS will give you a tax credit for your continuing educational tax expenses.
Web Site: http://www.irs.gov/newsroom/article/0,,id=156866,00.html

Retirement Tax Credit

Retirement Plan Saver's Credit   (2008)

The saver's credit is designed to help low- and moderate-income workers save for retirement. A taxpayer probably qualifies if his income is below certain limits and he contributes to an IRA or workplace retirement plan, such as a 401(k). Income limits for 2007 are:

- $26,500 for singles and married taxpayers filing separately
- $39,750 for heads of household and
- $53,000 for joint filers

Also known as the retirement savings contributions credit, the saver's credit is available in addition to any other tax savings that apply. There is still time to put money into an IRA and get the saver's credit on a 2008 return. 2008 IRA contributions can be made until April 15, 2009. Form 8880 is used to claim the saver's credit. Enter the amount of the credit on Form 1040 (PDF), or on Form 1040A (PDF). You cannot use Form 1040EZ to claim this credit.

For more information on eligible contributions to an employer-sponsored retirement plan or to an individual retirement arrangement (IRA), you may be able to take a tax credit. The amount of the saver's credit you can get is based on the contributions you make and your credit rate. Refer to Publication 590, Individual Retirement Arrangements (IRAs), for more information.

Credit for Qualified Retirement Savings Contributions
Form 8880: http://irs.gov/pub/irs-pdf/f8880
Go to http://irs.gov or call 1-800-829-3676 or write the IRS to place your order.

Individual Retirement Arrangements (IRAs)
Publication 590: http://www.irs.gov/publications/p590/index.html
Go to http://irs.gov or call 1-800-829-3676 or write the IRS to place your order.

U.S. Individual Income Tax Return
Form 1040: http://www.irs.gov/pub/irs-pdf/f1040.pdf
Go to http://irs.gov or call 1-800-829-3676 or write the IRS to place your order.

U.S. Individual Income Tax Return
Form 1040A: http://www.irs.gov/pub/irs-pdf/f1040a.pdf
Go to http://irs.gov or call 1-800-829-3676 or write the IRS to place your order.

Free IRS Tax Services

- Volunteer Tax Assistance
- Toll-Free Telephone
- Walk-in Assistance
- Outreach Programs
- Identity Theft

The IRS sponsors volunteer assistance programs and offers help to taxpayers in many community locations.

The Volunteer Income Tax Assistance Program (VITA) offers free tax help by trained volunteers to low to moderate income taxpayers. VITA sites are locally available at community locations, and provide free basic income tax return preparation to individuals. To see if you qualify, see Publication 910 (PDF), IRS Guide to Free Tax Services, at our website, www.irs.gov. Volunteers prepare Form 1040A (PDF), Form 1040EZ (PDF), and Form 1040 (PDF).

IRS Guide to Free Tax Services
Publication 910: http://www.irs.gov/pub/irs-pdf/p910.pdf
Go to http://irs.gov or call 1-800-829-3676 or write the IRS to place your order.

U.S. Individual Income Tax Return
Form 1040A: http://www.irs.gov/pub/irs-pdf/f1040a
Go to http://irs.gov or call 1-800-829-3676 or write the IRS to place your order.

U.S. Individual Income Tax Return
Form 1040EZ: http://www.irs.gov/pub/irs-pdf/f1040ez.pdf
Go to http://irs.gov or call 1-800-829-3676 or write the IRS to place your order.

U.S. Individual Income Tax Return
Form 1040: http://www.irs.gov/pub/irs-pdf/f1040.pdf
Go to http://irs.gov or call 1-800-829-3676 or write the IRS to place your order.

Trained volunteers can help you with special credits such as Earned Income Tax Credit (EITC), Child Tax Credit and Credit for the Elderly or the Disabled, which you may qualify for.

In addition to free tax return preparation assistance, many VITA sites offer free electronic filing (e-file). Individuals taking advantage of the e-file program will receive their refunds in half the time compared to returns filed on paper – even faster if you have your refund deposited directly into your bank account.

Learn the locations, dates, and hours of the volunteer sites by calling the IRS toll-free at 800-TAX-1040 or 800-829-1040.

Free Tax Help For The Elderly:

— Tax help sites in libraries, churches, community centers and other locations are staffed by trained volunteers. Taxpayers who earned less than $39,000 and file a simple tax return can call 1-800-829-1040 to locate the nearest Volunteer Income Tax Assistance Program site. In addition, senior citizens can take advantage of the free IRS Tax Counseling for the Elderly program by calling 1-800-829-1040 or AARP's Tax-Aide counseling program at 1-888-227-7669.
Go to http://irs.gov or call 1-800-829-3676 or write the IRS to place your order.

IRS Identity Theft Hotline

You should contact the **IRS Identity Theft Hotline at 800-908-4490** if you ever believe:

- Your tax records are currently affected by identity theft and you have not been able to resolve the matter, or

- You may be at risk of identity theft due to a lost/stolen purse or wallet, questionable credit card activity or credit report, etc.

Additional information regarding identity theft and your tax records can also be found at the IRS.gov website: http://www.irs.gov/individuals/article/0,,id=136324,00.html

For information on VITA and TCE locations and times, or to volunteer for any of these programs,

Order IRS Forms And Publications By Mail Or Phone.

If you need a prior year form or cannot locate an IRS product, visit the IRS Forms and Publications page to download products or call 1-800-829-3676 to place your order or write the Internal Revenue Service, 1111 Constitution Avenue, NW, Washington, DC 20224 and specify the number of the publications and forms you would like to order.

How to Order IRS Products

You may order up to 10 different products from the IRS and you will receive two copies of each ordered form and one copy of each ordered publication. The IRS will automatically include applicable instructions in your order. (If you need more than the quantity allowed, please call 1-800-829-3676 to place your order.) **Be aware that not all tax products are available through the IRS Web page and that quantities are limited.**

To place an order, enter the product number or a keyword in the search box. For example, if you need Form 2441, Child and Dependent Care Expenses, you could search for 2441, child, dependent, etc. Your search will produce a list of products matching the search criteria. Check the box next to the product and follow the instructions to finish your order or select more products.

Please allow 7 to 15 days for the IRS to process and ship your order. If a product is not available when you place your order, the IRS will send it as soon as it becomes available. Please do not place another order.

Internal Revenue Service
1111 Constitution Avenue, NW
Washington, DC 20224
Web Site: http://www.irs.gov
Toll Free: (800) 829-1040 (Tax Information)
Toll Free: (800) 829-3676 (Forms & Booklets)
Toll Free: (800) 829-0433 (Criminal Investigation)

Web Pages For Internet Form and Publication Articles and Indexes

- IRS Forms And Publications: http://www.irs.gov/formspubs/index.html
- IRS Forms And Publications Article: http://www.irs.gov/formspubs/article/0,,id=128717,00.html

Chapter 17

More Unclaimed Money & Cash Refunds From The Government.

Many companies go out of business with your money. Money with your name on it then goes to the federal government. Check to see if you are owed a tax refund or even a banking or mortgage cash refund or even stock shares in your name that are unclaimed. Check these sources and see if you have money coming to you.

IRS Refunds

Tax Refund Status call center and web site.

Call 1 (800) 829-1040 or visit web site to check the status of your income tax refund.
https//sa.www4.irs.gov/irfof/lang/en/irfofgetstatus.jsp
or
http://www.irs.gov/

A 2008 Letter From The IRS

IRS Seeks to Return $266 Million in Undeliverable Refunds And Economic Stimulus Payments to Taxpayers

IR-2008-123, Oct. 23, 2008

WASHINGTON — The Internal Revenue Service is looking for taxpayers who are missing more than 279,000 economic stimulus checks totaling about $163 million and more than 104,000 regular refund checks totaling about $103 million that were returned by the U.S. Postal Service due to mailing address errors.

"People across the country are missing tax refunds and stimulus checks. We want to get this money into the hands of taxpayers where it belongs," said IRS Commissioner Doug Shulman. "We are committed to making the process as easy as possible for taxpayers to update their addresses with the IRS and get their checks."

All a taxpayer has to do is update his or her address once. The IRS will then send out all checks due.

Stimulus Checks

It is crucial that taxpayers who may be due a stimulus check update their addresses with the IRS by Nov. 28, 2008. By law, economic stimulus checks must be sent out by Dec. 31 of this year. The undeliverable economic stimulus checks average $583.

The Where's My Stimulus Payment? tool (Note: no longer available) on this Web site is the quickest and easiest way for a taxpayer to check the status of a stimulus check and receive instructions on how to update his or her address.

Taxpayers without internet access should call 1-866-234-2942.

Regular Refunds

The regular refund checks that were returned to the IRS average $988. These checks are resent as soon as taxpayers update their address.

Taxpayers can update their addresses with the "Where's My Refund?" tool on this Web site. It enables taxpayers to check the status of their refunds. A taxpayer must submit his or her social security number, filing status and amount of refund shown on their 2007 return. The tool will provide the status of their refund and in some cases provide instructions on how to resolve delivery problems.

Taxpayers checking on a refund over the phone will be given instructions on how to update their addresses. Taxpayers can access a telephone version of "Where's My Refund?" by calling 1-800-829-1954.

Unsure Of Check?

Taxpayers not sure of which type of check they may be due should check on a potential economic stimulus check first because of the looming deadline. See instructions above.

Checks Returned

The vast majority of checks mailed out by the IRS reach their rightful owner every year. Only a very small percent are returned by the U.S. Postal Service as undeliverable.

Through September 2008, the government distributed 116 million economic stimulus payments with only about 279,000 checks being undeliverable. Meanwhile, the IRS has distributed more than 105 million regular refunds this year with only about 104,000 being undeliverable. In both cases, well under one percent of refunds or stimulus checks were undeliverable.

Avoiding Future Problems

The IRS encourages taxpayers to choose direct deposit when they file their return because it puts an end to lost, stolen or undeliverable checks. Taxpayers can receive refunds directly into personal checking or savings accounts. Direct deposit is available for filers of both paper and electronic returns.

The IRS also encourages taxpayers to file their tax returns electronically because e-file eliminates the risk of lost paper returns. E-file also reduces errors and speeds up refunds.

IRS Refund Year Articles

Tax Year 1999

2.5 Billion Dollars In 1999 Unclaimed Money Refunds
http://www.irs.gov/newsroom/article/0,,id=10 8836,00.html

Tax Year 2000

IRS Has 2.5 Billion Dollars For People That Have Not Filed A 2000 Return.
http://www.irs.gov/newsroom/article/0,,id=12 0309,00.html

Tax Year 2002

IRS Has 2.0 Billion Dollars For People That Have Not Filed A 2002 Return.
http://www.irs.gov/newsroom/article/0,,id=15 4625,00.html

Tax Year 2003

IRS Has 2.2 Billion Dollars For People That Have Not Filed A 2003 Return.
http://www.irs.gov/newsroom/article/0,,id=16 8422,00.html

Tax Year 2004

IRS Has 1.2 Billion Dollars For People That Have Not Filed A 2004 Return.
http://www.irs.gov/newsroom/article/0,,id=18 0280,00.html

Tax Year 2005

IRS Has 1.3 Billion Dollars For People That Have Not Filed A 2005 Return.
http://www.irs.gov/newsroom/article/0,,id=20 4931,00.html

Tax Year 2005

IRS Has 2.0 Billion Dollars For People That Have Not Filed A 2005 Return.
http://www.irs.gov/newsroom/article/0,,id=13 4886,00.html

Tax Year 2006

IRS Has 1.3 Billion Dollars For People That Have Not Filed A 2006 Return.
http://www.irs.gov/newsroom/article/0,,id=21 9727,00.html

Banking & Mortgage Refunds

Federal Deposit Insurance Corporation (FDIC) Unclaimed Funds
The Federal Deposit Insurance Corporation insures bank depositors to a specified limit in case of a bank failure. If you have lost Money because of a bank failure contacts the Federal Deposit Insurance Corporation.

If a financial institution is closed by a regulatory agency, the FDIC is appointed as Receiver and is responsible for the payment of insured deposits and the liquidation of the remaining assets. Search this site for unclaimed deposits and dividends held by the FDIC.
Web Site: http://www2.fdic.gov/funds/index.asp

ADDRESS:
Federal Deposit Insurance Corporation
550 17th Street, NW
Washington, DC 20429
Web Site: http://www.fdic.gov

National Information Center For Bank Information
Federal Reserve System has information on bank information that you may find useful. Get information about banks no longer in business as well as banks that have merged with other banks.
Web Site:
http://ffiec.gov/nicpubweb/nicweb/SearchForm.a spx
or
Web Site: http://www.ffiec.gov/nic

ADDRESS:
Federal Reserve System
20th Street & Constitution Avenue, NW
Washington, DC 20551
Web Site: http://www.federalreserve.gov

Credit union unclaimed stock shares
The National Credit Union Administration pays members when federally insured credit unions liquidate.
Web Site:
http//www.ncua.gov/Resources/AssetMgmtCent er/Unclaimed.aspx

Credit union unclaimed member shares.
National Credit Union Administration lets you search a list of unclaimed member shares in a credit union. [PDF]
Web Site:
http://www.ncua.gov/resources/assetmgmtcente r/files/unclaimeddeposits.pdf

Unclaimed Money From The National Credit Union Administration
Web Site: http://www.ncua.gov

ADDRESS
National Credit Union Administration
1775 Duke Street
Alexandria, VA 22314
Phone: (703) 518-6300
Web Site: http://www.ncua.gov

Treasury Department

Damaged Money
Many business establishments may refuse to accept your damaged currency. Most banks can exchange your torn or damaged currency for new currency, but the Treasury Department will also exchange your mutilated or damaged

money currency for new or clean currency.
Web Site:
http://moneyfactory.gov/damagedcurrencyclaim.
html

Savings Bonds Calculator
Bonds go up in value each year. You can go to this web site to find out what your bond is valued today.
Web Site:
http://www.treasurydirect.gov/BC/SBCPrice

Savings Bonds Interest
Some bonds have stopped earning interest. Go to this web site to see how much interest your bonds earn for you.
Web Site:
http://www.treasurydirect.gov/indiv/research/sec
urities/res_securities_stoppedearninginterest.ht
m

Savings Bonds Recovery
The treasury department will cash or even replace your lost, stolen or even destroyed savings bonds.
Web Site:
http://www.treasurydirect.gov/indiv/research/inde
pth/ebonds/res_e_bonds_eereplace.htm

Unclaimed Bonds
You could own unclaimed bond that you had forgotten or abandoned. Go to the US Treasury web site for Unclaimed Assets.
Web Site:
http://www.publicdebt.treas.gov/sec/secuncld.ht
m

Treasury Hunt For US Savings Bonds
Got to U.S. department of treasury website to search for matured US Savings Bonds issued by the US Treasury.
Web Site:
http://www.treasurydirect.gov/indiv/tools/tools_tr
easuryhunt.htm

Federal Unclaimed Property
Search for unclaimed property at the US treasury website.
Web Site:
http://www.ustreas.gov/opc/opc0039.html

ADDRESS
Department Of The Treasury
1500 Pennsylvania Avenue, NW
Washington, DC 20220
Web Site: http://www.ustreas.gov
Phone: (202) 622-2000

Security Exchange Commission

You money returned to you. – "Investors Claims Funds" and Class Actions Suits
Make a claim with the Securities and Exchange Enforcement cases where a Receiver, Disbursement Agent, or Claims administrator has been appointed and funds have been awarded to you.
Web Site:
http://www.sec.gov/divisions/enforce/claims.html

ADDRESS:
Security And Exchange Commission
100 F Street, NE
Washington, DC 20549
Phone: (202) 942-8088
Web Site: http://www.sec.gov

Department Of Housing

Mortgage Insurance Premium or Insurance earnings REFUNDS. (HUD/FHA mortgage)
You may be eligible for a refund from your HUD/FHA insured mortgage you may be eligible for a refund on part of your insurance premium or a share of the earnings.. Search by name or case number. To obtain additional information regarding refunds on FHA loans, please call the Federal Information Center at 1-800-688-9889 go to the website..
Web Site:
http//www.hud.gov/offices/hsg/comp/refunds/ind
ex.cfm

HUD Unclaimed Money from the Department of Housing and Urban Development.
Written correspondence only for unclaimed money claims. Enclose your FHA case number in your letter.
Attn: Disbursement Branch,

PO Box 44372,
Washington, DC 20026-4372.
Web Site:
http://www.hud.gov/offices/hsg/hsgabout.cfm.

ADDRESS:
Department Of Housing And Urban Development
451 7th Street, SW
Washington, DC 20410
Web Site: http://www.hud.gov
Toll Free: 1-800-688-9889

Pension & Retirement Money

Unclaimed Pension Funds By Company and Employee.
You may be entitled to pension money if the company that employed you went out of business and ended it's benefit pension plan. Contact the PBGC that may have funds in their accounts that have been transferred by your former employer.
Web Site: http://search.pbgc.gov/mp

Find Your Unclaimed Pension Money or get more information on your unclaimed pension money.
Web Site:
http://www.pbgc.gov/MissingParticipant/missingParticipantSearch.jsp

ADDRESS:
Pension Benefit Guarantee Benefit Corporation
1200 K Street, NW
Washington, DC 20005
Phone: (202) 219-8776 (PWBA)
Web Site: http://www.pbgc.gov

Civil Service Retirement Unclaimed Money. Civil Service Retirement System

ADDRESS:
Retirement Operations Center (OSOPM)
Boyers, PA 16017.
Phone: (202) 606-0500

Federal Employees Unclaimed Retirement

Money. Federal Employees Retirement System -

ADDRESS:
Retirement Operations Center (USOPM)
Boyers, PA 16017.
Phone: (202) 606-0500

Unclaimed Money Databases

National State Sponsored Database of Unclaimed Property . Listing of all 50 states and Canadian Provinces for locating unclaimed property records..
Web Site: http://www.missingmoney.com

National States' Unclaimed Property
National Association of Unclaimed Property Administrators. Search for unclaimed property nationwide. Check state offices in charge of reuniting property with its rightful owner.
Web Site: http://www.unclaimed.org

National Unclaimed Property Database to Search For Unclaimed Money. Search the database by all States.
Web Site: http://unclaimedmoney.org

Native American Unclaimed Money

Unclaimed Money For American Indians
The Office of the Special Trustee for American Indians is seeking current addresses for the Individual Indian Money account holders listed on their site. All accounts have funds to be disbursed to the rightful owner. Please contact the Office of the Special Trustee for American Indians site to see if you are an account holder.
Web Site: http://doi/gov/ost/iim/index.html

Unclaimed Money with Bureau Of Indian Affairs (BIA)
Web Site: http://www.doi.gov/bureau-Indian-affairs.html

ADDRESS

Department of the Interior
Bureau Of Indian Affairs
1849 C Street, NW
Washington, DC 20240
Web Site: http://www.doi.gov
Phone: (202) 208-3100

U.S. Postal Service Refunds

Postal Refunds
The U.S. Post Office offers refunds for lost or stolen money orders issued by the United States Postal Service for a cost of only $5.40.

Web Site: http://www.usps.gov

ADDRESS
U.S. Postal Service
475 L'Enfant Plaza, SW
Washington, DC 20260-2200
Web Site: http://www.usps.com
Toll Free: (800) ASK-USPS or (800) 275-8777/(877) TTY-2HLP (877) 889-2457 (TTY)

U.S. Veterans Unclaimed Money

U.S. Veteran Unclaimed Money.
The U.S. Veteran's Administration may have money waiting for you. Contact the Veterans Administration for unclaimed money.
Web Site: http://www.va.gov

ADDRESS
Department Of Veterans Affairs
810 Vermont Ave. NW
Washington, DC 20420
Web Site: http://www.va.gov
Toll Free: (800) 827-1000

Federal Information Center

Unclaimed Money Information From Regulated And Federal Agencies.

ADDRESS:
Federal Information Center,
PO Box 600,
Cumberland, MD 21501-0600.
Toll Free: 1-(800) 688-9889.
Web Site: http://www.info.gov

Department Of Defense

Unclaimed Property From The Department Of Defense.

ADDRESS:
Management Information and Analysis Division,
Defense Manpower Data Center,
99 Pacific Street, Suite 155A,
Monterey, CA 93940-2453.
Phone: (408) 655-0400

Social Security Administration

Unclaimed Money From The Social Security Administration.

ADDRESS
Social Security Administration
6401 Security Blvd.
Baltimore, MD 21235
Phone: 1-(800) 772-1213.
Web Site: http://www.ssa.gov
Web Site: http://socialsecurity.gov

Government Benefits

Free Government Money
The government gives away billions in free benefits to companies and individuals every year. You are eligible for many agencies that offer free government money. Contact this web site and see how much money you are eligible for the benefit programs the government offers to Americans in need.
Web Site:
http://www.benefits.gov/benefits/browse-by-category

Chapter 18

Special Million Dollar Information

Additional Bonus Report

I have a secret to share with you, one that will show you how you can make a lot of money an amazing free product. I am talking about vital information. Information is the most valuable product known. Some information in books is worth millions of dollars. I will show you later in this chapter where to get the most valuable sought after information that is easily worth thousands of dollars. What's more, I will show you how to get these special rare books for free. They will be yours so that you will have your very own million dollar product. Let me reveal more of my secret to you.

Use this this book as your guide to success that will show you how you can sell extremely valuable information on the internet and through direct mail. But what's more I will sweeten the pot. I will give you the valuable information. Extremely valuable information worth millions that has been passed down through the ages will be yours. This is information that millionaires desperately need. This is information that transforms people's lives. This valuable information is here in this chapter. This highly sought after million dollar secrets will be exposed to you, but this is only the beginning. This valuable information will be yours so that you own it. This highly sought after million dollar information will be yours to keep, absolutely free. I will even give you elaborate systems that you can use to sell this million dollar information. Read on and see what I have to offer you.

Many self-made millionaires have used the systems in this book to make their fortunes. You can now do the same. Because you have bought my book and are reading it, the secret is yours. This secret is yours use to make your own fortune. If you are poor, as I once was, this secret will make you rich; if you are already rich, this secret will make you richer. You can drive a Mercedes convertible, swim in your own pool or live in a mansion on the sandy seashore. Your search is over for money. You have just found what you have always sought. You are on your way to the big money you always wanted, and this section of this book is the key. I will explain to you a step-by-step formula that has, without fail, created wealth for some of the wealthiest people on earth. This system is simple you will offer everyday people valuable information that I will give you for free. This rare and valuable million dollar information is yours free. Use the free information that I will give you to make yourself rich. Make yourself filthy rich.

My secret will change your life. It will help you get whatever you want, and more. In addition, you will have the satisfaction and pride of knowing that you did it on your own. You are on the verge of a brave new world, and I will guide you every step of the way. I will show you how I and others created fortunes. I will show you how to do the same with extremely valuable information that is only known to the select and few. Take this free information I will give you and make a fortune. Now you can enjoy tremendous success while at the same time calling your own shots in your own business. But, above all, you will have the freedom to spend time with your loved ones. You can spend time on your hobbies and the pleasures life has to offer. You can have all of those riches only the rich enjoy, all of this with a product you will get for free.

There Is Magic In Belief

A wise man once told me that you will never get rich if you work for someone else. The only way to get rich is by having a vested interest in a business. You must be taking in a share of the profits to get rich. You do want to be a millionaire, don't you? There aren't enough days in a year or years in a lifetime for most people to become millionaires while working for others. On their own, though, they can do it in remarkably short order. So how much money do you want? Name your figure: $4,000? $40,000? $400,000? How about $4 million? You can get this money with the secret I will reveal to you.

Trust me for I have a plan that will make you succeed. First, you must have faith in yourself. To earn a lot of money you must believe in yourself. With faith in yourself you can make your first million. With faith, you can buy a beachfront home, a lakefront cabin and a nice shiny luxury car while still only working 4 hours a day. Believe in yourself for I will make it easy for you to succeed by revealing the secrets that will make you rich.

People think they have to work hard and deprive themselves to make money. This is not true. Working smarter not harder will make you rich, but hard work is always necessary when making big money. Money isn't everything but with money you will have the greatest gift of all; you will have your freedom. With freedom you can decide your own life. You will be able to do whatever you want whenever you want. Only money can buy your freedom so that you can do what you want. Take the afternoon off. Take the day off and lay out by the pool. Take the whole year off when you have money.

Freedom will make you happy. Do you want to be happy? Do you want success? Success is yours if you believe. If you believe, if you have faith in my method, you can end up very rich and very happy. Of course, success means different things to different people. To some, it means buying a long-desired possession, like a large home by the beach. To others, it means love and friendship. What does success mean to you? Do you want a loving family? Do you want a large home with an outdoor swimming pool? Whatever it means - wealth, recognition and freedom. If they are important to you then knowing my secret and acting on it make you achieve success. In this chapter I will reveal the secrets of earning your freedom and also helping you become rich.

What can stop you getting what you want? Only the limitations you put on yourself. How do I know this? Time and again I have seen people who could have done well, but didn't. Do you know why? Because they believed they could not do it. You can do it, all you need is this book. I will show you how to make it big and become very wealthy. Reach for the world. When you limit your expectations, you limit the amount of money you can make. Follow my steps to becoming very rich. I will show you everything I know to guarantee you will make it big.

I Didn't Believe In Myself. For many years I worked a hard laborious day job, in banquet hall and in an office. I was barely getting by. I had no belief in myself and just didn't think I could make money on my own. It was only when I had belief in myself that I started to do well. One day I decided I was tired of the 9-to-5 rat race. I was able to scrape up a few hundred dollars and put my plan into action. I used a special method to sell a book. The same system I will reveal to you.

It was a sunny Monday afternoon. I ran home to my mailbox to see if anyone was interested in my $6 book. When I got to the mailbox, I couldn't believe my eyes. It was so stuffed with letters that the mailbox door wouldn't close and I had trouble carrying all the letters. Each envelope contained a check. I spent four hours opening my mail. I just couldn't believe I could make so much money in so little time, but the evidence lay in front of me. Why didn't I make so much money earlier in my life? Why didn't I make money the poor man's way? The mistake was mine for not believing in myself.

Let me ask you a question: Do you believe in yourself? I urge you to follow this simple advice: BELIEVE IN YOURSELF. Don't go through life making peanuts when you should be making cashews. The choice is yours. Take the bull by the horns and believe in yourself. Belief, in yourself and in my secret. You may be skeptical and asking yourself: "Why should I believe?" I ask you this one question: "Why shouldn't you?" You have nothing to lose. I guarantee your success. Learn my secret, the same secret that made millionaires out of people just like you. Follow my program, and you will do well. If you don't try it, your life will not change. You will do much better with my secret? Is that what you want? YES, you do. Take what I am giving you so you will become rich.

I am giving you the chance of a lifetime. Most people feel they will go nowhere in life; they lack motivation. Good intentions don't move you ahead unless you have a vehicle. You have the vehicle, it is this book. I am offering a free race car. You can consider yourself lucky. Very lucky. You have the vehicle-which is this book and your belief in yourself. You see that pinpoint of light at the end of the tunnel and you move toward it in large, confident strides - without fearing the dark, without turning back, without doubting yourself.

Do You Have The Desire To Be Rich?

First, you must have the desire to be rich. Not just a normal, everyday desire, but a burning, all-consuming desire. A desire that makes you want to become rich so badly you are willing to learn new ideas, accept new ways, strike out on your own and reach that light at the end of the tunnel. Do you have such a desire? I know you do, because only a person with this desire would buy this book. Your desire to get ahead will get you ahead. Use this book to get yourself ahead.

Examine Your Own Beliefs So You Can Start A Business

I urge you to examine your business beliefs. Do you have any beliefs that are negative? How do you feel about people or any relationships you have? How do you feel about money and other material things? What are your beliefs toward happiness and love? Examine your beliefs. Sit down and look at yourself carefully, then ask: "What am I like? What do I believe in? Do I truly believe I will be rich?" Just being able to see yourself can help you recognize beliefs you should keep and those you should discard or change.

Ask yourself another question. Ask: "Why are my money skills this way?" This will start you thinking about the reasons your beliefs are the way they are. When you know, you can work on them. To succeed, you must believe. As the old proverb says. "Believe you have it, and you will have it." If others like you did it so can you? If I did it, so can you. If you believe you will make it too. If you really want a million dollars you must make certain changes like starting a small business from your home.

Take A Chance

What you risk is your time and effort; what you gain is wealth and freedom. Venturing out on a whole new path may scare you a bit, but It will tear you free of your fear of success or whatever else it is that holds you back from enjoying the finer things life has to offer. Remember what President Franklin D. Roosevelt said: "The only thing we have to fear is fear itself." How right he was! The only reason you limit yourself is fear, fear of rejection or loss. It is one of the greatest de-motivators. But failure is also one of the best teachers. Every time I suffer a setback, I pick myself up and continue. I figure out why I fell, then I push forward stronger than before. The truth is that failure helps me learn. If you learn the lessons of your failures, you will become a better person; you will also get rich. The Hindus say that "you will make the same mistake over and over again until you learn your lesson." Learn from failure - it's a great teacher. I have successful system of making money. I will show you the correct way to make your fortune. Follow my system and you can make it big too.

Why Sell Extremely Valuable Million Dollar Information?

The secret to becoming a millionaire very quickly is to buy very cheap and sell very high. You need a product that will cost you a few pennies that you can sell for hundreds of dollars. Your penny investment should give you high dollar returns. How will you be able to do this? What could you possibly get for a few pennies that people will demand you sell them for hundreds of dollars? Is there such a product? I must be in the clouds if I this is true. Well it is true. This secret I will show you. You will be providing extremely valuable million dollar loopholes and secrets to other people that will make them rich. The finest information that makes millionaires salivate will be in your possession. This extremely profitable product will cost you pennies but you will sell this product for hundreds of dollars. Everyone that pays you will tell you that the words you sold them were well worth every single penny. This information is mouthwatering joy, to anyone that wants to make money. I will show you this fantastic product in this chapter.

Why Start Your Own Business

So, apart from the huge profits you can make, why should you start a business?

1. First, you are your own boss. You make the decisions. In this new business, you work at your own pace and for how many hours a day you wish. And when the profits start rolling in, you will have the freedom to spend time with your family and friends. This increased leisure time can be spent any way you want.

2. Second, you will not fork over your life savings to anyone. Some places charge you an arm and a leg to set you up in your own business. I am not going to do that to you. I am going to show you how you can start your own business easily on your own, with almost no money. I will provide everything you need for practically nothing. You will do your very best with me.

3. Third, you avoid the frustration and possible rejection of approaching strangers and setting up accounts with vendors and other companies. I will tell you how to set up your own business and who to contact for your business needs. Even if your business is successful, you will have to be happy with a measly 5% profit on sales. The other 95% goes to high priced middlemen. I won't do that to you. I will show you how to take all of the profits so that you can put the money in your pocket. I will not show you how to make other people rich, while they gouge you and eat your profits. I will show you how to keep all the money for yourself. When you start this business my way, 100 percent of the profits go to you. That is every penny is yours. What more motivation do you need?

4. Fifth, you have a tremendous opportunity to make friends and enjoy customer responses. As a businessman, your customers will respond directly to you. You will enjoy the positive feedback and learn from the negative. Also, you will deal with businessmen and businesswoman, so you have ample chance to build strong business ties.

Alternatives To Writing

I am now going to show you how to get a free product. A free product that could make you millions. I am talking about words. Mere words are worth millions of dollars. The words are free, but people will pay you thousands of dollars for their meaning. I have seen one person save another person a hundred thousand dollars from 25 words. These twenty five words were priceless. Arrange your words correctly and you can make it big. Sell a free product which is words. Sell this free product on the internet and by mail. People will pay you a lot of money for this valuable information called words. Let me know show you how to arrange your words so that people buy your words for a lot of money.

Very few people like writing. I don't mean to be negative but, you may find, after struggling over your typewriter for a few hours or a few days, that writing is not for you, or that you don't have the time or the inclination to write. If you feel this way, don't worry; there are some excellent alternatives for you in this chapter. The best alternative is number one. I recommend you start your business with the first option. I am giving you the other options so that you understand the business you are in.

1. Get the reproduction rights
2. Ghostwriters
3. Go to a bargain wholesaler
4. Find remainder products
5. Get hold of expired copyrights.
6. Government supplied publications

A Business That Will Make You A Fortune

What is the key? What is the secret to all the success stories I've told you about? How did I and many others strike it rich? We did it by selling by the internet and by the mail. They had an amazing product and carried it through, and reaped the rewards. In this chapter I will offer you an amazing free product. An extremely valuable product you can call your own. A product that will make thousands for other people, yet it will be yours to sell. Think of all the good you will be making with your new product that I will offer you. You too can sow the same seeds and reap the same rewards as millionaire legends that you see in the magazines.

Making a fortune with valuable information doesn't stop here. You have to take the horse by the reins and keep right on galloping with wind in your face. Take it and run. You know English. English is one of the world's most widely used languages and there is a huge market for English products outside the United States. They love Americans all over the world. You can be an international bigwig tycoon and market to other English speaking people. That's right, of course. There is a huge market for material written in English, both inside and outside this country - in Canada, Europe, Australia, even in Africa.

Books with reproduction rights

Some of you may not have the time, skills or money to write your own books. What do you do then? Use David Bendah's system of striking it rich with information. You will have the reproduction rights. You can copy the book for pennies then sell the book for hundreds of dollars. You can only do this if you have the reproduction rights. David Bendah is offering you a product that will cost you nothing, but yet you can sell this valuable information product for hundreds of dollars.

Use David Bendah's System

David Bendah offers an e-book, audio book, print media Self-Publisher's Opportunity Kit, available for those who are serious about making money selling information by the internet or by mail… You can copy the books that David Bendah sends you. You will be sent reproduction rights. Make a copy of each audio book, e-book or printed book for you customers. Every time your customer buys a book make a copy. It only costs 20 cents a CD to make a copy of an audio or e-book. It would only cost you pennies to copy the paper books. It is so cheap to be your own publisher. On the internet you pay no money to give anyone a copy of the book. It is all electronic. You make a book for no money then you sell the e-book for thirty dollars. The internet is fantastic for selling a product that cost you no money. I am offering you, your very own book that people order on the internet. Just keep a copy of the book I will send you on the internet. Every time your customer orders this book, you get paid. Your customer just downloads your e-book or audio book for free. The book costs you not one cent but you will be able to earn twenty to thirty dollars from each e-book, audio book or printed book that you sell. You will be making this thirty dollars from free books. You can even give these books away as a bonus to get internet and mail order sales of other products.

Become Your Own Publisher With Your Own Books

When people visit your website you must sell them a product. You need a product that cost you nothing, but yet is very valuable. The product that will make you rich is extremely valuable information that costs you nothing. Extremely valuable information that people pay hundreds of dollars is an excellent product to sell. This is information that millionaires desperately need. This is information that makes people rich. This highly sought after million dollar secrets will be exposed to you, but this is only the beginning for I will offer you nine different valuable audio and e-books and print books for you to sell. You will love this rare and valuable information.   But there is more, you will have the reproduction rights to this valuable information so that you own it. This highly sought after information will be yours to sell for nothing.

You Will Get Nine Audio Books

People love listening to seminars and lectures. Listening to audio books is like listening to music. People can listen to audio books in the garden, in the home, while they are driving or even while they are exercising. It is great to lose weight while you are learning fantastic money making concepts. The audio books are yours. You will have nine different audio CD seminars with this program. The audio books will cost you twenty cents to make. Put your name and address in the audio book program and give away the audio books to promote your internet website or to sell other books. The audio books are electronic so you can put electronic audio books on the internet. Electronic audio books cost you nothing. They are a free product you can sell for a lot of money on the internet. I will include nine audio books on CDs for you to reproduce and sell.

You Will Get Nine E-Books

E-books are electronic books that will cost you nothing. I will give you these e-books so that you can sell books electronically. Pay nothing for the e-books, yet watch people pay twenty dollars for your books on the internet. These e-book sales will pile money in your bank account. Some people have earned $30,000 a month from e-book sales. You can do the same. An e-book is a free product that you sell for a lot of money. This is electronic book sales that don't require inventory. Yet money is transferred to your bank account every time you sell an electronic e-book. To sell an e-book you need a website and the e-book. I am offering nine different fantastic e-books for you to sell on the internet.

All websites need traffic. You need visitors to your website to make money. Visitors make internet companies money. It may cost $1 a hit to get people to visit you web site. One dollar is a lot of money when you have a lot of visitors. It is very expensive. There is a great way to get traffic to your website at no cost to you. You must absolutely give away a free product. Advertise a free e-book for anyone that visits your website. How much will an e-book cost you. An e-book will not cost you one cent. The e-books are free with my program. If you have an internet site you absolutely must have a free e-book product. With a free product you can direct traffic to your website for nothing. Anyone with an internet website must have this e-book program.

You Will Get Nine Printed Books

You need a free printed product to give away. Giving away free books will get you cash paying customers. The printed version of the 8.5" x 11" "The Self Publisher's E-Books & Audio Books Opportunity Kit" is 284 pages. All nine books have been typeset in one large book. You can take sections of this large 284 page book and copy them into nine different books. These books can be sold in a paper format to your customers by mail or as a free bonus when they order products from you.

You will get:

1. Nine different E-books on CD to sell on the internet.
2. Nine different printed books to sell by mail.
3. Nine different audio books on CDs to sell to by internet or by mail.
4. A total of twenty seven different audio, e-book and print media products.

You will get nine different books in three different formats. You will get a total of 27 different valuable information products to sell by the internet or by mail. You can then reprint each book for as little as pennies at your local printer or you can copy the books for nothing on the internet. The electronic e-books sell great. You will get nine different e-books. But that is not all, you will also get nine different audio versions of these books. Make copies of these audio CDs for twenty cents and sell them for twenty dollars each.

The kit contains nine extremely valuable books, but twenty seven different products that are yours in electronic, audio and printed format. All of these books have all been tested and are proven sellers with a large audience. Each book comes with a copyright agreement that allows you to reprint and sell as many copies as you desire. These books will cost you pennies to copy. Put these books on your website and pay nothing to copy them. Your customers pay you money every time they download your books. This very valuable million dollar product will cost you nothing to make but will make you a lot of money.

Use the self-publishing kit with complete step-by-step instructions on how to market these books for the greatest profit. You will also receive a very effective sales letter that will move your books immediately. In addition to the sales letter, e-books, audio books and printed books you get proven-effective classified ads to use to promote your books. These classifieds employ the best sales techniques available.

Description Of The Nine Books

Here is a brief description of each of the nine books in the "The Self Publisher's E-Books & Audio Books

Opportunity Kit".

1. How to Get Free Grants (audio book, e-book and print book)

Do you know that the government and foundations give out billions of dollars in free grants every year? Some of this could be yours, easily - all you have to know is how to get it. This book will show you how to get free grants.   The book tells you which institutions will give you money and how best to apply for the grant so that you are sure to get the free money.

Some highlights of How to Get Free Grants are:

- A detailed collection of 250 private foundations that await your grant application.
- How to get some of the billions of dollars given away each year by corporations seeking tax deductions and write-offs.
- Foundation grants for community development, education, religion, Christianity.
- Grants for students that want academic scholarships and fellowships.
- How to get your foot in the door for corporation grant money that must be given away.
- Wiz through the grant application with a marketing plan to get your grant.
- Grants for women academics in science and engineering.
- Cash grants for global health, climate, environment, urbanization, social and economic security.
- Money disbursements to improve the lives of women.
- Programs for the legal advocacy for people over 50.
- Grants for affordable homes for working families.
- Free grants for home ownership and wealth creation.
- Complete, step-by-step methods of applying for free grants: how to fill out the application; write the letter of appeal, and other support data.
- Grants for gay, lesbian, bisexual, transgender, HIV/AIDS.
- Cash grants for agriculture, aviation, conservation, art and education, health/biomedical waste.
- Grants for black men and boys, African American women's fund, black girls.

All this free grant money can be yours. Apply for free money at any of the foundations in the book. This free money can be yours, just for the asking. Won't you stake your share of free money?

2. Importing - Your Key to Success (audio book, e-book and print book)

Do you know that you can buy virtually any product made in the United States for much less money abroad? There is a great profit potential in importing from countries all over the world. If you enjoy traveling – this a great way to deduct all your vacations as well as making a profit by going overseas.

Highlights of Importing - Your Key to Success, include:

- Details of products you can bring into this country and pay no duty.
- U.S. Customs Service loopholes to use when shipping products in to this country.
- A list of foreign companies that will drop-ship mail order products to you.
- How to receive FREE products from almost any manufacturer, just for asking for them.
- How to determine if the product you choose will make you a fortune.
- How to travel FREE, with the foreign manufacturers of products paying your way to their countries.
- A list of FREE publications from countries all over the world.

- Getting FREE publicity to sell your imported products
- How to make millions in commissions for locating suitable products for interested firms.
- How to use all the importing tax breaks to reduce your taxes.
- How to get government agencies to help you import your product.

This guide is more than a book, it is a complete manual to importing success. Use it to create an importing empire.

3. Getting The Job & The Promotion (audio book, e-book and print book)

Do you have the job you want? Or are you overworked and underpaid? This book will help you in your search for "job happiness." Learn how to apply for a job and be hired as the top candidate. Move up the ladder of job success with ease and get promoted. Win over your supervisors and fellow employees. Impress your boss so much that he gives you bonuses and raises. Moving up in a company can be so simple and rewarding. The secret to know what to do. This book tells all.

Some highlights of Getting The Job & The Promotion:

- How to get that interview with ease at the company of your choice.
- What you should and shouldn't say at the interview.
- Confidential methods of getting a six digit salary.
- Steps needed to get your series of raises.
- How to master the art of difficult office politics.
- How to win your superiors over to your way of thinking.
- How to get what you want at work with the unique "assertiveness training" method.
- How to increase your productivity on the job while working less.
- How to be liked and admired by your supervisors and coworkers.
- Many methods on how to get a raise and promotion in no time at all.
- How to prepare persuasive and result-getting resumes.

Getting ahead on the job has never been easier. This book can show you how to make more money while working – working smarter, not harder.

4. Making a Fortune with Real Estate (audio book, e-book and print book)

Millionaires are created every day with real estate. You, too, can make big money in real estate with "no money down." This manual tells you how to spot instant moneymaking investments. Isn't it about time you got your share of the real estate profits?

Highlights of Making a Fortune with Real Estate are:

- How to spot foreclosure bargains, sometimes at 20% of their market value.
- How to buy real estate with no money down, then sell the property to make an instant profit with no investment.
- How to get the best financing possible with creative financing techniques.
- Geographical areas that give you the greatest return on your investment.
- How to spot property that sells for half its true market value.
- How to use other people's money for your investments.
- How to reduce your tax bill to almost nothing with real estate investing.

- How to triple your initial investments within a year.
- How to get low-interest government financing just for the asking.
- How to create a positive cash flow with the real estate you buy.
- Where to find rural land bargains you can get for 10 cents on the dollar.
- How to buy land at a fraction of its cost at tax auctions.

It is a myth that you need money to buy real estate. Anyone with no money and the right instructions can become a millionaire through real estate acquisition. Start accumulating hundreds of thousands of dollars of real estate with this book.

5. The Secrets of Raising Money (audio book, e-book and print book)

Getting a loan can be hard, or it can be very easy. If you do the right things to the right person, you have a much better chance of success. I not only show you how to get that extra money you need, but I also show you how to clean up a bad credit history and how to get the lowest-interest loans possible. Do you know that you are eligible for government-subsidized, low-interest loans? These and many other available sources of money are yours, waiting only for you to apply for them.

Some of the highlights of The Secrets of Raising Money are:

- How to wipe out your debts without bankruptcy.
- Get any credit card you want and use this credit card for any purpose
- Establish credit and get thousand dollar loans when you have a bad credit rating.
- An 11-step method that turns bad credit ratings into AAA-1 ratings.
- Confidential methods of negotiating with the loan officer.
- Getting loan approval for a $100,000 business venture loan.
- Get the lowest interest financing regardless of your credit.
- How to avoid paying taxes forever, legally, with this proven, eight-step plan.
- How to borrow $50,000 on your signature, for any purpose.
- How to raise $200,000 in 24 hours with no collateral.
- Raise two hundred thousand dollars by having a stock offering of your corporation.

Getting the right loan is a matter of proper timing and know-how. This book teaches you both. Learn the techniques for getting low-interest money.

6. Take Over A Going Business With Zero Cash (audio book, e-book and print book)

Some highlights of Take Over A Going Business With Zero Cash:

Buying a large business is easy. Pay nothing for the business then re-organize by making payments to creditors. Sweeten the pot even greater by issuing stock for the defunct business in your name. Earn ten to twenty million dollars in your stock without putting a cent in this business. Sell the stock for millions on the stock exchange while you take a salary to take the company out of debt. Even if you can't solve the companies' money problems you are still millions of dollars richer.

- Over 300 Venture capital firms that will finance your business with hard cold cash
- Venture capital firms that will finance the stock offering to give you millions in stock.
- Buy the company for zero down then split the company into separate firms, then sell stock for

both companies to reap millions.
- Exactly what to do to increase business value and put cash in the bank.
- Make the offer that includes no cash. Settle with creditors for the debts. The stock and inventory is yours. Refinance business and issue more stock.
- Restructure inventory and products to your "zero down" business, so that this business it is worth millions.
- Use the corporate take-over by offering stock instead of money.
- How to get up to $1 million from private investors for your investment project.
- Become a millionaire by selling company divisions and unneeded inventory with after a "no cash" company purchase.

Buying a business with zero cash down is easy when you have Venture Capital companies that will loan you money to refinance loans and make changes to the company.

7. The Millionaire's Secrets of Growing Rich (audio book, e-book and print book)

Millionaires make 100 times what you make, but they aren't 100 times smarter than you. What do millionaires do that you don't? They use a special plan. You could use the same plan. Imagine what you could do if you used the same systems they use to make themselves wealthy. You can with this informative, wealth-building book that reveals systems used by millionaires.

Some highlights of The Millionaire's Secrets of Growing Rich are:

- The art of making complicated decisions in five easy steps.
- Exposing your hidden talents with "self-evaluative psychology" and put them to good use making money for you.
- How to unlock your potential to make you millions.
- Goal setting time schedule to win your goals.
- A five-step procurement process that will get you virtually anything you want.
- Effective time management, which allows you to do twice as much in half the time.
- How to solve any problem with the Downy seven-step problem solving schedule.
- How to turn the negative aspects in your life into profitable opportunities with "adversity reversal" techniques.
- "Networking," and how it can get you to the top.

Millionaires use systems to make money, To do the same, all you need are those systems, and this book has them all.

8. How to Influence People and Win Them Over (audio book, e-book and print book)

This book will show you how to understand and get along with people so that they enjoy and desire being with you. After using the influencing techniques, you will find that people feel good around you for you will understand their needs and fulfill your own needs. People will like you. Winning others over to your way of thinking has never been easier.

Some highlights of "How To Influence People And Win Them Over" are:

- "Transcendental" influencing skills that make it easy for you to influence others.
- How to get maximum self-disclosure from others after perfecting the art of listening and talking.
- How to apply "projection analyzation" used by psychiatrists to win over defensive people.
- How to persuade others to give you what you want by using "assertion techniques."
- Thirteen confidential systems that get people to like you.
- "Criticism-reversal" techniques to get the better of overly critical people.
- How to use the five-step "self-promotion" method to get people to know you quickly.
- How to analyze people correctly and understand their needs.

The ability to get along with all people is priceless. Winning people over has become a science, and this book gives you the step-by-step instructions you need to master the art of being liked by other people. It's easy to understand and apply.

9. How to Get $400,000 in Benefits from the U.S. government (audio book, e-book and print book)

We all pay taxes, but how many of us get all the money from the government that we should? Very few. A recent survey shows that the average American receives only 11.8% of the money for which he or she is eligible. Do you get your share?

A few highlights of How to Get $400,000 in Benefits from the U.S. Government are:

- How to get up to $67,500 from HUD to buy a condominium.
- How to get up to $5,000 a year for your education, as long as you make less than $20,000 a year.
- How to get a guaranteed $50,000 loan if you live in a rural area and would like to improve living conditions.
- How to get a guaranteed loan of up to $1.5 million for your fishing vessel.
- How to have the government send you money every year to pay for your education.
- Details on low-interest business loans of up to $500,000.
- How to buy U.S. government surplus equipment and supplies for 10 cents on the dollar.
- How to buy land through the U.S. Department of Land Management for as little as $10 an acre.
- How to secure $92,000 for home improvements.
- A list of U.S. government departments that award grants.
- Government organizations that help low-income people get financial help.
- How to get cash grants of $5,000 just for having a low income and for going to college.
- How to get a $250,000 grant for being a woman in business.
- How to get up to $3 million in grants if you are a minority in business.

The government set up these programs for all of us, but few people take advantage of these priceless cash opportunities, mostly because of lack of information. This book tells you about hundreds of programs and how you can get what the government owes you in grants and loans.

How to use your kit

You will receive by return mail "The Self Publisher's E-Books & Audio Books Opportunity Kit" which includes nine books in three formats which is twenty seven professionally prepared books. You will get nine audio books, nine e-books and nine print books. In addition, you receive reprint rights that allow you to sell as many books as you like for as long as you like. Each paper book, audio book or e-book is 8.5 by-11 inches and is made to be easily reproduced. Reproduce the audio CDs or the e-books on your computer for only pennies. Take the books to your local printer and have them printed for pennies a copy. Everything you need is in your kit. Use the sales letter and the specially written classified ads to sell your books.

Here is what you receive

Nine well-prepared books written by leading authors, all specialists in their fields. The twenty seven audio, e-book and printed books are yours to reprint and resell as many times as you want. They are:

The nine books are:
1. How To Get Free Grants
2. Importing—Your Key To Success
3. Getting The Job & The Promotion
4. Making A Fortune With Real Estate
5. The Secrets Of Raising Money
6. Take Over A Going Business With Zero Cash
7. The Millionaire's Secrets Of Growing Rich
8. How To Influence People And Win Them Over
9. How To Get $400,000 In Benefits From The U.S. Gov't

You Will Also Receive:

- A certificate entitling you to full reprinting rights for any or all of the nine books.
- A well-written sales letter for good results.
- Classified ads for you to use are also included.
- You will also receive a guarantee with your Self-Publisher's Opportunity Kit. If, for any reason, you are not satisfied with your kit, return it within 30 days for a full, unconditional refund.

"The Self Publisher's E-Books & Audio Books Opportunity Kit" with twenty seven audio, e-books and printed books, certificate of reprint rights, step-by-step instructions, sales letter and classified ads, is only $129, plus $12 for shipping. Hurry because reprint rights of audio, e-books and print books are limited to a select amount of dealers. This program may not be offered anymore by next month. If you order after 35 days I may have to decline your order and you will not have the e-books, audio books and print books. I am sorry to have to do this but I must curtail the demand for this very valuable product. If you delay you will be left out. You must act now if you want to be ahead of the game. Send all orders to:

David Bendah,
914 E. 8th Street, Suite 110, Dept. B6
National City, CA 91950
(619) 474-9200

A certificate entitling you to full reprinting rights for any or all of the twenty seven books in audio, e-book and print format. A complete set of instructions that shows you how to sell your books for the most profit. Directions on how to handle all types of small business and publishing situations are also included.

If you would like to see the light at the end of the tunnel, let me show you how to take the first step toward it. Read and study this book. This book will show you everything you have to know to make big money with the internet and mail. The following are other alternatives for those that want to sell books by the internet or by mail.

Ghostwriters

Hiring a ghostwriter is a good idea if you don't feel you have the time or talent to write your book. But just because you hire someone else to write your book doesn't mean you can hoist all the responsibility for your book on to the ghostwriter. Remember, it's still your book. You will have to write an outline of your book, detailing what information you want in what chapters. If you are an expert on your subject, work closely with your ghostwriter - tell him where to research, relay to him information and experiences that only you, as an expert, know. In addition, while the book is being written, look over the ghostwriter's shoulders - make sure he writes what you want and is not going off on tangents. But you must recognize the fact that your ghostwriter is a professional and probably knows what he is doing. Listen to his suggestions.

Last but not least, make sure the writer you hire is good. Read carefully some of the books or articles he has written. Make sure the ghost writer has the type of style and personality you want, because style will be reflected in your book. If he is a negative person, your book will have negative overtones. If the writer is arrogant, your book will seem arrogant to the reader. Be concerned about this - it may make the difference between a best seller and a flop. Remember that the copyright is yours because you have paid another person for your own book to copyright. When you hire a writer you will own the copyright for the book written by the writer. For available ghostwriters and advice on how to pick one, see this section of the internet or college newspaper classified section. If you consider this ghostwriting option, remember that it is the most expensive option of writing a book that is open to you.

Wholesale books

You will have to buy books for at least 70% off the original cover price to make a good profit selling wholesale books by the internet or by mail order. Occasionally books offered at wholesale prices are good books that were badly promoted.

There are several companies that sell many, many titles at wholesale or discounted prices. You might try these:

BookCloseouts.com - The Bestseller in Bargain Books

Wholesale Sources for Name Brand Books and Accessories.
www.bookcloseouts.com

BookNook.com - Discount Book Store

Discount Book Store discount books, quality service, searchable catalog, recommended reading selections, Best Seller lists, online book ordering, book watch notification.
www.booknook.com/

DollarDays.com - Wholesale Books, Book Distributors

Wholesale bulk book distributor items and Discounted Books.
www.dollardays.com/

Remainder books

Remainder books are a real bargain. In some cases you can buy them for less than the cost of printing these books. Remainder books are books that usually didn't sell well and the publisher is trying to unload them. If it costs a publisher $3 to print a book and you buy it for $1.50, you have a good remainder deal. But there is a catch - you may have to buy several thousand copies.

Remainder books can require a heavy investment and, while the book may have been poorly promoted, it is probably out of print for good reason. Several companies offer remainder books, as well as promotions, closeouts and overstocked titles of every conceivable type, up to 90% off their original list prices. If you are interested, contact these companies. Be very careful when buying any remainder book:

Wholesale discount and Remainder Books

Remainders, wholesale graphic novels, discount books, wholesale book assortments, cheap books, overstocks, hurts, mixed assortments, bargain books.
www.rhinosales.com

Remainder and Bargain Books

Bargain and remainder titles. They carry nearly every subject from antiques to young adult, but they specialize in fiction. We also carry CDs and DVDs.
www.daedalus-wholesale.com

Wholesale Discounted Remainder & Overstock Books

Highly discounted remainder and overstock books for volume wholesale purchase. 80% to 98% off list price. Wholesale supplier to dollar stores &, book stores.
bookblowouts.com

Books with expired copyrights

The old copyright law before January 1, 1978 gave a book 28 years of protection before the copyright expired. If you can get a book that is older than 33 years (before 1978) and its copyright hasn't been renewed, you can reprint it with no royalty fee. If you get a book that is older than 89 years, it is usually in the public domain. Books in the public domain belong to the general public, and you have every right to reproduce them.

To sell books with expired copyrights, you must first reproduce them, which can cost you lots of money. Unless you can finance reproducing these books and you know for sure they will sell, don't undertake this venture. Don't forget that few books that old have material that is applicable and useful to readers in the 2012s. The biggest advantage you will get from books in the public domain is the ability to copy pictures, paragraphs and quotes for inclusion in your own book. Contact the U.S. Copyright Office, Library Of Congress, 101 Independence Avenue SE, Washington, DC 20559-6000. www.copyright.gov, for information on the copyright status of a particular book.

Government publications

The U.S. government is the biggest publishing house in the world, and anything it puts out is public property and is in the public domain, so you can use, copy and reproduce it at will. You can reproduce any government publication or book in its entirety, or you can just pick out interesting bits of information. However, you can't just reproduce a government publication and sell it for profit.

Some people use government publications for the research portion of their book. The amount of material you can glean from the government and the many studies its agencies conduct is amazing, and you should take full advantage of it.

If you would like to receive government publications that are of interest to consumers, write Consumer Information, PO Box 100, Pueblo, CO 81002, www.pueblo.gsa.gov, 1 (888) 8 PUEBLO and ask for the free catalog. Many of the publications are free and the rest can be purchased at cost.

Using Words To Create Your Riches

"The Self Publisher's E-Books & Audio Books Opportunity Kit" with twenty seven audio, e-books and printed books, certificate of reprint rights, sales letter and classified ads is perfect for anyone that wants to make a lot of money on the internet or by mail. But while it is costly and difficult some of you may decide to publish your own book. You will learn in this chapter how to put together a successful book of your own. Follow the steps I have outlined, which are the same steps I and other successful authors take, and you could have a best seller on your hands.

Choosing Your Topic

Big publishers look for topics with mass audience appeal to meet and justify huge production and promotion costs, but, as a self-publisher, you are not so restricted.
Topics successfully exploited by self-publishers fall into two categories:

1. Those of general interest to a large, easy-to-reach audience, for example: books on human relationships, fitness and general health care, pop psychology, moneymaking and personal finance, etc.

2. Those of special interest likely to appeal to only a narrow audience, for example: books on Mongolian cooking, wood-burning stoves, Early American quilts, pre-War German coins, waste disposal systems, white-water canoeing, handwriting analysis, etc.

Note that neither category includes fiction or poetry. Some poets and authors are successful self-publishers, and they have a flare for writing, for characterization and plot, for making the abstract concrete.

Poetry and fiction have the highest failure rate of any type of book. Writing poetry or fiction is not easy. As the famed New York Times columnist, Red Smith, once noted: "There's nothing to writing. All you do is sit down at the typewriter and open a vein."

So, be warned: The self-publisher generally does better selecting a likely audience and concentrating on supplying the buyers with specialized non-fiction information. Virtually anyone who can think clearly and has a rudimentary knowledge of grammar can write non-fiction. You don't have to be Hemingway. Writing form isn't that important - content is important. People buy self-instruction books not for their literary style, but for the know-how and information they convey.

However, if you don't feel you can manage the project, if you lack the desire to write or simply the time, there are profitable alternatives like "The Self Publisher's E-Books & Audio Books Opportunity Kit". In the next section there are a few titles that give you an idea of the wide variety of marketable topics, the first section appealing to a massive market, the second to a specialized one.

Massive Market Book Titles:

I Can If I Want To, Your Erroneous Zones, Never Cooked Before Cookbook, Decorating, How To Prosper During the Coming Bad Years, How to Get Out of Debt, How to Fall Out of Love, Dress For Success and *I Haven't a Thing to Wear.*

Special-interest Market Book Titles:

The Old-Fashioned Recipe Book, The Whole Earth Catalogue, How to Keep Your Honda Alive, Professional's Guide to Public Relations Services, The Zucchini Cookbook and *Postal History of Spain.*

If you know a lot about a subject - perhaps you've rebuilt the engine of your Honda four times - it is a natural topic for your book. If you think you don't know enough about any particular subject or issue, choose one that has always interested you. Of course, you can always tailor your subject so that it appeals to the desires of a wide audience. Let me help by showing you what people want.

People want:

- To be in better shape and have the chance of a longer life
- To have more comfort and luxuries.
- To have more money.
- To be more popular and attractive.
- To have more leisure time.
- To have security for their old age.
- To get praise.
- To save time.
- To be good parents.
- To be fashionable.
- To be influential.
- To have fun.

And there are hundreds of topics under the "how-to" category: *How to Win Contests, How to Borrow Money, How to Collect Stamps for Profit, How to Be Healthy and Live Longer, How to Move A House, How to Write Classified Ads, How to Design and Write Internet Ads, How to Improve Your Personality, How to Get Raises and Promotions, How to Play the Guitar, How to Become a Fund Raiser, How to Make Money With Your Camera, How to Hypnotize, How to Buy and Sell Antiques* - the list is endless. Whatever your topic, the next step is in the direction of your local library or internet to do research.

Research

Use the internet to view and read books still in print so you can read books on the internet or find resources to get copies of books. Remember, the librarian and internet is your friend, and the library/internet is perhaps your most valuable tool. Use all the libraries in your area - employees of public, city and county, community college and university libraries are more than pleased to help researchers. It's their job and they probably enjoy it. Look through the library's title index file for titles of books dealing with your chosen topic that the library carries or can obtain for you from libraries in other cities. Also, check a copy of Books in Print - it lists all books still in print by subject, author and title. Perhaps the library or internet has some of them; others you can order from the publisher or browse through or buy at your local bookstore.

Often, by the time a book gets to print, its information is out of date or the methods it advocates have been improved. The internet usually provides the latest information available on any given topic, so look through internet and magazines, which lists articles on thousands of subjects and tells in which issue the article was printed. If you can't figure out how this essential internet or magazine system works, ask your librarian. Magazine articles also supply you with the names of experts in the field you are writing about - call or write them for information; if they live near you then request a face-to-face interview. They, in turn, will know other experts and can lead you to other information sources.

Some of the material and information you collect will come from copyrighted pieces, so if you use large sections of the work, word for word, ask permission and acknowledge the author. Most authors are delighted if you use their work in your book. It gives them added exposure and prestige. In fact, you'll notice that exhibits in many books come from other books.

The key to the copyright law, which prevents the author's work from being used for profit by others without his permission, is that it protects only the order of printed words, not the ideas expressed. If you express another person's ideas in your own words or relay the same information using different words, you should be OK. A rule of thumb is to make sure you don't copy from another's work more than three or four words in a row. Gather far more information than you will use - you will throw out the excess baggage as you write and end up traveling light.

Outline: Initial Organization

By now, you will have a pretty good idea of what you want to say, so figure out the logical order in which to say it. If describing a step-by-step or chronological process, the order is obvious; if not, one order - perhaps dealing with increasingly complex instructions will be better than all others. Write up a table of contents, listing chapters in order and the information to be covered in each; then collect all your notes and research, assembling them in separate piles for each chapter.

Writing

If you have a computer word processor, all the better, but a typewriter is fine. Go through your research for the first chapter and organize that in a logical order. Type out the information, but don't worry about perfection on the first draft - just get it down on paper. You will have ample opportunity to correct, add and delete.

No one can teach you style or how to write, but there are guidelines:

1. Use short, strong Anglo-Saxon words, rather than those of Latin origin; i.e., use "gut," not "intestine."

2. Avoid fancy words. Most people use fewer than 800 of the 26,000 available words in the English language, and so should your book. Remember: You are trying to communicate, not impress.

3. Use nouns and verbs that express action; avoid superlatives and use adjectives and adverbs sparingly.

4. Show rather than tell. Use words that allow the reader to "see" what you are saying by describing the response of the five senses. The reader can paint a mental picture if you introduce sight, touch, taste, sound, smell.

5. Use lively quotes and humorous stories and examples to illustrate your points.

6. Organize paragraphs. Each paragraph is like a chapter - it must have a clear beginning, middle and end. The first sentence of a paragraph (the topic sentence) should both state the subject of the paragraph and link it to the preceding paragraph (a transition). The final sentence should link the paragraph to the next.

7. Write naturally. Write like you speak, using words and phrases that come readily to you. Pretend you're writing to a friend.

8. Relax.

Chapter by Chapter

Finish the first draft on each subject and chapter one at a time - this will help you concentrate and organize your thoughts. When a chapter is finished proof-read and edit the chapter, cutting out repetition, rephrasing awkward sentences and, if necessary, reorganizing the material.

Professional Help

It is difficult for an author to edit his own work, so get a friend or pay an editor to read through your material. For a list of ghostwriters, freelance writers and editors, contact writers magazine like Writer's Digest, which lists some available writers? If you have a hard time finding someone you feel will do a very good but inexpensive job editing your book, consider hiring an English or journalism major at a university or junior college near you. You won't have to pay a student much for quality work, provided you hire the right person. Place an ad in your local college newspaper. Once your book has been edited at least twice, type the final version on paper or on a computer disc.

Choosing a Title

A good title will boost book sales drastically. Some catchy, highly successful titles that have become standard phrases are: *I'm OK You're OK, The One Minute Manager, Your Erroneous Zones, Zen and the Art of Motorcycle Maintenance, Rich Dad Poor Dad, Catch-22, Real Men Don't Eat Quiche and the South Beach Diet.* There are hundreds more.

A good title arouses curiosity, plays on words, is titillating and prompts people to buy the book. A dull title will hurt your sales and probably damn your book to failure. Here is a tried-and-true method that will help you select a good title.

1. Look at the section on advertising headlines. A good headline for an ad will usually be a good title for your book. After all, they both serve the same purpose of enticing a person into reading further.

2. Make sure your title is aimed at your specific audience. If you are selling a book on a money-raising program for those looking to make money, why not call it *"How To Use Your Hidden Potential To Get Rich?"* Notice how the title arouses curiosity.

3. Use easy-to-understand words. If you use very sophisticated words, potential customers will think you are looking down on them. And if they think that, they won't buy your book.

4.   Gain credibility by listing specific information in your title. An example is a title of a book. The title could be, *"Making A Fortune On The Internet"*; instead, use a specific amount of money and a specific amount of time like one year. A book title could be, *"Making $500,000 A Year On The Internet"*.

No matter what title you choose, test the title. Ask your friends what they think of it. I write out a list of titles I like and then ask my friends to pick the one they prefer. Ask why your friends chose the title they did - this will give you insight into what people like and will buy. The better the title you pick, the more dollars in your pocket.

Advertising That Sells

The best ads ever written were well planned before they were created. Planning ahead is very simple and enables you to create impressive ads. The best advertising agencies use this method, and I'm showing it to you because I want you to create great ads. You may feel you already know all this information, and going through this process may seem unnecessary. But if it works for the best in the business, don't you think it's worth your time? It really is worth your time to plan ahead.

The following steps will put you in the same "mind set" as the big thinkers in the big ad agencies. There are several questions you must ask and answer, in writing: What am I selling? Who is my target market? What does my target market want? How can I reach my target market efficiently? Does my target market need and want what I am selling?

What am I selling?

You must ask yourself what you are selling. In your case, you are selling a book. Your potential customers will view what you are selling not merely as a book, but as a vehicle to realize their wildest dreams. You are offering them information that will dramatically change their lives. You are selling them words that will make them rich. You are selling them words that will cure their disease. You are not selling books you are selling riches and cures. You are helping them fulfill their dreams and desires and regain their health.

There are two ways to describe the product or service you are selling: by features or by benefits. If I describe a pen I am selling by features, I say it is made of plastic, it has a two-year warranty and the barrel is replaceable. Benefits, however, are what the features mean to the customer. A pen of plastic means that the pen will be durable, will save money, won't tarnish or corrode and is inexpensive. If the pen has a two year warranty, the customer will save money and have a reliable writing instrument. As another example, if I sell cameras, what am I' really selling? Not just a well-made machine with several ground-glass lenses. I am selling a device to make pictures that makes memories.

But what about books? If you are selling a book on how to make money, are you merely selling a 200-page book? No, you are selling a system for making money. Similarly, if you are selling a gardening book, you are not just offering a book with color photographs of garden plots and rows of vegetables, but a method of making carrots grow long and tomatoes grow fat - in effect, a system of creating better vegetables.

You have already chosen your book by now, haven't you? I want you to sit down and think. Think about what you are really selling in terms of customer benefits. Are you selling a product to make a lot of money or is it a product that miraculously heals people. Write down your findings on a piece of paper.

Who is my target market?

Find out who your potential customers are. Are they male or female? What are their jobs, their goals and desires? To whom does your book appeal? If your book is about gardening, your market is gardeners, of both sexes, probably single-plot owners who live in semi-urban areas. If your subject is computers, your market is less narrow, probably of medium income and encompassing a wide range of interests. If your subject is how to make money, your market is much larger - enormous, in fact, because everyone wants to know how to make money. If you know your book, you will know your market.

Just as in the previous exercise, write down who your target is. Think about it and write this down on a piece of paper below the previous answer.

What does my target market want?

Conversely, if you know your market, you know what book to write or sell. When you know who your prospects are, it isn't hard to know what they want. Just ask them what book they want to buy or find out what books they have bought. It's the reverse process of knowing who your target market is. I will give you an example of determining what your target market wants. First, let's say my target market is low-income people, aged 35 to 55, living in rural areas. Second, I know one of the things that low-income people want: money. What can I sell low-income people? A book on how to get low-interest government loans. I used this same technique to target my market for the book, $2,000 An Hour. I targeted this book to low-income people and, as a result, I sold about 250,000 copies of the book at $10 each book. That adds up to 2.5 million dollars in book sales. Write down what your target market wants, just below your observations for the previous exercise.

How can I reach my target market efficiently?

It is not enough to know who your prospects are - you must reach them. And if you can't reach them profitably, you can't undertake your advertising campaign. You can reach customers through the media. A medium is any vehicle that is used to reach prospects, such as the internet, emails, mail, magazines, radio, television, newspapers, etc. Internet sites and magazines that cater to the same specialized audience that your book is aimed at are your best bet. Only advertise on websites that specialize in a certain market, i.e. some websites caters to everyone who can read, so avoid them. Use a gun owner's website or magazine for gun buyers. Use an Japanese automobile website or automotive magazine for Toyota car part buyers. Use specialty websites or media which are aimed at your market.

Internet advertisements run in certain states will result in more sales per capita than those run in other states. The key question is, how many people per thousand in a particular state order by the internet or by mail? The state with the highest mail order response is Alaska. Why? Because many parts of Alaska are isolated, so it is more convenient for many Alaskans to order by mail. There is a simple way to find out in which publications you should advertise. Look at your competitors - in which websites or magazines do they advertise? If they keep advertising in the same websites or publications, they must be making money. If they are making money by advertising in a specific website or magazine or tabloid, so can you. Also, read the editorial content of websites or magazines - is it aimed at your market? If the website or magazine is full of stories about coin collecting, your book on pre-War German coins will probably sell well.

Does my market need and want what I sell?

You now know what you are selling; you know what your target market wants. You must now determine if the two match. Your target market must want to buy and read what you are selling. If you are selling a book on money then your target market must want a book on money. When you have finished this step you must decide how to sell your book. There are many alternatives - I will discuss each alternative in the next few chapters, but I'll tell you what they are now:

1. Sell your books directly from display ads in websites, emails, direct mail, magazines and newspapers.
2. Sell your books directly from classified ads on the internet and paper media.
3. Use a classified ad to entice your potential customer to write you for more information. You then send your customer your sales literature.
4. Obtain a list of potential customers and send them your sales literature.
5. Use the free publicity offered by the internet, blogs, face book, magazines, newspapers and broadcast stations.

Use a combination of any of the above advertising plans to sell your books.

Web Site Traffic

People will only go to your website out of greed. They will visit you if you give them something for free. If you give away a free product like an e-book or audio book you will have many people visiting your website. To earn website traffic you must give a free product away. If you give away free information for people that visit your website then you will have a lot of website traffic. Some people pay $1 a hit so that people will visit their website. It is so expensive to get internet visitors to come your website. A free product that you can give away, like E-books, audio books and print books are an excellent way to get customers to visit your website. Consider getting the "The Self Publisher's E-Books & Audio Books Opportunity Kit" offers twenty seven great e-books, audio books and print books that you can use to promote your internet website for only $129, plus $12 for shipping. Hurry because reprint rights of audio, e-books and print books are limited to a select amount of dealers. This program may not be offered anymore by next month. If you order after 35 days I may have to decline your order and you will not have the e-books, audio books and print books. Order e-books, audio and print books now to be assured of having a free product to give away so that you get heavy internet traffic.

Free Advertising For Your Products

Create good promotional materials to sell your products. Memorize and be familiar with all of the benefits of your product which you should also state in your promotional materials. Pay as little as possible for all of your advertising. Use blogs, face book and other forms of free advertising to sell your products. Don't pay for any advertising that you can get free.

Some social groups are set up just to network. Networking is a great avenue to sell your products. Any type of forum where you can write or speak should be used to sell your products. Always view a situation as a time to make money. Any party is a great opportunity to make money. If you are attractive and are presentable you will make more money. People always buy more products from attractive people then unattractive people, so dress for the part when you go out. Selling products to other people will keep you thinner, attractive and healthier. Use your time effectively to make money. When striking a conversation with anyone always talk about the product you are selling and give the prospect your business card. Keep promoting yourself as often as possible. You could make a lot of money selling products just going out and mingling with friends and family. Send e-mail, notes to friends, family and prospects selling your products. Any contact with another person is a great time to sell your products. Social circles must always involve making money.

Creating Successful Advertising

Advertising agencies

If you pay for advertising ask for as many discounts as you can get. When paying for television, radio, magazine, newspaper and billboard advertising, you can always get a discount of 15% if you own your own advertising agency. Ask for the discount even if another person created your advertising. If you create the ad you are called an "in-house" advertising agency. Always insist on your commission discount.

1. Regular Advertising Agency – Used for all types of advertising. For broadcast, print and internet advertising – this includes e-mails, websites, radio, television, magazine, newspaper, blogs, social media, and other electronic, print and space media.

2. Interactive advertising agencies – They offer web design and development, search engine marketing, internet advertising, internet marketing, e-business and e-commerce consulting.

3. Search engine advertising agencies – Called pay per click (PPC) and search engine optimization (SEO) companies. These agencies specialize in internet advertising where you pay every time a potential customer clicks on your internet advertising. Search engine optimization is to increase the amount of customers that visit your website.

4. Social media agencies specialize in promotion of products and brands in the various social media platforms like blogs, social networking sites, Q&A sites, discussion forums, microblogs, face book, etc.

If you are not a good ad writer you should hire an advertising agency. Make sure you can write good ads before you buy space in a magazine. If you don't feel confident, see what an advertising agency can do for you. If you do decide to pay someone to create your ads, make sure that person has had experience with advertising. Also, study the section on advertising in this book so that you can assist the ad writer with some ad writing expertise of your own. The structure of your ad is how you put your ad together. What you say and where you say it will make or break your advertising. Here it is:

Attention grabber

This is the headline at the top of your ad or the main caption in your advertising; it grabs the attention of the reader and draws him into your message.

Interest developer

With this, you interest the reader in what you have to say. For example, would you like to retire at 40 with a 4% return on your money? Or, you can start with an unusual or startling statement. For example, Mark Haroldson's ad for How To Wake Up The Financial Genius Inside you opens with: "Millionaires are not 100 or even 10 times smarter than you are, but it is a fact that millionaires are making 10 to 50 and even 100 times more than you." Another example is Charles Abbott's ad selling tips on low-cost legal advice, which opens with: "My name is Charles Abbott. I'm a lawyer myself and I may be cutting my own throat - but I'm going to tell you the truth."

Benefits of your book

Write down all the benefits your book offers your prospects. (Developing benefits is explained in the section titled "What am I selling?" When you have finished your list, rank each benefit according to importance. The most important benefit will be the theme of your ad; the secondary benefits will be secondary themes in your ad. Think of and include as many benefits as possible. First, emphasize the main benefit your book offers. Is it making money? In one advertising I stated I owned a million dollar home and a new Mercedes convertible hinting at the benefits of my system of making money.

Trust builder

No matter what you claim, if the reader does not believe your ad, you will not sell. One way to establish credibility is to use testimonials. For example, for an ad for another book I wrote, How To Use Your Hidden Potential To Get Rich, I had my financial advisor attest to my financial success. Under the words "Sworn Statement," he wrote: "I testify that David Bendah has indeed been able to secure an income of $8,254.41 in the first five days of using his systems. (signed) Virgil Holsinger, Financial Consultant, San Diego, California." You can also state your bank account and give references, such as your bank or Chamber of Commerce. In addition, you can use excerpts of letters written to you by satisfied customers, making sure you don't use their full names and addresses without their written permission.

Action

Your ad should end with a call to immediate action. In his ad, Karbo even goes so far as to call his readers fools if they do not respond immediately: "What's more, I'm going to ask you to send me 10 dollars for something that cost me no more than 50 cents. And I'll try to make it so irresistible that you'd be a darned fool not to do it . . . A month from today you can be nothing more than 30 days older - or you can be on your way to getting rich. You decide." Apart from urging them on, you can compel readers to respond by offering a limited-quantity offer (for the first 500 buyers), a limited time offer ("Good for two weeks only") or a special ("Free gift sent with all orders"). In addition, you can say that the price of the book will rise soon, due to increased costs, etc.

The Headline

The most important part of your ad is the headline; in fact, research shows, 80% of an ad's success depends on it. Your headline is your main attention grabber. So what in a headline makes it a success? What makes readers stop at your ad instead of flipping on through the web page or the magazine? The answer is that it must be interesting. It must arouse the reader's curiosity, appeal to his self-interest and stress the most important benefit of the book. Add to these characteristics words such as "free," "rich," "introducing," "new" and "easy" and your headline becomes a powerful psychological tool. You must understand the concept that "people want to know what you can do for them.". If there is nothing in your headline for them, they will not respond to it. The headline should tell your prospects what you are going to do for them; it must portray a definite benefit.

Here is an example of a poor headline, one that lacks reader benefit: It's Fun To Make Money The Easy Way. A person will read this, agree with it, perhaps think "no kidding," and move on to the next page. Compare it to this headline: You Can Make Big Money the Easy Way   Here are some successful heads: *How To Win Friends and Influence People, How To Flatten Your Tush, Everything You Always Wanted to Know About Sex But Were Afraid To Ask, The Power of Positive Thinking, The Amazing Diet, Secrets of a Desperate Housewife, How To Make love To A Single Woman.*

Another type of effective headline is one that not only appeals to self-interest but also asks a question.

The reader's curiosity moves him to read the ad. Here are some examples:
Earn $40,000 More A Year? The Secrets Of Earning $40,000 A Year?

Now that you know what factors make a good headline, how can you know what to put in yours? What should your headline stress?. It's simple. The most powerful benefit your book has to offer should be in your headline. That is why I wanted you to write your body copy before you wrote your headline. Pick out the major benefit mentioned in your body copy for a dynamic headline.

Words That Sell

Here are more words and phrases that, when included in your headline, will give it punch: free, guarantee, save, discount, money, make money, easy, profit, prosper, compare, announcing, special, now, you, introducing, modern, low cost, startling, advice, how to, why, value, wholesale, solution, sale, sensational, amazing.

If you are still not sure how to write headlines like the ones shown, study the headlines of ads that are repeated month after month on the internet, magazines or newspapers. You should also start a file of good and bad ads to give you a constant reference of "do's" and "don'ts."

The Subhead

The subhead is located just below or just above the headline, in smaller type. It is written using the same techniques as headline writing; its main purpose is to expand on the headline and further draw the reader into your ad. Examples are:

- Gold Jewelry
- Your Quick Way To Easy Money
- Big Profit Sales
- Get Moneymaking Benefits
- Work Part or Full Time
- Free Booklet
- Secret Methods Revealed

In addition to the main subhead near the headline, subheads are often scattered over the page. They break up large blocks of copy, and are therefore a useful design tool; they highlight the secondary benefits your book offers.

Capturing Your Target Audience

If you know your target audience, and by now you should, you can write your headline and subheads to appeal to that narrow market. The headline appeals to the prospects' self-interest and states a benefit; the subhead gives more detail and states a second benefit. For example, if your book is about pet care:
PET OWNERS CUT COSTS
New Book Shows How to Save Money, Keep Pets Healthy
The headline catches the attention of all pet owners and states the primary benefit: saving money. The subhead gives more detail and states the secondary benefit: keeping pets healthy.

Ad-Writing Tips

Of course, the advice I gave you on the structure of your ad doesn't cover the whole topic. Here are some more tips:

The "you attitude".

All your ad copy should contain the "you attitude." This tells your readers that you are interested in them, rather than only in yourself.

Here are some examples of sentences with and without the "you attitude":
- Without: Earn up to $50
- With: You can earn up to $50
- Without: I can make dreams come true
- With: I can make your dreams come true

Positive atmosphere

Never say anything negative in your ad. Never tell people what they can't do for them, but tell them what you can do for them. If you only have a red and blue product, not yellow and green, don't tell your prospects that you don't have yellow and green -tell them you have red and blue. Here are two examples of negative statements made positive: "You shouldn't be poor" should read, "You should be rich"; "Don't drive around an old clunker" should read, "Drive a new Lexis."

Present tense

Studies show that ads using the present tense have the greatest selling impact. Use the present tense in all your ads, not the past or future tenses.

Captions under illustrations

If there are any illustrations or pictures in your ads, put captions under them. A reader's eyes are automatically drawn to illustrations, so captions that go with those illustrations get high readership.

Simplify your writing

Avoid long sentences. Your ad should be as easy as possible to understand, so limit sentences to less than 20 words. Short sentences are better. Write as if your audience is a class of seventh-graders

Words to use

Every word in your ad should be understood by everyone who reads it, so use simple and familiar words that convey your message quickly. Here are some examples of difficult words commonly found in ads and their easily understood alternatives:
- Utilize - use
- Ascertain - find out
- Substantial - a great deal
- Majority - most

The same rule applies to phrases - make them simple and omit needless words. For example:
- Owing to the fact that - because
- In spite of the fact that - although

Again, if you have problems writing simply and with vigor, a good reference is Strunk and White's The

Elements of Style, available at bookstores for about $15.95.

Test your ad for clarity

If you are unsure whether your writing can be easily understood, test it out on an average 12 year old. Ask him if he can understand what you wrote; if he can't, ask which words, phrases or paragraphs confused him. Write down what he tells you and rewrite your ad.

Offer free information

It is difficult to get people to send more than $20 from display advertising unless they know who you are or have bought from you before. The amount of money you ask for is proportional to the amount of space you allow for your sales talk. If you are asking more than $20 for your book, even a well-written, display advertising on the internet may not bring great success. Instead, buy an advertising space and offer free information about a given topic. Give the prospect a free e-book then sell the prospect your product. You could offer a free book on stock trading for anyone that goes to your website. After they click to your website give them the free stock e-book then sell them your stock market service.

Ads offering free "how-to" information succeed because they arouse curiosity; they prompt a response because the reader has nothing to lose. E-books are a great product to give away free. Write an e-book and give it away free to prospects so that you can sell your product. "The Self Publisher's E-Books & Audio Books Opportunity Kit" offers twenty seven great e-books, audio books and print books that you can use to promote your internet website for only $129 plus $12 for shipping. Hurry because reprint rights of audio, e-books and print books are limited to a select amount of dealers. This program may not be offered by next month. If you order after 35 days I may have to decline your order and you will not have the e-books, audio books and print books. I am sorry to have to do this but I must curtail the demand for this very valuable product. If you delay you will be left out. You must act now if you want to be ahead of the game. Send $129 plus $12 shipping to David Bendah, 914 E. 8th Street, Suite 110, Dept. B6, National City, CA 91950. (619) 474-9200, for a large collection of twenty seven electronic e-books, print books and audio books you can give away free to your customers.

Be sure to put the offer of free information first, then the sales talk second. Offer your customers a free e-book or a free audio book. With a free product you will be able to entice your customer into buying your product. A fisherman would not catch fish without a worm on a hook. You need a lure to catch a big fish. With a free product you will be able to catch a big fish. If you want to make money in the internet or by mail order you need to reel people to your sales pitch. You need to entice the greed in people so that you can sell them. Put a worm on your fishing line so you can reel in the big fish. Give your prospects a free product, like an e-book or an audio book then you will be able to pull customers to your advertising. Fisherman always fish with worms and hooks. Act as a fisherman if you want large pile money stacking up in your boat.

Use long copy

As a general rule, the more copy you have, the more prospects you will get. But you won't be able to sell if you merely repeat the same ideas over and over - you must introduce new and different benefits. Write down all of the reasons your customers should buy your product then write in all of the arguments to convince your customers to buy from you. Long convincing copy will sell your products.

Make your copy dynamic

I have mentioned this before, but I want to remind you again to use short words, short sentences and short paragraphs. When you re-read and edit your ad, pare it down, cut unnecessary or repeated words, and write conversationally, as if talking excitedly to a friend.

Advertise your book only

Don't sell other people's products. Sell your own products. All of your advertising should concentrate on the customer buying your product. If my ad prompts more people to buy soft drinks, I have increased the primary demand for soft drink. If my ad gets more people to buy COKE, I have increased the secondary demand for soft drink. Don't increase the primary demand for books, all that will happen is that people will buy more books in general. Don't persuade people to buy books. Persuade people to buy just your particular book.

The point I am trying to make is that when you are advertising a book on dieting, don't talk about the merits of losing weight - talk about how your particular book can help your potential customer lose weight. Tell them that your book is the only book that will make them lose weight. If you just talk about losing weight in your ad, your potential customers will go out and buy another book and forget about buying your book. You must convince them that your book is the best solution to their weight problem. Tell them that only your book will remove their fat problem. Make sure your ads zero in on your book. Only your book is the solution to their problem. Your ad shouldn't promote all books that are of the same general topic as yours.

Professional touches

To give your ad that final professional touch, put your logo at the bottom. You may also consider including an order form or a click pad for your e-book on the bottom right corner of your ad. Click pads make it easy you're your customer to get your free book

Stimulate quick responses

Apart from a free-information, limited-quantity, limited-time or special offer, there is another popular method of getting readers to order your book as soon as they finish reading your ad. You may lose 40% of your sales if your customers don't act right away.

Offer a free, inexpensive, but attractive gift for all orders received within a certain time, say 10 days. It will increase sales because the lure of anything free prompts procrastinating prospects to order right now. You must force your customers to order your book right away. If they wait they will not order your book. Give your customers a free book if they order your book within seven days. "The Self Publisher's E-Books & Audio Books Opportunity Kit" offers twenty seven great e-books, audio books and print books that you can use to promote your internet website for only $129, plus $12 for shipping. Hurry because reprint rights of audio, e-books and print books are limited to a select amount of dealers. This program may not be offered anymore by next month. If you order after 35 days I may have to decline your order and you will not have the e-books, audio books and print books. If you delay you will be left out. You must act now if you want to be ahead of the game. Send $129 plus $12 shipping to David Bendah, 914 E. 8th Street, Suite 110, Dept. B6, National City, CA 91950. (619) 474-9200, for a large collection of twenty seven electronic e-books, print books and audio books you can give away free to your customers. You need a free product to make money with the internet or by mail order. Use e-books or audio books to convince your customers to buy your product. Anything that makes ordering more convenient will result in a quicker response, so include a coupon with your sales literature.

Money-back guarantee

Always offer a money back guarantee. It is a great way to generate more sales. I should say it is an excellent way to generate more sales. People want to feel that they can return a product that is unsatisfactory. Most people never return a product even if it is bad, unless they paid a lot of money for the product. Regardless, you need your customers. If your customers are happy they will buy from you again and again. Make sure your customers are satisfied and you will have repeat customers. The best marketers depend on repeat customers. Many businesses lose money on the first sale and make money on the second and third sale. Always offer a money back guarantee to generate more sales and to get repeat sales. I must add that a "satisfaction guaranteed" assurance and a "money-back guarantee" is now common and a standard with almost all companies so it is a necessary practice. You will experience few serious complaints or returns unless your books or products are of poor quality.

Conclusion

I'm sure you've heard of other people making big money with the internet or mail order. You have seen their expensive homes, luxurious cars, and everything else that goes with being wealthy. You deserve those same things. A lot of people just like you have been very successful using my confidential methods. Now honestly tell me that you have had the urge to join them. You can with your very own book. Consider using E-books, Audio books and printed books to make your fortune. Sales of this valuable product are limited. Not just anyone will have e-books, audio book and print books that they can give away. If you are left out of this program you will not be as successful on the internet and in mail order. Be successful on the internet and by mail. You need a good product to sell on the internet and by mail. You need a free product to get website traffic. Order the e-books, audio books and print books today. This is an excellent product for you. If you have any questions please contact: David Bendah, 914 E. 8th Street, Suite 110, Dept. B6, National City, CA 91950-2564, (619) 474-9200

Chapter 19
An Important Message

People have paid me thousands of dollars to get all of the information contained in my book. This book was written to help individuals make enormous amounts of money in a short period of time. Many people asked me if I could offer them additional information to aid them in making $2,000 an hour. I have contacts all over the country that keep me posted in reference to "unclaimed money" developments on the government and local level. These contacts and sources of information took me years to develop. I had to come up with a way to make this vital information available to you, and this indicated a definite need for an association. For this reason the "Money Finders" Association was created

This association will provide you with all the training you will need to make $2,000 an hour. It will also inform you of everything you need to know in order to make $2,000 an hour. This "Money Finder Association" is the best investment you will ever make in your life.

Free With Your Membership

1)   The Complete Manual To Finding Unclaimed Money, which tells you exactly in precise detail how to set up your money finder's business so that you can start making up to $2,000 an hour. This manual will show you how:

- How you can recover the unclaimed money before it goes to the states and how to recover unclaimed money in distant countries.

- Advanced methods and sources of searching for people.

- How to set up your money finder business and design your own office for the lowest price.

- How to minimize costs and maximize efficiency.

- How to budget your business for maximum profits, including how to set up your accounting system and business records.

- How to assess your employee needs, including how to determine when it's the right time to hire.

- How to develop a professional company image.

2)   Save in legal fees. Save hundreds of dollars is what it cost me to get the finder's fee contract prepared. This alone makes your association membership worthwhile. You will receive a revised legal contract which includes a power of attorney contract written up by two attorneys in different states. This contract is to ensure that you get your money, and has already been used to recover thousands of dollars.

3)   Detailed "States" report. Which states are the easiest to make money in? That question is answered in a 50 page detailed report (included in your membership package) on the laws regarding unclaimed property in every state. We personally wrote and called every state in the U.S. to find out which states are most cooperative and which states to stay away from. And did you know your vacations to other states can be tax-deductible? It's true! If you make money by finding a person in another state, you may be able to write off a vacation trip to that state.

4)   Receive direct mail proven winners. These letters have helped the sender recover hundreds of thousands of dollars. These extremely well-written letters are sent out—with contracts enclosed —to potential claimants; they are designed to convince the claimant to send you back a signed contract. Many letters have been tested, but none has had as successful a return rate as these extremely luring letters.

Join The Money Finder's Association

Join the association and watch your financial dreams become a reality—you'll be amazed at the return on your investment! You could always use an association that will show you where to find money. This association is an excellent investment. The legal contracts and the state reports on all 50 states and the direct mail proven winners is well worth at least $4,000 dollars alone. You will be getting $4,000 of tools you need for only $159 dollars plus $12 for shipping and handling. The small $159 plus $12 (S&H) is worth every penny. Hurry because there is a limit to the amount of people that we allow in our "Money Finder Association." It is the best association you will every join in your life. Join today.

This association is an amazing bargain right now. Send $159 plus ($12 for shipping and handling) – a total of $171 to join the Money Finder Association.

David Bendah
914 E. 8th Street, Suite 110, Dept. B1
National City, CA 91950-2564
(619) 474-9200

If you would like more information on this program, please feel free to contact me at (619) 474-9200. I will be happy to discuss this program with you.

Best Wishes,

David Bendah

P.S.   As an additional bonus, you will receive audio CD's that are part of the award winning *"Discover Tape"* series; telling you all about the quickest methods of obtaining riches.

Purchase More Copies Of This Book

You can purchase "The Secrets Of Earning Free Government Money" for only 19.95 for one to three copies and $17.95 for more than three copies. Please include $5 for shipping and handling for all copies ordered. Send all orders to:

David Bendah
914 E. 8th Street, Suite 110, Dept. B1
National City, CA 91950-2564
(619) 474-9200

Testimonials

$200,000 Claim

Dear David Bendah

I have used your book with great success. I have a dozen claims in with the states. One is worth $200,000. Your book is one of the most factual books I have read in years. It leaves nothing out and explains everything in great detail. Even after reading the book I was a little skeptical but I tried it, and to my surprise it works. It really works. The amount you can learn is almost limitless. I have tried almost all of the other get rich plans around, but this one is a real working system. This book is complete not like a lot of others that are sketchy at least. Buying this book has changed my life. It is the best thing that has ever happened to me. James, C MO

Secured $52,614.21

Hey Dave

I've spent at least $7,000 on money-making books and seminars. The difference between them and your method is that yours works! In less than three weeks (part time) I was able to secure $52,614.21 Thanks for a business that will easily make me $100,000 this year. If I can ever be of service just call, Dave. Steve S., CO

Contracted For $500,000

Mr. David Bendah

As a result of buying and using your course I have contracted for over $500,000 of other people's money in the last 100 days. I had a small business that had been in business for 7 years. But with the downturn of the economy I saw an ad for your book and responded to it. I am personally convinced that your book is the greatest invention since plastic. I found this one ladies money that I could not convince it was hers. I found out she was a church going lady and contacted her minister. He called her in and convinced her to take her money. It really makes me feel good to help people while making money. Often I get invitations to dinner and thank you from people I have helped. Nat H., TX

I Found $3,000 Of My Own Money

Mr. Bendah

I was in possession of your book for one day only when I found $3,000 that was rightfully mine. My father died in 1961 in Dayton, Ohio, and left a bank account that we were unaware existed.

David L., OH

Secured $24,685

Dear David

Thank you so much for the methods outlined in your book. I was able to secure $24,685 in just six hours of work. I have read just about all the other books but yours has to be the best.

Terrie, T., MI

Secured $299,700

Mr. Bendah

I have spent a lot of money on the many other "ideas", but this one has very definite potential. I have located over one hundred (100) people that are owed a combined total of over $299,700. By applying your techniques about four hours a day I have been able to find people.

Irvin J, VA

I'll Still Make $3,000

Dear David

I sent out 27 letters on August 17th and on this date I have received one answer. It is a wonder this person got the letter. The person had left the Arizona address over 7 years previously. On this one account, and living with the lousy Texas finder fee law, I'll still make almost $3,000 -- not bad for almost 14 hours work and a couple of bucks postage.

Al B., TX

Received $7,620

Dear Dave

It was great speaking to you on the phone the other day. I am enclosing proof of my having received $2,070.00 and an additional $5,550. As I told you, it was all possible from having read David Bendah's book. I credit this book with helping me to turn my life around. That's a pretty strong statement. Let me explain. A few months before graduation, both of my parents developed cancer, and my father subsequently died. My life was shattered. For the next two years, broke and discouraged, I worked odd jobs in order to pay the bills and take care of my mother who somehow survived. When I finally decided to return to school to finish my education, I was worse than broke and thousands of dollars in debt. But about that time, Mr. David Bendah's book came along and I learned about the various programs contained in his book. By using the techniques in David Bendah's book I received $7,620. My friends still can't believe it! If I can do it, anyone can, believe me. Since then I have eagerly recommended they secure a copy of Bendah's book for themselves....

Well I may not have made the "100,000 in 30 days" that all the get-rich-quick adds promise, I have found something that works. And it works very well. And I have a lot of thanks to give to Dave for helping a struggling young man turn his life around and make his dreams come true. Thanks again.

Chuck R., NJ

One $98,000 Case

Mr. Bendah

I purchased your book a few months ago. I have five cases pending ranging from $19,000 to $45,000 who I have the legal claimants for. At the moment I have found a missing owner for the amount of $98,000. My first account was a simple target for a lady who moved to Oregon after her husband died and I quickly located her at a new address at a new county. I used the Milton Freeman Telephone Directory and the easy logic conveyed in your book. This is probably the most effortless road I have traveled to gain success in my life with no huge outlay if any.

David C. CA

Earned $22,850 In Finder Fees

Dear Mr. Bendah

Since I purchased your guide in recovering unclaimed property, I have received a total of $22,850 in finder fees. For this I wish to thank you. Thank you for your time and effort.

Ian T., CA

Secure A Weekly Income Of $2,500

Dear David

Before I started your method, four months ago, I was deeply in debt. After using your method described in your book, I was able to pay off all of my bills and have money to spare. At first I was skeptical, not being over 21, I didn't think I would succeed at your program. Your method is in such an easy format, anyone can do it. After three weeks of working part-time, I was able to secure a weekly income of $2,500 and it is growing every week. The best things about this money is being able to buy luxury items, I could never afford before I used your method.

Tim C., IL

Earned $3,500 From Wheelchair

David Bendah

I am a paraplegic who must use a wheelchair in my work. If I can almost anyone can become successful. I worked part-time. The people have sent me $3,500 for helping them. The most unusual case involved return of a bank account to a widower. When he furnished his marriage license as proof of ownership. I immediately spotted the names of the mother and father of the bride. In all the father and his two daughters collected $11,000.

It is a pleasure to be in a business of giving money to nice people and also getting paid for doing this enjoyable work. Thank you David Bendah for getting me started in this business. The time spent reading your book surely can be valued at $2,000 an hour.

Herman J. L., TN

Found $20,197,323.97

Dear Dave

So far I have been able to locate and notify 421 people, worth $20,197,323.97 in unclaimed money. I followed the instructions in your manual and continued to contact people by phone and by mail. I was even contacted by a Texas ranger that thought I was running a scam. Later when the ranger understood what I was doing he told me I could use him as a reference. I have secured over $300,000 since I last wrote you Dave.

Herb H., TX

At 17 Earned A Total Of $36,846 But Earned $4,374 In Two Hours.

Dear Mr. Bendah

I have earned $4,374 the first week of applying the techniques explained in your course, so far I have earned $36,846 as a direct result of your course. I began making money at 17 in my last year of high school. I saw your ad for the book sent off for it then studied the methods in your book. It took a couple of hours to make the first weeks $4,374. At my age I had no background at this kind of work. My friends thought I didn't have a job yet I was making more money than they have ever made. With the money I made I bought a brand new car and the rest I am saving for college. It is the best way to make money while doing something good for other people. One person I located just before Christmas thought it was the best gift he had ever had for Christmas. Thanks Dave.

Vic H., MI

Join The Money Finder's Association

Join the association and watch your financial dreams become a reality—you'll be amazed at the return on your investment! You could always use an association that will show you where to find money. If there is money in the streets of New York City, the heart of Minnesota or in the suburbs of Dallas we will show you how to find it. This association is an excellent investment. The legal contracts and the state reports on all 50 states and the direct mail proven winners is well worth at least $4,000 dollars alone. You will be getting $4,000 of tools you need for only $159 dollars plus $12 (shipping & handling). The small $159 plus $12 (S&H) is worth every penny. Hurry because there is a limit to the amount of people that we allow in our "Money Finder Association." It is the best association you will every join in your life. Join today.

This association is an amazing bargain right now. Send $159 plus ($12 for shipping and handling) – a total of $171 to join the Money Finder Association.

David Bendah
914 E. 8th Street, Suite 110, Dept. B1
National City, CA 91950-2564
(619) 474-9200

If you would like more information on this program, please feel free to contact me at (619) 474-9200. I will be happy to discuss this program with you.

Best Wishes,

David Bendah

The End